MEYER'S UNIVERSUM

IN HALFMONTHLY PARTS

ILLUSTRATED

WITH

ENGRAVINGS FROM DRAWINGS

BY

THE FIRST ARTISTS.

VOLUME I.

CONTAINING 48 PLATES.

THE LITERARY DEPARTEMENT

BY

J. MEYER.

ENGLISH-AMERICAN EDITION.

PRADO. MADRID

NEWYORK:

HERRMANN J. MEYER, 164, WILLIAM STREET.

1852

MEYERS UNIVERSUM

OR

VIEWS

OF

THE MOST REMARKABLE PLACES AND OBJECTS OF ALL COUNTRIES,

IN STEEL ENGRAVINGS BY DISTINGUISHED ARTISTS,

WITH DESCRIPTIVE AND HISTORICAL TEXT,

BY

EMINENT WRITERS IN EUROPE AND AMERICA.

EDITED BY

CHARLES A. DANA.

VOL. I.

NEW-YORK:

HERRMANN J. MEYER, 164 WILLIAM STREET.

1852.

LIST OF ILLUSTRATIONS.

PROSPECTUS.

Now that American Commerce and Enterprise are so rapidly embracing the Globe in their wide-spreading relations; while millions of immigrants from every region, with their sturdy industry, their capital, the hoard of laborious and economical generations, and a thirst never yet satisfied, for public liberty, and law-guarded order, come to augment the resources, the prosperity, the independence and the power of the United States, the publisher of "*Meyer's Universum*," hopes that he will only meet a great and increasing want of the American public, by laying before it a work designed to afford a living and intimate acquaintance with the natural scenery, historical monuments and social peculiarities of every people.

All persons desire to know foreign countries, but few are able to command the means and the time necessary for distant travel, while even that few must still leave many of the most interesting and instructive parts of the world unvisited or unexplored. This desire "*Meyer's Universum*" is intended to supply; it will contain views of the most remarkable cities, public edifices, and natural scenes in every zone and on every continent; accompanied by letter-press descriptions, which, while conveying the most accurate and trustworthy information, will seek to clothe the dry details of facts and figures with something of the vitality of nature, and to enable the reader while he observes historical and political phenomena to gain some insight into the causes from which they spring.

"*Meyer's Universum*" has been established in Germany for years, and has appeared in nearly every language on the European Continent. In Germany, especially, it has met with a degree of success demonstrating its plan to be one answering a universal public want. No other periodical publication in that country has ever approached the circulation which the "*Universum*" enjoys, in spite of the restrictions and opposition of the existing monarchical governments.

In commencing the issue of the work in America, the publisher, while preserving its original plan, will aim to give it such a character as will be adapted to the requirements of the American public. Extensive and costly preparations have been made to present in it the fullest collection of views, not only from every section of the United States, but from all parts of the Continent. For above a year past, artists have been engaged in exploring the most romantic regions of this country, Canada, and Central-America, for the special benefit of this work and its readers, and the engravers are now occupied on above one hundred views of North American scenery alone, which in due time will be laid before our subscribers.

These will be illustrated by descriptive and historical articles from the pens of some of the most popular writers in the country. In addition, the publisher will use the engravings appearing in the German edition, which will enable him to give to every number of the work the most varied interest, by presenting at the same time desirable views from countries the most remote from each other and the most unlike in laws, religion and social habits.

"*Meyer's Universum*" will be published regularly on the 1st and 15th of each month. Twelve numbers will compose a volume. Each number will contain four steel engravings, executed in a high style of art, with about twenty pages of letter-press. The vast and increasing sale of the work in Germany, and the confidence of the publisher in an equal or greater demand for the American edition, encourages him to put the work at the low price of $3 the volume, or 25 cents for a single number. All subscribers paying for Vol. I in advance, will be entitled to receive, as a premium, the superb Plate, engraved on steel, size imperial folio, "JACK IN OFFICE," after the celebrated picture of F. Landseer, engraved by G. Metzeroth, which will be delivered with the last part of Vol. I. Editors noticing the work will be entitled to receive all the numbers of the volume noticed.

Orders and Subscriptions may be addressed to

HERRMANN J. MEYER,
164 William Street.

G. R. 1851 DEL. JOHN POPPEL SC.

NIAGARA-FALLS

(HORSESHOE-FALLS)

Published for HERRMANN J. MEYER. Nº 164 William-Street NEWYORK.

NIAGARA FALLS.

To the ancients the larger and fairer portion of this globe was a more profound mystery than was the expanse of the heavens. It was reserved for the Genius of modern times, the Spirit of Inquiry, to unlock the wonders of one half of the world. To the present generation not a corner of our planet is concealed. The human mind roams, unhindered, from pole to pole, without fear of straying, and with the Lamp of Science penetrates into the most remote countries, transports itself among the most distant people. This faculty gives us a great advantage over the ancients. From its exercise arises a source of manifold gratification, a gratification most beneficial, when we employ it to escape the sorrow arising from external circumstances and occurrences, or to forget all intercourse with men who are irksome or odious to us, among whom, however, we are obliged to live. Then, if the foreign object which we contemplate, appears to us in fairer colors and outlines, if the scenery is more enchanting, and men happier, we rejoice thereat without envy; if we behold the reverse, however, it reconciles us with the spot upon which we dwell, and in the sorrows of our distant brethren we find consolation and strength to bear our own the more lightly.

It is in this fact that the chief reason is to be found, why descriptions of foreign countries and people excite so general and yet so very peculiar an interest. This would be still more vivid, were it always in the power of words to portray men and nature with perfect fidelity, and with that freshness of coloring in which they appear to the mental and bodily eye. But what man is such a master of language that he can claim the ability to describe perfectly the majesty of the Ocean, the sublimity of thè Alps, or the splendor of flame-vomiting Etna? Who could think himself equal to depict the wonders of vegetation in the tropics, or the beauty of the rivers and dales in Greece and Italy? In vain does the describer call Art to his aid, and, when words are insufficient points to a picture. Still he but places shadows by the side of shadows.

A walk along the Niagara to its Falls, „that wild billowy Titan of America" displays to us one of those pictures of Nature, which language is incompetent to enclose in a fitting frame. Imagine a river, as broad as the Hellespont and as blue as the sky, flowing through the midst of dense forests; imagine all the wonderful gradations of light and gloom, which fall from the gigantic trees, that cast their shadows along the shore. Here we see mighty willows, prostrate from age, bathing their gray tops in the flood; there, tall plane-trees, mirrored in the waves, from whose branches creeping vines droop caressingly to the stream; here stand, in groups, the Canadian fig tree; there, in long rows, the Virginia poplar; yonder moss grown pines, robbed of their tops by time and tempest, look down sadly from the black precipice upon the dark rushing waters of the depth below. Now a stream, breaking forth from the gloom of a tall and glorious wood, wooes, in grave earnestness, the waves of the majestic Niagara; then a brook, in youthful frolic, leaps from the lofty precipice, a mad cascade, into its broad arms, hiding their union in a veil of spray. Here the shores recede, there they gracefully advance; now the bed of the river grows broader, now narrower; at one place naked rocks overhang the flood on which the foliage of shrubs casts its shadow, at another, the tops of huge trees dive into the watery abyss. The tinkling bells of grazing herds, the barking of dogs, or the echo of the destroying axe, now and then remind the wanderer of the neighbourhood of human beings. The solitary hunter, the flying roe and the timid deer, which, at times, he meets; the eagle, which, soaring high above the waters, watches for its prey, or having seized it, devours it upon a rocky pinnacle, — are objects far from being disturbing accessories in this picture of silence and repose, or from lessening the enjoyment of the solitude. — Amid highly cultivated landscapes imagination labors in vain to soar to a lofty pitch. Civilization which it meets on every side, weighs, as it were, like lead upon its wings. But in those still fresh and primeval spots the soul can bathe in the ocean of forests, rock upon the waves of the streams, and blend with nature in unfettered freedom.

Imagine a traveller wrapped in such feelings, when suddenly he hears a strange, hollow murmur, an awful tone, like far distant thunder, now returning, now ceasing. With beating heart he stops and listens, until suddenly, upon the wings of the breeze, borne from solitude to solitude, the solemn roar of „The Falls“ breaks upon his ear. It announces the end of his journey, toward which he speeds with winged feet.

That the reader may clearly comprehend the nature and causes of this grand spectacle. I will endeavour to describe the topographical features, to which it owes its existence.

The Interior of America north of the source of the Missisippi is an elevated plain, from which flow countless rivers. Those which run eastward, collect themselves in and around Canada in five broad basins, and form the largest lakes of the western Continent: — Lake Superior, Huron, Michigan, Erie and Ontario. They are connected with each other by the descending river, which, as it emerges from lake Ontario, takes the name of the St. Lawrence, whose waves, for a distance of more than seven hundred miles, roll majestically towards the Atlantic ocean. The channel that connects Lake Erie with Lake Ontario, [the latter lies about three hundred and fifty feet lower, than the former,] is called the Niagara. The neck of land between the two is a mountain-ridge, which, at first, inclines gently to the plain, but terminates in a rocky perpendicular wall from two to three hundred feet in height. Through this dam has the Niagara forced a passage, and its plunge over the wall into the plain below, in a width of nearly four thousand feet, forms, about fifteen miles from Fort Niagara, the most magnificent of all Cataracts in the known world*).

---

*) It is perfectly clear to the eye of the geologist that the Niagara-Falls have backed up all the way from Lake Ontario. The rocks are beds of sandstone, cracked in every direction. „The Falls“ must gradually (in the course of some thousands of years) recede to Lake Erie and disappear.

About a mile above the Falls the bed of the river inclines to such a degree, that, looking up the stream, the spectator seems to behold a mountain of water, which, with indescribable rapidity and force, urges its hundred thousand waves towards the yawning mouth of a deep abyss. But before reaching its verge, its waters are scattered in white spray, apparently as dense and lustrous as crystal. The water is divided into two falls, of unequal width, by a black, rocky Island, which, threatening to plunge down the precipice, bends its broad, wood-crowned head, far over the billowy chaos.

For a long while this island was thought to be inaccessible; but an attempt made many years ago to rescue some shipwrecked Indians, who had clambered upon the rock, and seemed destined to perish by starvation, led to the discovery that, on one side, the stream could be passed, and after indescribable labor, the garrison of Fort Niagara succeeded in driving iron posts into the rocky bed, from shore to shore, upon which a bridge was laid, and by this means they attained the object of their humane efforts. Afterwards this bridge was firmly secured, and it is now crossed without danger by those who wish to view the magnificent and fearful spectacle of the battling waves, from the height of a tower, erected in their very midst, upon the verge of the principal fall [Horse-Shoe-Falls]. Formerly dizzy stairs led down from the brow of the rock to a vaulted cavern, over which the waters plunge in a wide arch. A few years ago, however, the force of the flood tore away this portion of the island, [Table-Rock] and hurled it down into the abyss.

The mass of water which falls on the American side, arches itself like an enòrmous bow, at the instant when it thunders over the verge of the precipice, and then rolls downward like an avalanche, gleaming in the sunlight, with all the colors of the rainbow. The British Falls upon the Canadian side, by far the largest, descend perpendicularly into the chasm. For miles around the earth trembles with the recoil of the mighty torrent upon the bottom of the deep, whence it is hurled aloft in whirlpools of foam, which, soaring above the woods, resemble at a distance, pillars of smoke, as from burning cities. The wall of this glorious cataract is studded with gray rocky pinnacles which look forth from beneath the white veil of waves like fearful spectres, and with each moment seem to change their shape. Above and below the falls the banks are overgrown with hickory-trees and pines, robbed of their tops by age and storm, while on the right shore, stretching far into the land, stands the tall and majestic forest. Eagles and vultures, in search of prey, hover over the abyss, into which the billowy vortex draws, with irresistible might, every thing that ventures within its reach. At all seasons of the year the waves cast upon the shore, below the falls, numbers of dead deer, which have endeavored to swim the river above, but too weak to withstand the current, have been hurled down the precipice*).

The desire to see Nature's grandest Scenery in the New World, now leads annually more than a hundred thousand travellers to the Niagara. Towns and villages are springing up in the vicinity of the falls, while splendid hotels, furnished with every convenience, afford all the luxuries of civilized life. Turnpike-roads and railways traverse a Landscape, where forty years ago the guidance of an Indian was necessary through the trackless wilderness. The heights on both sides of the river are studded with the elegant country-seats and mansions of the opulent. On the American side a town is laid out, which promises to grow up to a splendid city, having for its environs a park, the grandeur of which defies all description.

---

*) I advise all people going to Niagara to suspend making a note in their Journal till the last day of their visit. You might as well teach a child the magnitude of the heavens by pointing to the sky with your finger as comprehend Niagara in a day. It has to create its own mighty place in your mind. You have no comparison through which it can enter. It is too vast. The imagination shrinks from it. It rolls in gradually, thunder upon thunder, and plunge upon plunge; and the mind labors with it to an exhaustion, such as is created only by the extremest intellectual effort. I have seen men sit and stare upon it in a cool day of autumn, with the perspiration standing on their fore-heads in large beads, from the unconscious but toilsome agony of its conception. After haunting its precipices, and looking on its solemn waters for days, sleeping with its howling monotony in your ears, dreaming and returning to it till it has grown the one object, as it will, of your perpetual thought, you feel, all at once, like one who has compassed the span of some almighty problem. It has stretched itself within you. Your capacity has attained the gigantic standard and you feel an elevation and breadth of nature, that could measure girth and stature of a seraph." — WILLIS.

THE TOWER OF LONDON.

„Rule Britannia!" The heart of every Briton beats proudly at these words, and every nerve in his frame echoes „Rule Britannia!" But if a Sybil should unlock the secrets of the future, a humiliating appendix would not be wanting. Signs speak. Most certainly England has passed the Acme of her power. The days of old age are coming, and America, her daughter and presumptive heiress', steps into the foreground. The young giantess whom England, as a mother, nursed, has become not only her peer, but the source of her apprehensions also; and when fear is once harbored by the leaders of an empire its fall has already commenced.

Nemesis has lifted the sword over England, visible to all. She will not restore it to the scabbard until she has completed the work of retribution. The day of judgment dawns, and it will be a trial such as has not yet been. Ireland, her natural sister, the child of woe clad in rags, arraigns the queen of the earth for an immeasurable debt of crime. In vain the latter purchases respite upon respite with her treasures. The treasures pass away, but the debt is not diminished. All is too late and all is useless. Neither does it avail that England, with selfish greediness, continues to grasp every thing that her long arm can reach. Ireland hangs upon her, as a dead, putrifying limb upon a living body; it taints her vital juices, and saps her full-flushed strength. England can never recover health. The causes of her slow decay are no longer to be removed; their action and reaction continue, and the final result can be no other than death and

The TOWER of LONDON

Published for HERRMANN J. MEYER 164 William-Street, NEW YORK.

That this catastrophe will come is certain, but the time thereof no man can determine. England's empire is so strong and firm a structure, its foundations are laid so deep and so enduring, its beams are so nicely fitted, that centuries, perhaps, may pass, before History writes its last page. What storms must rage in coming time, what tempests howl, what events stir the nations to their lowest depths, before the colossal edifice of British sway shall fall in ruins and the sentence of that tribunal which is now inditing its first summons, shall find its execution!

The Tower of London is the classic ground of British history. In its stately halls the Magna Charta was drawn up and confirmed by many kings. Stirring events of the past, intimately connected with the fortunes of the kingdom, had here their scene of action; — deeds of honour and of joy, of misfortune, of sorrow, and of crime.

When the star of Rome set in Britain, anarchy and confusion oppressed the forsaken land. The people were lacerated by civil war, and the feuds of the Nobles devoured their strength. The Anglo-Saxons, called from Germany by the vanquished parties, came to their aid, and in the disorder the guests made themselves the masters of the land. With the Saxon rule, a new aera dawned upon Britannia. The kingdom was reconstructed in all its parts upon the principles of ancient German freedom. The rights of the people were completely secured and guaranteed by their share in the legislation. The Saxon empire continued to flourish for four hundred years, and in Alfred the Great the world beheld one of the most enlightened of princes, whose wise institutions, in part, continue operative even at the present day. In the tenth century, the sword of foreign conquest once more triumphed over England. The masters became servants, the Saxons were made the serfs of the Normans. Their duke William, as king of England, declared the liberties of the Saxons forfeited, put down their law and overburdened them with duties and services as men who were to be held down with an iron hand. He declared himself the sole proprietor of the entire soil of England. He divided it into sixty thousand fiefs, which, after having reserved fourteen hundred as domains of the crown, he bestowed upon his Norman knights and on those Saxons, who had voluntarily submitted, or who had won his favor by their servility. Thus sprung up the British Crown-fiefs, and their possessors, originally about eight thousand, composed the feudal nobility of England, which, in various gradations of rank, rose from the baron to the duke. The principal obligation of this new-born aristocracy was military service. Bound, at the crown's command, to raise sixty thousand horsemen, this powerful institution of defence augmented the dignity of Royalty, and increased the strength of the empire. Yet the Norman conquerors, dispersed as landed proprietors over all England, proved, in the course of time, too weak to maintain their ascendency against the powerfully developed nationality of the Saxons. Before the elapse of two centuries after the conquest, the Saxons had regained the upper hand, and the greater portion of the fiefs fell, partly by the favor of the crown, partly by marriage or purchase, into Saxon hands. In the year 1215 England obtained from the crown its patent of freedom, the Magna Charta. By this charter Saxon liberties and Saxon laws were restored, and institutions which had been wrecked in the storms of the Conquest, emerged again into light and life. The reestablishment of Saxon vitality became complete when the old Norman nobility, with the exception of a few families, had perished in the wars of the two Roses. The despotic Henry VIII. crushed the last remnant of the feudal pride of the Norman barons. At the same time he weakened the power of the Pope by favouring the Reformation and by the suppression of monasteries and religious Orders. The crafty tyrant gave the greater part of the immense property, which he confiscated, to the protestant clergy, who erected the structure of the English church upon the ruins of Catholicism.

The middle-classes in the cities and towns had gradually risen to importance and power. In the party-wars of the two Roses the city of London had more than once decided the issue. In return the valiant burghers obtained those privileges which raised the corporation of that community almost to a state of independence. Other cities followed the example of the capital, and availed themselves of every opportunity to enlarge their liberties at the expense of the crown and the nobility. Such corporations obtained the right, in the persons of their delegates, to sit in the chamber of representatives with the barons. In later times they established a distinct house of their own — the House of Commons, which, by degrees, secured to itself the initiative in legislation. Thus the aristocratic element found its counterpoise, and Democracy stepped forth as a legal power in the Constitution. The old Saxon right had now shaken off the last chains of foreign oppression. At a still later period, stirred to its very depths by the tempest of religious war, the Spirit of Freedom broke through all bounds when Charles I., by treacherous and ill-timed measures, roused the people to resistance. England shook off the yoke of monarchy in disgust and became a republic. A daring experiment! It started into life with Oliver Cromwell, and with this great man it died again after having sent the criminal-king to the block. The restoration of monarchy brought back the Stuarts; not the public peace. That ill-fated race was then to England what the Bourbons are now to France: and not until the Stuarts were expelled, and the nation succeeded in a compromise with the new dynasty, by the Declaration of Rights, which completed and enlarged the Magna Charta, did the crater of the Revolution close. These two compacts compose the Constitution, in which the greatness of the English people has its foundation. This Constitution has justly been an object of admiration to all nations. It has outlived six centuries, and what a proud structure has it supported! Its like is not to be found upon the wide globe, and if the wonderfully growing power of North America is gradually casting it into shade, yet it should never be forgotten that England is the mother, and that, without the mothers constitutional freedom, the glorious liberty of the daughter would not exist. —

In the British Constitution, whose vital power, in spite of its age, is not exhausted, the three gradually developed elements of the government appear balanced with care and wisdom. Monarchy is the centre. But the British monarchy is only a name for the *government of laws*. They bind the Executive to the very letter, and with their bearing the people are most profoundly penetrated. Royalty, supported by the national church, is controlled, in the first place, by the inherited power of all the wealth and dignity in the nation — the *House of Lords*; in the second place, by the national intelligence and industry assembled in the *House of Commons*; and over all watches *Public Opinion*, which is powerful, in proportion as it is independent, honored, in proportion as it is deserving of honor: for the free press ceases to be esteemed by the people of England, so soon as it indulges in passion, insolence and license, to do which, however, it has entire liberty. Shall we not admire a people like this, upon whom, in the enjoyment of perfect freedom, the law acts like an enchanter, and penetrates all ranks from the king's son to the pauper? I saw one day the king's brother descend from his carriage in the public street during a shower of rain and follow the officer, who arrested him for a forgotten debt of five shillings sterling, which he owed to a day-laborer; and another day I saw a crowd of ten thousand men disperse and retire before the blue staff of a constable, — men, who, a moment previously, had uttered a vote of censure against certain measures of the government, and whom the discourses of popular orators seemed to have excited to the highest pitch. Admirable people, in which, though divided into a hundred sects, all honest men agree in the belief, that *Religion* is the corner-stone of all vitality in the state and of all legislation, the consecration of each worldly endeavor, the source of all that is good and venerable in man! Even in their aristocracy the British people might yet find an element of freedom. The British aristocracy is a body in which worth, splendor and dignity balances the splendor and dignity of monarchy, a body adorned with historical reminiscences, girt with the fame and honor of England, and in which noble pride, independeuce of thought and firm self-reliance find their constant expression.

Guided by liberty and wisdom, and controlled by public opinion, the *Magna Charta* written down six centuries ago in the Tower, has advanced in steady developement until the present day, and even the storms of the Revolution have ventured against it no deed of violence. The constitution is looked upon by the Britons as a sacred compact, not to be dissolved at the pleasure of either party, a compact concluded between past and future generations, the great compact of all compacts, the source of all particular agreements, a sacred trust confided to the nation inherited from their fathers, and to be transmitted unimpaired to their children.

And with this venerable, vigorous, developing constitution has England attained her unparalleled greatness. A state has grown up surpassing in extent more than four times that of Alexander or that of Rome, ruling over a population of twohundred millions, swaying empires in all quarters of the globe, and covering all seas with proud fleets. The constitution is for England a coat of mail, in which the nation has defied and baffled the most terrible assaults and the greatest dangers. Revolt and emancipation of the most important colonies, a thirty years war with the rival powers of Europe and with the greatest hero of modern times, the exclusion of the British trade from the Continent, the immense destruction of property, the maintenance of numerous armies, the dangerous insurrections in India and Ireland, years of scarcity and offamine, disturbances in the manufacturing districts called forth by the despair of hundred thousands of men crying for labor — all these dreadful crises have passed away without lasting damage to the state. Under the discipline of the constitution, the British national character has acquired that stamp of firmness, boldness and security, that proud self-consciousness which nothing can bend and that steadfastness and perseverance, which is the envy of other nations. „Every English cabin-boy sailing round the globe, knows that, should foreign authority venture to touch a hair of his head, his government would not hesitate to procure him perfect satisfaction, either by negotiation or by force“. These words of Canning's, uttered in parliament, are words which every Briton bears in his heart; they stand written upon his proud brow, they are his passport of safety in every corner of the earth. This feeling of security ennobles his enterprising spirit, and makes all portions of the world, which his sword and trident have not subdued, tributary to his commerce and industry.

But alas! at this glorious tree worms are gnawing, and destruction peeps forth from countless buds. Within the last twenty or thirty years, the British aristocracy has been undergoing a transformation which seriously threatens to impair its worth and dignity. It rots, as it were, in the exuberance of its vital juices, it is becoming inactive, proud, supercilious, presumptuous, common place; it brings itself more and more in hostile collision with the middle classes, it is separating itself from the people. The clergy of the State-Church are likewise on the decline. Estranged from their former position and forgetful of their high calling, they become daily more and more entangled in the affairs of the world. They are drawn down into the life of political faction, and becoming prosaical and profane, paying a blind homage to hypocrisy in matters of faith, they present the aspect of a priesthood more despised than respected. British Science, enslaved by the church, is weakened in her creative powers, and, with a few exceptions, has of late brought forth little for the advancement of civilization. The universities are stagnating in pedantry; their learning has become insipid, stationary, dead, mechanical. Legislation is on the decline. It heaps up its acts mountain high — mass upon mass — so that no man can longer see through the chaos of countless contradictions, in which pettifogging lawyers can ensnare the clearest rights, or defend themselves against them. Even the middle classes are slowly degenerating to the worse. They are no longer that compact mass, full of honesty and strength, with a sense of independence in every bosom. Since Capital masters Industry, since manufacture by machinery, upon a gigantic scale, occupies the place of human skill and independant labor, the heartless class of mill-owners has sprung up, who, each in his sphere, exercises a more oppressive tyranny over thousands than that of the knights in feudal times over their serfs. The artizans have, for the most part, been rendered subject to the manufacturing capitalist of the present age, and the relation between master and apprentice, once so respectable, has changed and deteriorated into that of principal and servant: — a band destitute of moral check, which has no other aim than that of private advantage. It brings both parties into endless contention and perpetual strife, in which craft and deception play their revolting parts. A long peace and the inconsiderate habits of the labouring classes continue to favor the increase of population, and, at the same time Invention and Science endeavor to render human hands less necessary by the Automatons of Mechanism, which, are becoming more and more the masters in the workshop. Of the soil of the land, the property of the aristocracy, every spot, capable of culture, has long ago found its cultivator, and as industry and trade gradually weaken by the competition of other nations, and are more and more unable to receive and employ all those who desire labor, a fearful enemy is growing up to society, an enemy who is becoming more menacing and more terrible every day. It is Pauperism. Pauperism is not only recruiting among the millions of the manufacturing districts, but also among that numerous class of small farmers, whom the aristocracy, since they have discovered the secret of obtaining greater rents by the selfmanagement of their estates, yearly drive by thousands from the soil which their fathers and grandfathers have tilled and cultivated. As the aristocracy of the soil works thus to the increase of pauperism, so does the aristocracy of capital, those men, who without subjecting themselves to any kind of labor, make their money work for them in the national debt. These lazy people have but one interest in the state, viz: that the interest of the public funds should be regularly paid, and their greatest anxiety is, lest this should fail to be the case. They are therefore opposed to every improvement that requires an expenditure of public money, to every grand, but expensive national undertaking, and they form a phalanx against the government, so soon as it appears inclined to engage in enterprises, which advance a claim, in any manner, upon the national treasury, and thus prejudice their interest in the state: — the paymens of the interest of the national debt. For this reason the plan for transforming the paupers into agricultural colonists and landed proprietors, by means of emigration to Canada and Australia at the public charge, often as it has been agitated and recommended by statesmen as a radical cure for pauperism, has never been adopted; for the fifty millions Sterling, necessary to its execution, could not be raised by the Government without creating apprehension among the stock-holders. This influential class of men, is always a ready advocate of every hard measure, of every tax which oppresses and exhausts the people, provided external and internal peace be preserved and the public revenue secured requisite for the payment of their rents.

The old saying proves true: „only the man who works for the people, and with the people has a heart for the people.“ The British stock-holders, who, by the permanent increase of the national debt, are continually growing more numerous and powerful, that class, which already thrust one half of the revenues of the kingdom into their pockets, will always judge of the welfare of the state, solely according to the price of Stocks. The more there is exacted from the people, the greater the amount of the national revenues, so much the more contented do they feel, and their own comfort is, according to their views, identical with the happiness of the state. „L'etat c'est moi“ says the capitalist of England at the present day with as much truth as a Louis XIV. said it in France.

Pauperism, this demon of our days, which, like the spirit of vengeance and retribution, stalks abroad in the old monarchical state-structures of Europe, is, as it were, a people grown up without doors. It no where finds a chamber left for it, for every room in the state was bestowed and occupied long before its birth. In the domain of rights it finds no right, for the old Constitution of England could not provide for that which was not yet in existence. Pauperism is the foundling of our epoch, abjured and abandoned by father and mother. Bare of rights as it is, so much the more resolutely does it advance its claims to an equality of privilege, and clamorously demands admission to the great compact of the nation. British pauperism, generated by the heartless oppression of Capital and landed Property, a slave to demoralization and given up to the rudest animal passions, is a terrible power, a power which is increasing in a fearful degree, and presses onward to a social revolution even more irresistably than the proletariat of France and Germany; for in England the contrasts stand out more abruptly and irreconcileably. The most haughty, colossal wealth confronts the destitution and misery of the masses with more insolence, mercilessness and defiance than elsewhere, and fills the popular mind with unbounded bitterness. The landed Aristocracy allied to the tyrant Capital, alarmed by the pressure of the poor, concentrate their strength in that Oligarchy, which, under the party-names of Tories and Whigs, govern the land alternately. They are never at a loss as to the means for the preservation of their power; they oppose to the assaulting masses the rampart of the law, of the standing army and of all the various other instruments of state-power. As the demands of the poor rise, so does their obstinacy in resistance rise. Aristocracy and Capital are now sacrificing — and this *must* lead to a rupture, and render a catastrophe unavoidable — to the principle of *conservatism* even the principle of *improvement*. By this means the organic developement of British state-vitality is checked, and stagnation has stepped into its place. It is evident to all, that in such a condition, a state cannot remain, in which a power so fresh and mighty as that of British pauperism stirs and works without intermission. A social revolution, which will upturn all things, will as surely come in England, as it will come in France and Germany. Toryism, which is again at the head of affairs, will hasten the catastrophe; the explosion will shake the world, and the demolished structure will cover the earth with its ruins. As the crisis draws nearer to its climax, the stadia grow shorter, and such is the feverish state of things at present, that the poor and pennyless majority need but a few bold, able chiefs to bring on the mighty outbreak, and with it to call forth a contest, which, though it be many times repressed, will not end until the grandest and most admirable work of human wisdom, a work for whose formation a thousand years were necessary, has disappeared from the earth.

From the preparations for this mortal strife of the elements of British Society, the eye turns back to that quiet, peaceful picture, the cradle of all this menaced greatness and splendor, the starting-point of my reflections.

The Tower of London was the residence of the kings of England for some centuries after the Norman conquest. The palace proper, the so called White Tower, is that lofty quadrangle with the four flanking turrets. It was built by William the Conqueror, in the year 1078, upon the spot where once stood the castle of the Roman governors, and a very aged structure is still standing, which bears the traditional name of Caesar's Tower. The Tower stands at the eastern extremity of the city proper, separated from the Thames by a narrow rampart. It is surrounded with walls, bastions and a deep moat, which receives water from the river by a canal. Besides the old palace it contains a barrack for the garrison, and the dwellings of the numerous functionaries. These buildings form a couple of short and narrow streets. The shape of the ground-plan is round; its diameter is about 1100 feet, its circumference nearly a mile. The little garrison whose number can never be augmented without leave of the city-council, is changed daily. More numerous than the soldiers are the cannons and mortars which from the loop-holes of the walls, and from the bastions, point their black mouths against the city and the harbor. Upon the terrace fronting the Thames stand sixty pieces of large calibre. „They are good old fellows who will do nobody any harm“, says the London burgher, and, in truth, for three centuries, amid all the popular insurrections and tumults, they have announced only the births of princes and princesses, or roared at coronations, or accompanied toasts at national festivals. In England the people are not without ceremony regaled with grapeshot, as are the people at Paris, Berlin, Vienna, or Munich, when they are rioting. During my stay in London in the year 1817 I saw the democrat Hunt march with two hundred thousand of his men through the streets of the city, groaning before the palaces of the ministers and breaking their windows. The barrack-gates were closed, the ministers paid for the broken glass, and not a soldier was to be seen; on the following day no one even spoke of the matter; it was thought a thing of course and — forgotten. I was present when the then all-powerful Lord Castlereagh accidentally met a public meeting of democrats. I saw them take the horses from his carriage, and amid the „hellish laughter“ of the countless crowd, raise him upon a hogshead, which stood upon an overturned cart, opposite to Hunt, their leader, that he might make a speech — and the prime minister, with the star upon his breast, complied with a smiling face. While he spoke he received a shower of foul oranges from the mob with more coolness than the Lind receives bouquets and wreaths of flowers. And when he had spoken, he listened firmly, calmly, and with folded arms, to the reply of his radical opponent, who, a blackguard, stood opposite to him upon a cask, and, with clutched fist, gesticulated towards him like a champion of the ring. The minister replied and then retired amidst the cheers of the meeting. Not a word was heard of sabring and cannonading, of imprisoning, of indictments and courts of law. The same evening I heard Lord Castlereagh in parliament, and he spoke as calmly as if he had come from the privy-council. On the following morning Castlereagh, „the mob-orator,“ was seen „selling for a penny“ in all the caricature-shops of London; the people laughed, and the affair was forgotten.

The Tower has for several centuries ceased to be the residence of royalty. The halls and chambers of the palace serve now only as a military magazine; the stock of arms stored here is sufficient to equip a quarter of a million of soldiers. In a single chamber, formerly the banqueting-hall, which is 345 feet in length,' weapons are stacked that would arm 150,000 men. Other halls contain the trophies of British victories in all quarters of the globe, and in every time; in one is preserved the armor of the English kings and generals from Edward I. (1272) down to James II. (1685). The true „Lion“ of the Tower, however, is the Jewel Office, where the regia insignia are preserved, and shown to all who wish to see them. It is a dark vault, to which lead narrow passages, secured with strong iron gates and constantly guarded. These are closed behind every visitor. The jewel office itself is brightly illuminated, but divided in the middle by a strong network of iron wire, behind which stand the guards, who exhibit to the spectator without the sparkling tinsel of monarchy, as it lies in compartments upon tables covered with velvet. There may be seen the golden rods of chastisement for the people; imperial globes, sceptres, and golden spurs by dozens, crowns in heaps, together with imperial swords sufficient to arm a company of the militia. No lack is there of golden table furniture, salt-cellars, chalices, boxes for the holy wafers, and even the emerald bowl for the holy oil is not missing, with which the King or Queen „by the grace of God“ is anointed. Nowhere in the world is there to be seen such a treasure of costly stones as here. In the light of the tapers they shine in all colors; of course not with half the beauty, in which, on a clear, cold Christmas morning, the new-fallen snow sparkles in the rays of the rising sun. It is useless to say, the diamonds in the crowns of Royalty will last longer than those of the frozen water; for did they last even a thousand of years, what are these but seconds upon the dial-plate of Eternity? Quite as glorious, and, it may be, more glorious, were the regal treasures of Cyrus, of Alexander, of the Assyrian and Egyptian rulers; and where are they now? They have disappeared with their empires and their palaces, and nothing remains but the gravemounds of their cities, and a few withered leaves in the book of History. — A time will come too, when those jewels will be broken from the crowns of the British empire, those sceptres and globes find their way into the crucible, and when goats will graze upon the ruins of the Tower of London, and herdsmen sing strains in languages yet unknown.

HOHENASBERG

Publish'd for HERRMANN J. MEYER, 164 William Street NEW YORK

THE HOHENASBERG.

Near Ludwigsburg, in the kingdom of Wurtemburg, upon the of top an isolated mountain, that steeply towers from the plain to the height of about 700 feet, stands a strong castle, called Hohenasberg, once the cradle of a long forgotten race of counts, to whom it gave its name. Records of this castle date as early as the tenth century; in later times, it came into the possession of the counts of Tubingen, and the first duke of Wurtemberg enlarged and adorned it for a princely dwelling. It was this great and good prince who used to say — „I can lay my head in the lap of the poorest Wurtemberger and sleep quietly“ and who once remarked to his ministers — „If my rule has been hard and unjust to any of my subjects, that man shall step forward and be fully indemnified out of my private property and if my God and Creator be not content with this — He may inflict punishment on my soul and body“. — Then and now: what a contrast! If the millions of sighs of the wretched, which, from the dungeons of the Hohenasberg, ascend to heaven, if all the tears of silent sorrow and deep woe which have been shed there, should descend as a deluge, to sweep Cruelty from off the face of the earth: — where could it look for rescue? where could it find compassion? — The celebrated poet Schubarth, who edited a journal for the instruction of the people, was imprisoned, and made dumb and silent upon this mountain, seventy years ago; and at present instead of this one, seven editors of popular, liberal journals are confined there, and say their prayers so much the nearer the stars. How strangely sounds this „Da Capo!" after an interval of seventy years! Even the Almighty's thunder has not awakened the crowned sleepers to humanity and reason, and the bolts of the revolution have fallen near them in vain.

Well, well, sleep on, you kings and dream your last dream! —

Demoralization is the curse of mankind, corruption penetrates all classes, and this most melancholy phenomenon in our disgraceful time is calculated to fill the minds of the weaker patriots with discouragement, the hearts of the stronger with disgust. Yet it should not perplex any body. The same has happened before this and within our lifetime. To the yoke of the Corsican conqueror and his Confederation of the Rhine, succeeded the uprising and triumph of the German nation from 1813—15; to the Carlsbad decrees, the quaking of Absolutism in the year —30; to the later oppression of the people and persecution of the patriots, the revolution of—48. The result of the prohibition of the German colors by the German diet was the planting of the three colored standard upon the palace of the princely union itself, and the fettering of public opinion ended in the famous decree: „the German press shall be free for ever!" Thrice was I an eyewitness of the ebb and flow in the affairs of Germany; thrice have I seen the waves of freedom and of servitude alternate; thrice have the people rent their chains, and thrice have they again been manacled. — Is all ended with this „thrice?" Will the nation die in her new fetters, or will she burst them once more? The conviction stands firm in my soul, that the subjugation of the German people, as it is planned by absolute Monarchy, will never be successful. Absolutism may attempt it, it may resolve to try to choke the stream up to its very source — but it will be all in vain! Though true greatness is not to be found in this age of exhaustion, yet the champions of Tyranny are the feeblest of all. The popular aversion is too general, too vivid. Princely absolutism cannot effect its object. The rulers are preparing their own destruction. The people was surely very stupid to attempt a half-revolution which forced Authority into the opposite path. But the material for resistance is losing no strength by oppression, and the decomposing elements have thereby rather gained than lost in efficacy. I can never believe that bare Absolutism is to be the end of the stirring of so many nations. Even the present dissolution of the old parties is not death, but rather the herald of new life. It is evident that the spirit of future society can not suit the old forms, and that it cannot be contented with the old party ideas. New wine requires new bottles. The democracy of —48; the constitutionalism of —49, the reaction of —50 and of —51 are agents that wear themselves out entirely, and all the men of moderate or feeble capacity, who represent those parties, are already so completely ruined in public opinion, that, if they should venture upon the stage of the future, they would most certainly be hissed from it. There is no fear of the permanent sway of Reaction in Europe. As the temporary holder of material force, it can lay claim to a certain respect so far only, as it is vivified by intellectual greatness. But its actors are fortunately mere pygmies and in the whole company, with all their craft and trickery, there is not enough sound common sense, to know that the dead may be galvanized, but not restored to life. I repeat, the cause of Tyranny has no chance; it is a hopeless cause. The cause of the People, on the contrary will be lost only then, if the nations themselves should abandon it; and yet, even then the cause of Humanity would not be ruined, for this is guided by God. The reconstruction of society however — that problem to be solved by the future — is the cause of Humanity.

Germany, it is true, has never before seen days of greater humiliation. The enormity, the wretchedness, the cowardice, the destructiveness, the wickedness of Napoleon's Confederation of the Rhine, when we consider the mental and political greatness of the conqueror, was in its day not so contemptible as that policy of the present, which does not blush to call on a barbarian autocrat as an umpire in the affairs of Germany, and to send German statesmen to Petersburgh or Warsaw to fetch the wisdom of the modern Pythia with mustachios and knout. Upon the heels of these shameful doings punishment will follow so closely, that, ere long, that path will be forsaken. But whether this happen sooner or later, it is always a subject of regret, that, even but for a short time, Russian maxims of state-policy, so hostile to humanity, should have been permitted to exert influence in Germany. Destiny will avenge the fact and history will pronounce its sentence.

What have the German patriots to do in the present condition of the country?

I answer: Look up to the starry firmament — the world of the Future; and look down into the past — the world of Experience: it is written in both. What the patriot ought to do, each one should know; for, what was coming, each one saw long in advance. It strikes no one unprepared, no one unexpectedly. And the end is concealed to none. The calm eye of the observer following the furious progress of Reaction, clearly sees its grave — the abyss! The path into which it has turned, with its heavily laden carriage, is so steep in its descent, that no power now can hold it back, and rescue the driver and the passengers. Avenging destiny has grown stronger than all human might. And if, in patriotic self-sacrifice, we should cast our bodies before the down-rushing wheels, we could not check their course; they would pass, crushing, over us, as the car of the Jaggernaut-Idol over the victims of fanaticism.

Tyranny is hurrying to a catastrophe, which will engulf it, and the catastrophe must be awaited as something unavoidable. Its final outbreak will call all true patriots upon the stage. Not until then, when the fire blazes up in a thousand quarters, and the fuel, heaped high as heaven, bursts forth into flames, and a general conflagration threatens to devour, with all that is evil, all that is good, with the tinsel, the treasures, with absolutism, the dearest privileges acquired by centuries of civilization: — I say, when it would plunge Arts and Science with the bearers of their honors, and all men in high stations, without distinction and without trial, into one common grave: — then, resolved to risk our life in the defence of what we deem holy, we must cast ourselves, boldly and calmly, against the wild powers of desolation. The pledge of victory must be our unity. And a more glorious and righteous league, the earth will not have seen!

It is this purpose which is to be aimed at by all patriots, firmly maintained, and widely spread abroad. Upon its realisation hangs the fate of Germany and of Society in general.

How great or how small the number be of those who bear within their bosoms sufficient courage and self-devotion in the decisive moment to venture, resolutely and joyfully, upon the attempt to still the billows of destruction, and after sufferings and oppressions without equal, to rescue our unhappy country from the ruin of Anarchy: — this enters not now into the question. Great social catastrophes have always begotten great men. Single as they now stand, the faithful and true, they will not remain single when the hour of danger has struck. At present it is their urgent calling, to fill the vocation as teachers of the nation, to bring it, calmly and dispassionately, to a clear comprehension of its situation, to strengthen it in the belief of the justice of God, to foster a sense of right and honor, to keep it awake to the greatness and independence of Germany, to point out coming and unavoidable dangers, to loosen, with a gentle hand, the bands of hereditary prejudices and antipathies, to combat individual selfishness by instruction, to elevate the minds to a sense of the general good, and thus to scatter the seeds for the nation's regeneration upon the principles of universal humanity. It is for them to collect and to carry to the building-ground stones for the future structure, while Despotism, blinded by a conceit of the durability of his house, with his own hands tears up the foundation, upon which it stands. And of the means alluded to for successful action in these sinister and frightful times, the hardest measures of leagued Tyrants cannot entirely deprive the patriots.

Thus then, let us labor, friends to humanity! so long indeed, as any room for labor remains. Divested of passion, blending moral earnestness with mental dignity, our aim and our instruction must unceasingly be directed to the civil, religious, and moral elevation of the people. There is no danger in the despotism of the rulers, for it is suicidal. But there is great danger in the ignominous state of the people. To rescue the Fatherland from a despotical sway and to rescue its Freedom: — we must in the beginning rescue the nation from the fetters of ignorance, rudeness and dishonour.

FINGAL'S CAVE in IRELAND

THE ISLANDS OF IONA AND STAFFA. THE CAVE OF FINGAL.

In the immeasurable space of the universe, man appears to himself like a May-fly, sporting in the evening-sun over the stream of eternity. The huge globe itself seems but a leaf in the forest, which buds, unfolds, fades, falls, and perishes. But a deeper contemplation convinces us, that nothing is dead in God's creation. All that appears to the corporeal eye as perishing or lifeless, is, in fact, but another state of existence, and every form, the dew-drop as well as the ocean, the valley as well as the hill, the thundering cataract as well as the flaming volcano — all, from the smallest mote in the sun-beam up to the milky way, — that sphere which embraces the life of millions of suns — count back infinite generations of change, since the moment when the Almighty uttered the creative word for his universe. An infinite consolatiou lies concealed in this thought. It is the surest warrant of our immortality.

Therefore Nature, in all her forms, is sacred to every man of sense, and never are we happier, than, when removed from the busy crowd and its weary cares, we ascend the summit of a mountain, or take a walk in the silent forest that girds its base. There, in the midst of a life, which kindly welcomes each visitor that brings with him a feeling heart, we behold in every blade of grass, in every shrub, in every tree, in every worm that crawls across our path, in the towering rock and in the tumbling brook, in the low, green mound, as in the blue- clad mountain-ridge near the horizon, a life full of beauty and full of love. Every flower and every insect reflects the benign form of that glorious Being whom all creatures name and extol as their Father.

Such happiness is seldom my lot. But why grope in the labyrinth of my own sorrows? the rehearsal would but weary the reader. Rise, eternal soul! lift thyself from the clod, to which thy body is chained down, soar above the mountains, beneath which rage the storms of life; for thou shalt now tell us of the island of the Poet who, two thousand years ago, thrilled the hearts of nations.

Far away in the Atlantic ocean, near the coast of western Scotland, are situated the islands of the Hebrides, the Ultima Thule of the ancient geographers, beaten for ages by the foaming billows of the sea, and by unbridled tempests. To this group belong two small isles, called Iona and Staffa. They tower aloft above the rest, like great men above their humbler brethren.

Iona and Staffa are the sanctuary of the fables and myths of the north. Upon their pinnacles Ossian sung his immortal songs, the Druids taught their wisdom and the Celtic gods had their altars. The holiest traditions of the people being there centered, the customs and language of the ancient celtic race were there preserved in their utmost purity. Iona, er Icolmkill, was once, in the western world, the sun which shed light in a wide circle of darkness and of barbarism; Religion, leagued with Science, was here cultivated long before the Roman legions planted their eagles upon Scotlands frontiers. Iona was the common burial-place of the kings of northern and western Europe, for to those interred in the sacred ground, a devout faith promised preservation in the day of general destruction. Upon the grave-stones remaining, are the names of sixty four kings of Scotland, France, Ireland and Norway, carved in Runic characters, legible still, and many more have been defaced by time. In one grave of unusually large dimensions an entire race of kings was interred. We tread with every step upon the dust of crowned heads, on the fragments of monuments erected to the great men of extinct nations, of heroes and bards once honored and adored, of whom posterity has not even recorded the names. Iona was filled with the places of druidic worship. On the site of the chief temple the first Christians built, in the sixth century, a chapel, whose ruins still exist. They are, as it were, the link which connects Pagan with Christian antiquity, for the priest of the true faith made of the great pagan God a saint, and dedicated to him the new church. And not in St. Odin's (Ovan's) chapel alone, do we behold the types of pagan worship strangely mixed with those of the christians; many more monuments confirm this fact; several basreliefs for instance, upon which are scenes from Biblical history by the side of representations of Odin's sacrifices, and the cross is carved upon an altar that is covered with pagan symbols. The present inhabitants of the island, probably the direct descendants of the old Druid race, support themselves by rearing flocks of sheep, and catching the sea-birds, which hover, in countless numbers about the rocky coast. A clergyman comes, once every year, across from Mull, to preach the gospel, to baptise, to join in wedlock, and to bless the graves of the departed. The youth grow up, from generation to generation, without instruction, and the renowned seat ot Druidical learning, is, at the present day, an abode of ignorance: — a bad testimony surely for this age of improvement and general education.

Staffa, the sister island, is not inhabited. Its natural wonders, however, bring crowds of travellers every summer to the lonely rock. Speculation has in vain attempted to rear a hotel for the convenience of visitors. Twice the buildings were completed, but as often the wintry

Atlantic blasts swept them away, and hurled their ruins into the ocean. Staffa rises perpendicularly out of the sea to the height of one hundred and forty feet. It is the summit of an extinct volcano, from whose sides those streams of lava rushed into the flood, to which we owe the most wonderful basaltic formation that can be found upon the earth. The entire southern façade of the island, in a breadth of almost half a mile, resembles a fairy palace of indescribable majesty. In various places the pillars are built, as it were, in stories, rising one upon another; in others they form projecting portals, in others wide gates, along whose inner sides stretch rows of pillars, and whose roofs are tessellated as regularly, as if by the hands of an architect. Numerous as are the caverns already known, yet new ones are found every year, and it is probable that the whole interior of the island is filled with them. Fingal's Cave is the most splendid and celebrated of all. Situated on the western shore of the island, the ocean guards, as it were, with jealousy, this wonderful work of the Creator. It is only during a fresh west-wind possible to approach it, owing to the dangerous currents and the terrible breakers. It often happens that crowds of tourists wait for weeks for the favorable moment and nevertheless in vain. I myself experienced this misfortune; and I must therefore let a friend speak in my place in the following description. — „Our little Steamer started off with a favorable western breeze in the morning. The weather was beautiful. At noon we approached the island, which majestically started from the deep, crowned with the most magnificent colonnade in the world, and its top encircled with a halo of the sun's glorious light. In the colonnades the gradation of hues, from the deepest shadow to the brightest silvery tints was indescribable. The steamer dashed through the breakers; when about a hundred fathoms distant, sideward from the Cave, it stopped. Each hastened to be the first in the boat that was lowered into the water. A few moments of anxious expectation (for the waves dashed over us at each hard pull of the oars) brought us to the entrance of the cave of Fingal. Our anticipations of the splendor of the spectacle had been great; but they sank into nothing. What mortal can describe it! Poetry herself is insufficient and prose is indeed too feeble. On either hand, lofty pillars, fifty feet in height, stretch onward to a distance that the eye cannot measure. Between these a colossal porch, one hundred and seventeen feet in height and forty in width, forms the entrance to the cave. The ground is uneven; the tops of the basaltic pillars that compose it, give it however, the appearance of the finest tesselated work. Column upon column of shining, black basalt, stand in rows along the sides of the porch. The waves dash far into the cavern, and the dazzling white foam dances up along the walls like spectral shapes. The entire length of this natural temple is three hundred and seventy feet. Three lofty clustered columns support a roof that rivals the proudest domes in the world. The forms and proportions of this work are entirely original; and the whole is in the sublimest harmony. Farther onward the ground descends, the waves completely cover it, with the exception of some stumps of pillars, upon which, with great toil indeed, one can step onward to the very end. Such an attempt, which is not entirely devoid of danger, has something terrific in it. On either hand roar the breakers in the black abyss; no where is there a support to grasp at. The greater number of our company tried, but returned intimidated. Following the example of the most courageous, I removed my shoes, that I might proceed more safely upon the slippery fragments of pillars, and, with beating hearts, we reached in safety the extremity of the cavern, the spot where are heard those mysterious symphonies, which have rendered Fingal's Cave so renowned. We listened in breathless silence, and, for a long time in vain, until, at last, we heard, distinctly, the unearthly music, — at first softly, then swelling to grander volumes of tone, at last to the rolling of thunder, that made us all turn pale and tremble. These transitions depend upon the manner in which the acoustic fibres of the structure are touched by the waves, as they dash and break against the walls of basalt. In several places of this glorious temple, men, former visitors, have carved unknown names. We could not but smile upon these childish efforts of vanity and continued to listen in awful silence to the of song of the foaming waves. How overwhelming must be these hymns to the eternal God in a night of tempest, when the mountain-billows of the angry ocean kiss the gable of the gigantic porch, and the surf bathes the tessellated vault! This music is destined for the ear of the Almighty alone. No mortal has ever heard it, for in tempestious weather it is impossible for man to approach the Cave of Fingal. —

The ROYAL EXCHANGE

LONDON

THE LONDON EXCHANGE.

Change is the stamp of time and men. Every epoch has its own Idol and its own miracles. Those temples, hewn in the mountain's gloom, those colossal pillars at their feet, those sphinxes, stammering in hieroglyphs, those pyramids and obelisks, towering to the sun, Balbec, with her colonnades, the splendor of Susa and Babylon, Hellas' light lofty temples, Rome's triumphal arches, and the imposing cathedrals of the Middle ages — all are speaking witnesses of the ideas which prevailed in their several epochs. Our age also shows much that is great and will be admired in times to come; but its Idol is of a peculiar stamp. One might say it is the Judas among the Gods. It is the paymaster, that is skilled in the management of his affairs, that knows how to reckon, that heaps interest upon interest. Man's endeavors are now, for the most part, directed to the Profitable, and his powers of activity are turned chiefly to Gain. Making money is the cry of the world. The arts and sciences perform the service of handmaids to this Idol, light him down into the bowels of the earth, level mountains, fill vallies, and assist to advance the gigantic shapes of his dreams to the light of reality.

The old favorite of that Idol is Britannia. Planting one foot upon her national soil, the other in the midst of the ocean, she bears her head aloft, above all the other kingdoms of the old world. Mightier than Rome, and wealthier than Carthage, she calls half the earth her own, nor is the other half able to escape her influence. In Liberty, she guards her golden fleece, in Industry, she protects the basis of her greatness, and Commerce is the breath of her nostrils.

Rome required eight hundred years to complete the conquest of the world with the sword alone. By Trade and Industry England has effected more in three centuries. Similar means lead to similar ends. — America has copied her example, and the world views the result with astonishment.

The hour has not yet struck; but it will certainly arrive, when America's glorious republic will enter into possession of all the immeasurable advantages which the British empire owes to her flourishing manufactures and commerce. Let her beware, however, how she seeks these upon a false path! It is not the spirit of enterprise, it is not foresight, it is not activity, it is not the power of money and political strength, which has given the preponderance to England's manufactures and traffic; but rather the cool sagacity, the good management, and the honesty of her men of business. If ever the enterprising citizen of the Union should neglect these virtues, we may be certain, that, notwithstanding the protection of the most powerful fleets, notwithstanding the calculation and foresight of the most profound political shrewdness, American vessels, repulsed from every coast, would soon disappear from those seas, upon which they now exchange the treasures of the world for the treasures of their home.

I dwelt on the soil of old England in the most glorious days of her fame. It was then an elevating employment to me to study the character of the English manufacturer and merchant, in whose society I passed so many years. Observation invariably led me back to the conviction, that the insatiable desire, which dwells in every English man of business to crush and push aside his foreign rivals, never resorts to means, at which the man of honor would blush. A cool, determined, well-regulated activity, a prudent boldness, with which he ventures all with a prophetic calculation of accidents and results, a perseverance, which nothing paralyses, nothing shakes, and all those vigorous virtues, which dwell in a soul, the first impulses of which are public spirit, a sense of the national honor, and the pride of conscious honesty, elevated by the energy of the government, and the inviolable protection of the laws: — these are the qualifications that lead the English merchant and manufacturer to results, which, in the aggregate, have, in a comparatively short time, obtained for that country, that enormous wealth and power which are without parallel in history. To this single object is all the activity in the people and in the government continually directed; for this the treaties with foreign powers are concluded; for this purpose legislation is effectual; for this the floating fortresses of Britannia are sent to all seas. To protect the rights and property of the British merchant and manufacturer their government keeps watch on the circumference of the globe. A never-resting activity continually excavates new harbors, builds new docks for the merchant fleets, rears new light-houses in the abyss of the ocean, and deepens out the rivers; and all these great public works proceed from the people, which, on their part, desire nothing from the state, except protection all over the globe in their strife against foreign labor, and at home justice and liberty with the „Laissez faire“ in every thing else. And this „Laissez faire“ has, in the short space of eighty years, enabled England to expend three hundred millions of dollars for roads, five hundred millions for railways, three hundred and fifty millions for canals, and an equal sum for harbors and docks; it has founded innumerable depots of industrial and commercial activity, and raised the value of her soil by three thousand millions of dollars.

„Citizens, you have built an Acropolis“ said Peel, the prime minister, at the inauguration of the new London Exchange „and we will hold it in honor, as Greece held in honor that glorious sanctuarium, of which those pillars so vividly remind us.“ — Words worthy, in truth, of so great a statesman! —

In the middle of the city of London, where Cheapside and Cornhill pour forth their noisy crowds, in the heart of English commercial life, are grouped those immense structures, which serve the purposes of commerce and industry; there are the Bank, the palace of the East India Company, and the Royal Exchange. The latter stands upon the site of the old Exchange, which, renowned in its time as the most splendid in the world, was, Jan. 16th 1838, completely burnt to the ground. On the 17th Jan. 1842, the corner-stone of the new Exchange was laid, and within less than three years, this splendid edifice was completed, an admirable representation of which is given in the accompanying engraving. From the noble west-front, with the Grecian portico, the frieze of which is adorned with sculptures, — (allegories of England's commercial greatness) — leads a magnificent flight of granite steps to „the Merchants walk". It is a beautiful arcade, which encloses the open inner court. This colonnade is the temple proper of the ruling god of the age. In the afternoon, from the hours of three to five, his priests and worshippers assemble here, the bankers and merchants by thousands, men of all complexions, all zones, all nations, and the stir and bustle of the world's traffic is heard humming in all languages. It is a great and impressive spectacle, and the Briton, as he proudly contemplates it, may well think the time immeasurably distant, when the words of the Roman philosopher will be applicable to England:

„*Fuit quondam Graecia, fuerunt in Graecia Athenae, nunc neque Athenae, neque in ipsa Graecia Gracia est.*" *)

---

*) „There was a Greece; there was in Greece an Athens; there is no more an Athens, nor is a Greece in Greece."

CONSTANTINE

Published for [illegible] 164, William-Street, New-York.

CONSTANTINE.

France stands a Rome in modern history, and it is bearing the fate of Rome. Avenging the inequity of martial conquest, the nations of Europe have in our own days met before the gates of her Capital, and wrested from the usurper's head the iron crown, which, with Cyclopean power, had been forged for universal empire. Napoleon sleeps quietly under the majestic dome of the Invalids; but the tree of social Reform, which in France, its native soil, is so deeply rooted, is extending its branches gradually over Europe. Although the imperial era of the conquering sword may be past for ever, yet an imperial era of those ideas may follow, which aim at the dominion of the world: — I mean the ideas of Liberty and Selfgovernment.

There is nothing like the French nation in the rest of the world. This people plays with their rulers and the forms of their governments as with puppets. They decorate and dandle, and crush them alternately, at their caprice and will. When the revolution of 1830 raised the craftiest of the Bourbons, Louis Philippe of Orleans, on the throne, that man contrived every means to give it firmness. In vain! Monarchy in France will never find a foundation to be relied on for a single day. The roots are loose, the vital elements are destroyed, and restored Royalty was barely a hollow frame, good for parties to play at hide and seek therein, an aggregate of mere outward existence, exposed to every accident, at all times dependent upon circumstances, which it could neither guide, nor sway, nor foresee. Engendered in incest, it was destitute under the house of Orleans of every dignity, even honest birth. Not supported by the nation, but by a party, from which it had received the mission to protect its interests by great sacrifices, to defend acquired rights, to uphold solemnly-made promises, it could last only so long as that fraction of the people held the supremacy, and so long as it performed its part to their satisfaction. Standing singly and alone upon the narrow, slippery basis of the Charter, the head of the new dynasty could defend himself against the pressure of parties only by leaning upon that one which happened to be the strongest, and in consequence he was compelled to adopt that treacherous system of policy, which roused the contempt of the nation. But while the enormity and craft of this system only increased the dangers it endeavoured to suppress, and the insecurity which it betrayed, those dark powers that lie as germs in every man's bosom ranged themselves in the phalanx of the enemies of Royalty. Many of its antagonists became fanatics. There was a class of men who considered the murder of a king, whose cup of crime was filled to the very brim, a deed of patriotism. Eleven times did the angel of death pass by the assailed, at once protecting and warning Louis Philippe; but — the warning of destiny passed unheeded by the Royal egotist. To his very fall, the head of the vile house of Orleans continued playing like a cheat with false cards, speaking with two tongues and a twofold language. Humbly seeking protection from without, by leaguing himself with inherited power, which, out of France, was firmly rooted in hereditary soil, he sought safety within, by drawing closer and closer the fences around the popular freedom, the mother of his power, and surrounded himself with that execrable dark and invisible apparatus of defence, called the state-police, an ear of Dionysius even in the army and in the colleges, a yawning lion's mouth in every tavern and every private dwelling: — that always and every where listening, prying, lurking power, that creeps about in the darkness, that catches at every word, investigates every project, and, for every mine, digs its countermine.

Louis Philippe's political shrewdness endeavored constantly to furnish an outlet for the vanity and thirst for glory so prominent in the French character. He ever was busy in opening to the chivalric, adventurous spirit of the nation an arena for its exercise in battle and the arts of war. The king well knew that the Gladiator, strengthened in the wars of the Revolution and of the Empire, now that no external enemy threatened, would lacerate his own bowels, if wanting a tourney field, for his superabundant strength. What the bloody sports of the Amphitheatres and Naumachiae were to old Rome, were to France Navarino, Antwerp, Algiers and Constantine in the days of Louis Philippe.

Constantine, the celebrated African fortress, is situated about one hundred and sixty miles from Algiers, at the foot of Mount Atlas, upon an almost quadrangular, table-formed rock, which rises perpendicularly on all sides to a height of from three to four hundred feet. Almost unassailable from its position, the city would be impregnable, were it not commanded by the neighboring heights. It is accessible only on the south-east side, where a splendid viaduct, a work of the Romans, leads into the city, across the intervening chasm. The country around is not destitute of attractions. From the summit of the rock, the eye roams over the vallies, clad with verdant meadows, which stretch up along the mountain, and which were once covered with Roman country seats, and villas, and palaces, the ruins of which are still every where to be found. The back ground toward the south and east, is formed by the towering peaks of the Atlas, and a long steep rocky ridge. The ancient walls of the city enclose the whole plateau, which is more than two leagues in circumference. Judging from this, the city must once have contained, at least a quarter of a million of inhabitants. Now, the greater part of its area is filled with gardens, and the population, including the French garrison, numbers not above twenty thousand.

It is to the Carthaginians that Constantine owes its foundation, and its ancient name, Cirta. While the Numidian monarchy lasted, this city was its capital, and under the sway ef the wealthy and powerful Massinissa, it saw its brightest epoch. The most splendid ruins now found there are those of buildings, which date their rise from this time. During the wars of Marius and Sylla, about a hundred years before the Christian era, Numidia was laid waste. Under Tiberius it became a Roman province and the once rich land was impoverished beneath the yoke of the greedy Roman proconsuls. Constantine, although favored and cherished as the residence of the Roman governors, never again attained its earlier splendor; yet as a chief point d'appui of the Roman empire in Africa, it maintained a high position, so long as this sway lasted. Two legions were permanently stationed here, designed to hold in check the restless mountain-tribes, and to protect the adjacent districts from their incursions and depredations. Numidia early receivcd the Christian faith. Very soon after the spirit of sectarianism took up its abode in the province, and the religious strife of the Arians and Donatists ended in civil war. Cirta, often the scene of bloody battles, was destroyed by fire. Between the years 340 and 350 the emperor Constantine rebuilt it, enlarged its defences, and provided the walls with strong towers, which still are in a perfect state of preservation. Since that time Cirta has borne the name of Constantine. The great aqueduct also, a masterpiece of Roman architecture, which brought water to the city from the district of Physgeah, fifteen miles distant, seems to date from this period. After having served for fifteen centuries as a quarry to the people of the country, after the hand of time has, for an equal period, aided in the work of destruction, sufficient remains to enable us to form an idea of the whole — an idea which resembles rather a gigantic dream than an image of reality. It seems the work of Titans, not of mortals.

The colossal empire of ancient Rome fell in ruins, and with it all her pomp and splendor. Palaces, forums, academies, temples and theatres passed away in Constantine. The barbarians, summoned to revive a world corrupted and withered by despotism, inundated Roman Africa, the Vandals invaded Numidia with the mission, to uproot the civilisation of the past, and destroy its signs. Terribly did they execute their mandate. Constantine was plundered, burnt and its inhabitants put to death. These desolators were followed by the Arabian conquerors, bearing at the sword's point a new faith to the subjected people. Constantine became the capital of the kingdom of Africa, now erected under the dominion of the Fatimites. It lasted two hundred years. The dynasty became extinct in the year 900, and the unprotected kingdom fell into the hands of the Jerytes, a race, who ruled over other parts of Africa. Constantine, now a provincial town, was henceforward of importance only as a fortress. In the year 1550 it fell, one of the last ruins of the Arabian monarchy, under the iron sceptre of the Turks. These formed of Constantine and its territories a Pachalick, and placed it under the Dey of Algiers. Owing to its situation in the midst of a fruitful country, between the desert and the richest part of Tunis, Constantine became the centre of a florishing trade. In 1780 Constantine contained from 50, to 60,000 inhabitants, and the caravans put in circulation more than 400,000 florins monthly. In the year 1782 a war broke out between Algiers and Tunis, and in consequence the trade of Constantine suffered most severely. War was followed by the plague. Nearly one half of the inhabitants of the unhappy city fell victims to this scourge. Many of the wealthiest families fled and never returned. In 1795 Constantine numbered only 15,000 inhabitants, and its former prosperity, to which the beauty of the streets and buildings still bear testimony, passed away.

Algiers, which in 1830 surrendered to the French arms, opened the widest arena for the occupation of the adventurous, daring spirits of the nation, and for the gratification of its love of fame. Bona was taken, and the conqueror's next glance was directed towards Constantine. A corps of seven thousand men, all picked troops, under the command of Marshal Clauzel, received orders to take the place. On the 12th November 1836, the expedition left Bona. No battle with the enemy could have been more terrible than their battle with the elements which commenced on the first day of their march. The rain fell incessantly and in streams, rendering the roads almost impassable; the artillery and an inumerable train sank into the mire, and with them the exhausted horses; but what the beasts refused to do, was performed by the inflexible spirit of the men. They dragged the wagons and artillery over the heights, and through swoln rivers; each ravine had become a stream. Not only did the clouds of heaven pour down their floods, but the fountains of the earth also. On the 17. of November the army reached the first plateau of the Atlas. Here a snow-storm overtook them. It lasted for twenty eight hours, and transformed the African landscape into a Siberian one. The old warriors were reminded of their winter-campaign in Russia. They were still two days march from the objeet of their expedition. But enthusiasm conquered all obstacles. Three days afterwards the army encamped before Constantine. In what a condition! A third part of the troops had perished from hardships, or had been rendered unfit for service, and the remainder were in a state ot extreme exhaustion. Proudly, like an armed giant, stood the rocky city before them, inaccessible, vulnerable only from a single spot, and this was defended by 9000 Arabs, who fought for their altars and their hearths. Napoleon's grey bearded marshal resolved to attempt an assault. The height opposite the bridge was stormed and the artillery drawn up. Yet it was found impossible to erect batteries upon a ground, that an eight days rain had transformed into a miry pool. The heavy guns sank in the marsh. Amid these fruitless attempts, the artillery of the place vomited its murderous fire against the unprotected ranks of the besiegers. A thousand men fell. Now the encouraged garrison ventured upon a sally; but with cool intrepidity the French repelled, by the bayonet, the furious attack of the Arabs, and pushed after them as far as the principal gate. There, before the very cannons mouth, an unexampled contest followed, which raged from morning to night. The want of artillery the French supplied by the butts of their muskets, and by their axes. With such means the intrepid besiegers endeavored to storm one of the strongest fortresses of northern Africa, and they were so far successful that they actually made themselves masters of the outer gate. A second inner one however withstood those weak instruments of assault, and all the efforts of the most undaunted courage to carry it were in vain. It had snowed during the whole day. Not a musket could be discharged. Chilled with cold, famished with hunger, and exhausted by the most terrible exertions, without hope of a better result for the coming day, night covered the little army with her mantle. Fires were blazing upon the heights around, summoning the sons of the desert, like vultures around the dying lion. In this desperate condition, the old marshal commanded the retreat.

If the French had thus far displayed the utmost fearlessness, it was now necessary to exert true heroism. One half of the troops took upon their shoulders the sick and wounded; the other half formed the guard which defended them. Thus, amid snow and rain, upon the most toilsome and trackless paths, continually exposed to the attacks of the Cabyles and Arabs, who swarmed around them in thousands, they effected a retreat worthy to figure in history beside that of Xenophon with his ten thousand Greeks. In Guelma, half way between Bona and Constantine, they met a small reserve, which had there entrenched itself. The army halted and took up a strong defensive position. Seing his troops safe, Clauzel hastened to France, to fetch a suffiicient reinforcement to insure the conquest of Constantine. France felt that this was indispensable to the honor of her arms. In the following autumn, an army, 20,000 strong, crossed into Africa, to perform what the old marshal had found impossible to effect with the force under his command; two sons of Louis Philippe's, accompanied the expedition, to participate in its dangers. Constantine was the prize — and it was gloriously won. The tri-colored flag has now been waving for twenty years upon the rock of Constantine. The place is the principal strong-hold of the French power in Africa, and it is, at the same time, the point from which France will develop her farther schemes of African conquest.

ST. CLOUD.

,,But where is he, the modern, mightier far,
,,Who, born no king, made monarchs draw his car;
,,The new Sesostris, whose unharness'd kings,
,,Freed from the bit, believe themselves with wings,
,,And spurn the dust o'er which they crawl'd of late,
,,Chain'd to the chariot of the chieftain's state?
,,Yes! where is he, the champion and the child
,,Of all that's great or little, wise or wild?
,,Whose game was empires, and whose stakes were thrones;
,,Whose table, earth — whose dice were human bones?
,,Behold the grand result in yon lone isle,
,,And, as thy nature urges, weep or smile.

In the idea of God all that is sublime dawns upon the soul; in the idea of Infinitude all human grandeur sinks into nothingness. Petty and powerless do we appear in the presence of Omnipotence. Yet the fact has nothing humiliating in it; on the contrary we feel ourselves elevated by the capacity to conceive Infinitude, and to comprehend God's unbounded greatness in his works. When reflecting on it the sense of the Sublime fills our soul. The visible order in the immeasurable structure of the universe, the paths, which the sun's satellites describe in the

PALACE and GARDENS of ST CLOUD

Published for HERRMANN J. MEYER 164, William-Street, NEW YORK

ether, the starry hosts, that pledge of our immortality — all these elevated objects we contemplate with unspeakable delight. At every manifestation of the All-powerful and All-wise, we feel a rapture, before which all discontent at our own littleness and weakness disappears.

As in the natural, so in the moral world. The truly great man, whose soul virtue and genius have stamped with the impress of heroism, stirs the bosom with a thrill of reverence, joy and pride. The mingled sense of our own insignificance has nothing discouraging in it; it awakens rather a feeling of self-esteem, for in the object of our admiration we behold a fellow being. We see, as it were, the reality of our own ideal. We look up to the lofty mortal, we measure his altitude, and great as it may be, we find it within the reach of human faculties. We behold, as it were, the connecting link between God and Mankind. The great mortal is the torch at which noble thoughts are kindled; he gives us light to guide us in a world of ideas; he awakes our mind to sublime purposes, he stands before the soul, a shining pattern, worthy of emulation. Such a man often exercises an almost supernatural influence upon whole nations. He becomes in the popular mind a mythic hero, and admiration and reverence are exalted to worship. The belief that a man of this description is actually of divine nature, or, at least, acts under God's immediate and especial protection, that all that he does is excellent, perfect, fraught with blessing, takes hold of millions, and becomes indelible. The people say of him: „He speaks, and it is done; He commands, and it stands fast.“ — Such a man, supported by such a prestige, can venture upon the greatest undertakings, and they will succeed; if he proposes to perform miracles, the miracles will be done. Such a heavenly mortal

> That upward soars,
> And passes o'er the thoughts
> Of humbly bending souls,

it always conscious of his strength and power. From this conciousness emanate his acts — that illuminate, fructify and give form and impulse to all below him. While the humbler man thinks only of the humble, and to this limits his endeavors, while the little man, even with the greatest means, effects but little: a great mind performs wonders with the bare idea, and with slender means he accomplishes what the world admires.

He sees the furthest objects lying near,
Which humbler mortals deem beyond all reach,
He plumes his wings to soar aloft to heaven,
He pathes himself in the red morning glow,
He saileth with the tempest-driven clouds,
And men and demons, spirits of earth and air,
Are servants of his genius. Future time
Lies all unrolled before his eagle glance,
Order he brings from chaos, light from darkness. —
But in his loftiest pride the hero towers,
When tempests howl and rage throughout his works,
When, 'neath the structure which his hands have reared,
The earth yawns wide and threatens to ingulf it,
When, in a twinkling, Destiny's mighty grasp
Hurls him from all his glory, headlong down. —
Then the great man, in truth, reveals himself,
A being native to a higher sphere,
He rises loftier from his fearful fall,
And, in redoubled glory now his deeds
Rise, a memento to his deathless fame.

Many great men — those of the commoner cast — display a dualism of nature. In contemplating their doings, reverence is mixed with terror. Such men are far more frequent than those rarest mortals, which, as messengers of God, appear, from time to time, upon the earth as the apostles of Religion and Virtue, and whose deeds live in reverence in the memory of man from age to age. — As the high, overhanging walls of a precipice, as the volcano in its destructive splendor, as the tempest in its desolating might, as the flame which consumes cities, inspires, at once, both admiration and terror, so is it with those men, in whose soul the Divine strives with the Demoniac.

The heroes of *military glory*, the *conquerors*, the *founders of empires* who, for six thousand years, have passed before us in history, belong, almost without exception, to this category. An Alexander, a Caesar, a Charlemagne, will always excite admiration by their *intellectual* greatness; but with our admiration is mingled our terror. We contemplate them with that pleasure, with which we contemplate the storm-beaten ocean, that piles billows upon billows, and makes the shores tremble. We take delight in the vastness of their power, and find enjoyment in the tumult of soul, which it excites within us; but they give us no foretaste of the joy and happiness with which we contemplate those greater men, *the elect of God.*

The last in the bright row of heroes and conquerors, was the man, who, about a life-time since, so often took his meditative walks in this garden, walks during which sometimes the fate of kingdoms and of nations was decided. St. Cloud and Napoleon are ideas as inseparable as Olympus and Jupiter. At that time Napoleon was at the pinnacle of his power. From St. Cloud the emperor ruled in the style of ancient Rome; here he sketched his great plans for the subjection of the world. It was in the solitary avenues in the park of St. Cloud, that he found repose for the reflections of the philosopher, the lawgiver, and for those works of deep political wisdom, which will encircle his head with glory when all his triumphal arches and columns of victory shall have disappeared from the earth. From St. Cloud he issued those decrees which entirely reorganized the administration of France, and gave to its machinery that simplicity of construction which can never be surpassed; in St. Cloud, after his reconciliation with the pope, he arranged the affairs of the Church, and, in spite of her resistance, rendered her the handmaid of his power, and the strongest, mightiest instrument of his will; from St. Cloud he regulated the education of the people, as an emperor and absolute master, not as the people's friend, not for the service of Humanity, but for the service of his unbounded Ambition; not for Freedom, but for Slavery; for the fashioning of a generation as mere automate of his will; a generation which of the dignity and independence of a citizen scarcely knew the name. — From St. Cloud it was, that he also arranged the administration of justice throughout his vast empire. He restored to it external gravity and dignity, he placed the courts of judicature upon a loftier tribune; and what was more — he gave stability, simplicity, rapidity, and cheapness to legal proceedings and by this he became a true benefactor of the nation which obeyed him. But lest the independence of the judges might be a restraining band to his despotism, he called into existence, at the same time, that terrible power, the secret police, at the head of which, his satellite, Fouché, held in his hand all the threads of public life, and, always ready to the emperor's nod, was ever prepared to execute the imperial will in the remotest corners of the empire. Napoleon spread his execrated system of secret police like a net over the land, and the diverging radii of telegraphic lines, which had their centre in St. Cloud, gave to his commands the celerity of lightning. He organized the bureaucratic hierarchy by a wonderful system of centralization, which rendered the servants of the state the unresisting and unfailing instruments of his will. — In like manner he reformed the financial department completely; it had become a chaos; he restored it to a state of order and simplicity. Napoleon managed the public property, like a good householder, and with a budget that scarcely amounted to a third of the sum, which the soi-disant Citoyen-King, Louis Philippe d'Orleans, consumed by his administration, the Emperor contrived not only to govern his vast empire, but also to raise the fleets and armies wherewith to conquer half the globe, and to erect those grand works of public utility, which future times and generations will view with wonder. But, sparingly as he dealt with his people's money, he was most prodigal of their blood. Napoleon wasted it without scruple; the lives of men counted for little or nothing in the calculation or his schemes. It was from St. Cloud, that dated the famous decree, which completed the system of military Conscription. Never has the earth seen a more effectual instrument for war than this. The flower of the nation belonged henceforth by law to the battle-field. Filled to intoxication with the thirst for glory, the French Youth marched as to a festival, to distant countries, where victory or death awaited them. The aggregate of Napoleon's incomparable activity gave to his empire that unity in which its main strength was concealed. Is was the prototype and envy of all monarchs and tyrants. It made the work of conquest easy. Many princes did not even wait for Napoleon's assault, but staggered like birds into the mouth of the rattlesnake; others were conquered by craft; the strong he overthrew in a succession of battles, and all resistance was scattered before his sword and his genius like empty chaff. Twelve short years sufficed to conquer half Europe. The nations lay in fetters, and Charlemagne's empire rose once more into existence. From the Dalmatian coast to the Pyrenees, from the Baltic to the bay of Naples, Napoleon's hand ruled absolute and unbounded. France, Italy, Holland, Germany lay as slaves at his feet, his allies bore the badge of vassalage, and as a reward to kings for having yielded up their independence to the foreign yoke, they were permitted to play the tyrant with their own subjects. Who would now think it worth while to turn over the leaves of the Diary of this palace, in which are bound up the foulest pages of European dynasties and of princely sway! Who would think it worth his while to relate, how, at that time, the new-baked sovereigns, clothed with the shreds, which the Man of the Island had thrown to them from the stolen mantle of the German empire, demeaned themselves in the antichamber of the emperor, and how he treated them? It is a fact that on one occasion a Persian ambassador took three German Highnesses for valets-de-chambre, and another time Napoleon's favorite Mameluke dismissed a king with the words — „The emperor commands the German majesty in waiting to call again to-morrow; to-morrow at eleven o clock precisely!“ — We men of mature years, who were contemporaries of that period of shame, we remember yet too well the sordid parts which proud heads of German dynasties played at that time! The German nation, now trodden down with scorn by their princes, will never forget the infamous traffic with the Corsican about the fragments of the

Imperial crown, and—with what were paid such fragments, the memory holds fast! We shall never forget who they were that willingly placed the despotism of the Corsican in the place of German freedom; how they levied the tithe of blood from our youth, in order to bring an offering to the foreign Moloch, and to forge an iron band around the nation, making obedience the acme of military honor, and by what means they degraded the German armies to despicable engines for despotism. We will never forget how they drilled the civil functionaries to servile bureaucrats put into livery like their jockeys, subjected to military discipline, and instructed to seek in princely favor and will the only source of their duty. No! Germany will never forget how every thing that opposed the system of despotism — national tradition, manners and customs, local and provincial rights, the liberties and privileges of classes and corporations, the power of usage and of popular habit, the pride of self-reliance and independent thought, were continually assailed in order that all power of resistance might be uprooted; how, at last, the sole aim of government was to conglomerate all classes of the people into a worthless mass of subjects, which were valued only as figures and numbers, according to the amount of the taxes levied on them. It was then, that, to creep into the favor of the foreign master and to content their own greediness, German princes applied the forcing pump to all the productive powers of the nation for the sake of extracting the marrow from burgher and from peasant, and create pauperism in all quarters, which, in the end, would drive Industry and Capital out of the land and leave nothing remaning except — wealthy princes and slaves without a right or a penny. Oh, disgraceful time not to be forgotten even in this present time so disgraceful! — Germany was then condemned to wear double chains; those of a foreign master, and those of her own princes, who, on their side, blushed at no slavish service. In the palace of our sovereigns was burning incense to the foreign master, his name shone in gold in the German Almanacs, and his name- and birth-days were officially proclaimed to the nation as joyful festivals! Was it a wonder then, that all sense of honor and national integrity was destroyed, and every feeling of civil liberty and independence was torn up by the very roots? This lot, it is true, did not fall upon Germany alone. The flood reached far out over its borders, it stretched from the pillars of Hercules to the shores of Finnland, and all nations and princes of the continent of Europe, England excepted, bent their heads before the Emperor Napoleon.

And it was in St. Cloud that a single stroke of the pen and a single moment annihilated the gigantic work of twenty years. Napoleon signed his second abdication in St. Cloud. Betrayed, forsaken, a captive, chained to a solitary ocean rock, the Hero transformed himself into the Prophet, and from the lips of the dying emperor the waves bore to the old world those words, which disclosed the future and have been fulfilled even to the present hour.

St. Cloud has several other interesting leaves in its chronicle. Here, July 1830, Charles X. signed those ordinances, which called the sleeping Revolution from its grave, and its spirits from the deep. It was from St. Cloud that Henry V., the heir to the crown, fled France to become the wandering knight of the restoration. The Republic opened the palace, park and gardens to the people — and the people, like a child, now laugh and jest there, where those plans were formed, which filled the world with blood and tears.

The palace of St. Cloud stands on the bank of the Seine, two leagues below Paris, situated picturesquely upon a hill, surrounded by splendid grounds, which cover the plains and heights for more than a mile. In ancient times it was a cloister, and was founded by Clodovic's grandson Clodovald, who died within its walls. Later it became a royal hunting seat, and Louis XIV. built the present palace. It consists of a main-building and two pavilions, and is less imposing by its magnitude, than by the harmony of its proportions, and the richness of its external embellishments. The furniture and interior ornaments bear the impress of Napoleon's grandeur of character. It is simple and noble. Napoleon scorned all display of the paltry tinsel of power. But the noblest works of art — trophies of his conquests and victories — rendered St. Cloud a Villa Hadriana. Many of these have dissappeared after the downfall of the empire, but enough remain to excite admiration. The former apartments of the emperor still retain, in part, their original arrangement and furniture. The Lilies, which during the Restoration, had thrust aside the Eagles, have faded away; the emblems of Napoleon's power and glory have, since the last Revolution, every where returned to their places. The people delight in these symbols. They are a legacy of their renown; on them the popular mind spins forth the thread which escaped the hand of the Dead, and it hopes of the future that it will complete what He began.

The gardens of the palace were laid out by Le Notre. They have always been kept in a state of the most careful preservation. Basins, fountains, statues of marble and of bronze, tall hedges of yew trees and parterres of flowers, offer a highly attractive picture. The most splendid feature is the grand cascade, the subject of the accompanying, and admirably executed engraving. The water descends over staffeling rocks, from an altitude of one hundred and eight feet into the large basin, from whose depths mighty jets ascend aloft to the height of a hundred feet. The whole bears that proportion to the great works of nature, to the Niagara-Falls or the Rhine-cataract near Schaffhausen, as the pasteboard-Vulcano on the stage bears to the flame-vomiting Etna — and the „staffage“, the lions, hyenas, snakes, and sea monsters, which spout water in each other's faces, call to mind the dreams of a maniac. It is only in spring and autumn that the works have their complement of water. But then the population of Paris streams forth every Sunday, and park and gardens become a rendezvous of pleasure. They roam through the

W. HEINE, NEW YORK, 1850, DEL. | JOHN POPPEL SCULPSIT.

NEW YORK-BAY

saloons o the palace; they think of the Pyramids, of Vienna, Berlin and Moscow; they fight over again the countless battles of their hero; they drink glory in full draughts. And on their way home they mock at the impostor in the Elysée, who wears the imperial hat as a fool's cap, and builds a house of cards to protect himself from the storms, which the Eternal justice is gathering over his head to avenge the deeds of a rascal.

NEW YORK BAY

FROM STATEN ISLAND NEAR THE LIGHT HOUSE.

America! star in the dark night, staff for millions of broken hearts, sole living hope when all others are dead and borne to the grave; land of promise for men and nations; last safe asylum for the civilization of the old world from the inundation of barbarism! — America! Were I a Solomon, I would sing a song of songs in thy praise, were I a David, I would celebrate thee in psalms.

In the nations of Europe there lives a great wish, never yet fulfilled; an irresistible desire, ungratified; an everlasting longing, with everlasting refusal; it is more than all that I could utter in words; more than all joys and all earthly good, and the pain of deprivation is more than all pains. This *great wish* is *the red thread* in the life of civilised nations. It will not suffer them to find repose, it pours bitter drops into every cup of joy; it places discontent, as a sentinel, at the door of every cottage, at the gate of every palace; it is the secret mother of that discomfort, which impels society, in the old world, from revolution to revolution; it is the architect, that labors ceaselessly at the heaven-aspiring steeple of the national woes, adding story after story. This wish has been called, sometimes by one name, sometimes by another: but no form of speech entirely suffices, none perfectly expresses the thought, even the best word compares with it, only as a temple compares with the universal temple of Nature, as the morning sun with the starry firmament, or sleep with death, or time with eternity. Give it what name thou wilt: call it the impulse toward *Freedom*, toward *Happiness*, toward *Progress*: it exists, it is living and operating every where, and where it does not step forth to clear consciousness, there it is active as a presentiment. Equally undoubted is the fact that the forms of European society occupy a position hostile to this wish. Old-age strives constantly after repose, and society, in its decline, naturally clings to the principle of Stability. It desires the preservation of an existing order of things, at the expense of the impulse toward change; it desires immobility, at the expense of movement; it desires the dead form, at the expense of the life, which fashions forth new shapes. This antagonism has, at last, become so powerful, and has so unhinged all the relations of society, that each one feels that matters *cannot* continue *thus* much longer. A catastrophe is near. It stands as a certainty before the mind. As at the time of the destruction of the classic world, as at the period of the corruption of Grecian and Roman society, when the nations of *the East* poured, like a deluge, over the continent, barbarism is on its march again. The East is moving against the West, and the Atlantic ocean is the high road, upon which the banished and the prosecuted are hastening toward their new home. A *new* emi*gration of the nations* has commenced across the Atlantic. The hundreds of thousands that have gone before will be followed by the millions, the poor will be followed by the rich, the rude by the educated and at last, the sciences and arts will leave the grave mounds of their old home, and close the march.

Westward speeds the fiery chariot of the prophets, that proclaim the return of a golden age! On this side the ocean nothing more is to be hoped for. The genius of our continent is suffering the last iron rings to glide through his fingers; what follows is the work of devastating demoniac powers, destruction and death. A new life is born beyond the sea; it lies in the lap of the new world, and smiles upon us like a young bride, and is endowed and ornamented by the Creator's hands with wondrous gifts, with fabulous treasures, with lavish costliness and splendor. Where is Nature developed in grander forms? Do not wonderful powers there fructify the bosom of the earth, and is not in America, the most luxuriant dream, at it were, becoming reality? Immensity — that is the true word for the riches of American nature in all her realms. Hhis superabundance is displayed before the glances of the oppressed nations of the world, and near by stands the Goddess with de Phrygian cap, in her bright, star-spangled robe, and spreadig out her arms, she calls: Come hither, and share in all my treasures! — —

The truly grand and enchanting spectacle, which unfolds itself to the glance on entering the Bay of New York, is faithfully represented in the accompanying engraving. A peculiar feeling of repose and happiness steals upon the mind as we contemplate the view. On either hand the neat country seas on Staaten Island, peeping forth from de rich, green landscape, appear like the dwellings of enviable mortals, who have taken up their abode in a haven of delight. Above us, we behold the vault of heaven, from which the star of day casts its brightness and its glow. Before us curls the glimmering sea, covered with countless vessels, from the fisherman's skiff to the proud ship and the mighty steamer, which convey hither the treasures of the Indies and of California, together with the merchandise of Europe.

Even the traveller who has roamed over the whole world, finds Nature on this Porta Europaea, as the Narrows may very justly be termed, wanting neither beauty, nor majesty; though he misses the romantic and the awe-inspiring features of the renowned landscapes of Europe. The feeling that he is upon the high road from the old world to the new one, acquires peculiar force and impressiveness; here the thought can best be grasped, that the neverending flocks of wanderers, foreboding Europe's winter, enter chiefly through this gate, like birds of passage, into the land of their hope, warmed by the sun of Freedom. This mighty gate of the Ocean, nearly 2000 yard's in width, leads into a harbor large enough to receive all the fleets in the world in perfect security. On the right hand, stretching eastward, lies Long Island, the natural breakwater against the billows of the Atlantic; to the left we see the river Hudson, protected as far as the eye can reach, by pleasant heights and rocky barriers against the west and northwest winds.

On either side of the harbor cheerful villages adorn the heights, and in the distance we have a glance at Jersey-City and Brooklyn, daughters of their mighty mother. Before us, upon an island, as in the arms of the noble river, lies New York herself, the Capital of the new world, with her countless docks and wharfs, — secure both against the violence of nature and of man; for on three small islands that dot the road-stead, Governor's, Bedloe's, and Ellis's island, strong forts are erected, whose batteries command the passage on all sides, and forbid approach to fleets coming on any other than a peaceful errand to the land of liberty and a self-governed people. — —

From the vessel's deck I looked at the proud star-banner of the forts, and gazed around — and the land appeared to me like a table spread for a feast of the gods. All gleamed with gold, everywhere there was prosperity, happiness, and joy! But as from joy to grief there is but a single step — I thought of my Fatherland — and tears of anger, of sorrow, and of shame fell, mingling with the hallowed waters.

THE WALHALLA

THE WALHALLA.

It is the especial province of *Architecture*, to execute *national monuments*. Sculpture and Poetry should serve only to *interpret* and *explain* her vast conceptions. It was in *this* spirit that the *ancient* nations of the *East* reared their monuments, that *Athens* adorned her Acropolis, that the *Romans* erected mausoleums to their Consuls and Cæsars, and that the Pharaos of *Egypt* built pyramids and temples. Where the personality of the hero occupies a limited sphere of action, a statue, the *Portrait* of the man, is suitable and appropriate; where it embraces minds of universal activity, however, the mere likeness must play a subordinate part. — When, in the beginning of this century, the Thuringians wished to erect a statue to *Boniface*, their apostle, in a lonely forest-nook, where he first reared the cross, the drawings for the monument by several artists were laid before the duke *Augustus of Gotha*, when presiding at his privy council, that he might decide between them. The high-minded prince, after looking them over, took up a pen, and, sketching the figure of a flambeau upon the cover of a letter, handed it over to his prime-minister, saying: *That is Boniface*. A *candelabra* was erected in consequence upon the height of the forest, visible far and wide, and the simplest peasant of the country understands its meaning. What should a statue of *Hermann*, the hero of independent Germany in the days of imperial Rome, be it ever so colossal, do in the forest of Teutoburgh? A German battlesword on the crest of the mountain, towering its colossal blade like an obelisk toward heaven, — that would be a fitter monument and the whole nation would understand and cherish it.

A kindred and equally comprehensive signification, has the glorious temple of German renown which a king has lately erected near Ratisbon. The Walhalla is the receptacle of the statues of the great man of the nation. Its eastern gable is decorated with a representation of Hermann's victory over the Romans. The western front represents Germany's latest liberation. The interior is illustrated by the art of the sculptor with the complete history of the land, the results and consequences of every contest for German independence.

The corner-stone of this grand temple of national honor was laid in 1830. The celebrated Klenze sketched the plan after the idea of king Lewis of Bavaria, and guided the architectural execution; the Sculpture, for which Rauch in part prepared the drawings, was entrusted to the immortal Schwanthaler, and his pupils.

The building represents a Doric temple of white marble, similar to the Parthenon on the hill of the Acropolis at Athens. Its dimensions are vast and imposing: — seventy feet in height, a breadth of a hundred, and a depth of three hundred feet. The roof is supported on each side by a row of colossal pillars, eight of which stand at the two ends, and seventeen at each side. The interior is a vast hall of marble, whose richly checkered ceiling is supported by two rows of Ionic columns. The frieze that passes around the hall, is decorated with bas-reliefs, executed by Wagner in Rome, which represent the ancient history of the Teutonic race, from the time it left the Caucasian country down to the diffusion of Christianity amongst them. Along the army walls of the interior hall, appropriate niches contain the marble busts of those men, who have been the pride of the German nation at all times — her heroes in war, in council, in poetry, in the arts and sciences. In an outer compartment are placed the busts of celebrated contemporaries who are considered worthy to be numbered with the heroes of the Walhalla. Of the one hundred and forty places extant, fifty are as yet unoccupied. All the busts are, so far as it was possible to obtain them, faithful portraits. In a subterranean hall, an archive preserves the biographies of those admitted into the temple. They are written on parchment. King Lewis himself was their biographer. The complete works of the literary celebrities are placed, superbly bound, in a library.

The Walhalla rests upon substructions built in the Cyclopean style. White marble steps of immense proportions lead up to the terrace of the temple. From the terrace the eye roams across the romantic valley of the Danube, and over the neighboring mountains, the nearest of which is adorned with the picturesque and imposing ruins of the ancient castle of Donaustauf. The cost of the building, although it was originally estimated far lower, was not less than three millions of florins, and it was paid out of the privy purse of the king, to whom impartial judges willingly give the honor of having, in this monument, led back Art to her noblest destination.

A WALK IN RICHMOND PARK.

„There he is, the rascal!“ exclaimed my friend, as, following the smooth gravelled walk, we turned round a huge oak, whose thinly leaved boughs cast flitting shadows upon the velvet sward of Richmond park — „there he is, the old usurer, that cheated God and man!“ and with these words he raised his cane, and pointed to an old man, who, with a stately dame in black upon his arm, and followed by two servants, was sauntering beneath the elms, which lined the bank of the small adjacent lake. „The scoundrel has betrayed his country and people, re-opened the crater of the revolution, whose fiery flood and showering ashes have buried the peace of a continent, and ruined the property and happiness of millions — and all this to gratify the filthy selfishness that reigned within him. He was the cause of my ruin also“ he continued — „may my curses follow him to Orcus!“ And with glowing face and rising voice, he cried aloud: „Let the spirit of retribution come, who will root out crown-wearers and usurers, and liberate mankind from the fiends of despotism! Matters will not mend until the whole accursed brood is sent into exile, and has holiday, like this Louis Philippe — or until the portrait of Brutus precedes the titlepage of every almanac!“ he added, after a short pause as if a happier thought had suddenly entered his mind.

SCENERY in RICHMOND-PARK
near London.

Published for HERRMANN MEYER, Nº 164. William Street, NEWYORK.

„Why, you would not make a saint out of Brutus?“ I said playfully, as he advanced towards the shady avenue, with lifted cane, and an air almost of menace.“ And if I did! — it would not be the least meritorious among those deeds which have obtained beatification. To slay a wolf is nowhere a crime. And, believe me, this old man still spins the threads of mischief, as well as that other one in Brighton, who sets the puppets dancing upon the scene in Germany. Politics are offered, ready-made, to the German nation, while they think they make them themselves. Metternich is still the oracle of the princes. I tell you, there is no salvation without a Brutus — even exile affords no safety against diplomatists and kings.“ — „And the fraternity of the black gown, what will you do with that?“ — „It is dying of the Aqua Toffana of Freedom“ replied Charles, laughing. „You doubt it? look at North America! Elevate man to the pride of the citizen; that is the whole mystery of a people's liberation. Be the Apostle of your nation when you return, preach this mystery in the market places and streets of your home. Why do you smile? are you not entitled to do so? have you not the right of association and assembling, patented by your sovereign diets? Why do you shake your head? Are the ports of your home closed? Or can you no longer recognize liberated Germany in her faded blouses? I tell you, you cannot miss: where tattered tri-colored flags stand in the dusty corners of the council halls, where the dungeons in every city and the casemates in every fortress are filled with patriots, where you find each court of justice crammed with indictments for hightreason, where martial law has replaced the common law of the land — there is your fatherland; and where the permanent state of siege enhances the glory of princes and the welfare of the people there is Germany. Hasten then home, my friend, and preach loyalty before the Ides of March. — Tell me, pray! Will the Genius of Germany again foster the nightmare, or play the lunatic in his search of revolution?“ Thus spake the scoffer. But I replied sullenly: „Germany will not re-act the part of 48 when the Ides of March come again.“

The first garden upon the earth was — Paradise, and the first prohibition, and the first disobedience, and the first judicial trial, and the first exile — were also in Paradise. And old as Paradise is, equally old is the strife of man against dictatorial laws and commands.

Man was driven from Paradise. Care and want seized him with cold hands, and led him into the arms of unrelenting Nature, who conceals her best fruits behind toil and danger. And well it was that it was thus. For henceforth man was free in his search after knowledge; to wrestle for the fruit of the once forbidden tree became a duty, knowledge a reward of toil, and virtue the path of the soul into the Eden of everlasting peace.

The true garden of Paradise is within man himself. — Those gardens which man plants around him are of another kind. They are the blossoms of high culture, and they are to be found only among the most civilized nations. Man must be advanced in the knowledge of Nature and of her gifts and powers, before he associates the beautiful with the necessary and useful, passes from want to enjoyment, and applies the cheerful rules of art to the fashioning of the landscape which surrounds him. He then seeks to bring in closer proximity those beauties, which lie scattered over wide tracts of country, the gardener creates landscapes, subjects Nature, who has thus far obeyed her own rules, to the dictates of his refined taste, and hence arises the thing, which we call a park — a union of Nature's beauties in a narrow space.

In the East, whither we involuntarily direct our eyes, when we look for the site of Paradise, we also find the first traces of imitations thereof by human hand. The rulers of the old Persian empire, in the period of its greatest prosperity, surrounded their palaces and castles with vast gardens, which formed, as it were, the intervening space between their splendid dwellings, and the land whose people bowed beneath their will. Still farther reached the arm of the „Sons of Heaven", — the Chinese emperors. Not only did they transform the fields around their residences into pleasant parks, embracing an extent of miles, but they covered also vast tracts of fruitful land, around populous cities, with pleasure-gardens. In later times this custom took root in the West, and first with the Romans; the gardens of Pompey, Hortensius, and especially those of Hadrian, near Tivoli, still excite our admiration whether we peruse the descriptions of the classic authors, or view their ruins.

All that we know of these gardens leads to the belief that they were any thing but a Paradise for the people, at whose cost they were arranged, but that they were a paradise merely for their masters, of whom indeed the people was instructed to believe that they had a right to lead on earth a life full of heavenly enjoyments.

It is a curious fact, that it did not occur to the ancient Greeks to lay out parks and gardens. Were they repugnant to their relish for nature's beauties, or to their refined taste in matters of art? Did their architectural works need no landscape-enclosure, laid out after rule and method? Were their arts so much the very children of their land, that the two, of themselves, formed a harmonic whole? Did nature in her simplicity suffice? The learned may answer these questions; it is a fact that the Greeks knew nothing of landscape-gardening.

The parks of the present day, which we see, now, laid out as vast gardens, extending over meadows and woods, there enclosing some magnificent country-seat, there embracing winding roads connecting the palaces of princes with their country-castles, had their origin in England. They were at first enclosures for game, mere hunting-grounds. When cultivation with spade and plough broke up the original forest, when villages and towns grew up, and roads intersected the country, when woods were thinned, and lakes and ponds drained, the great lords of the land saw their field-sports put in jeopardy, and were seasonably provident to secure for them an undisturbed place of refuge. If the old chronicles speak truth, Henry I. of England was the first man who invented hunting-parks. He enclosed, near Woodstock in Oxfordshire a portion of a forest that abounded in game, with a stone-wall seven miles in circumference. The royal example found imitators. Nobles and prelates enclosed their hunting grounds in great numbers: the bishop of Norwich alone owned fourteen of them. The invention of the British nobility found quickly passage into foreign countries; the park made its way into Germany, that second home of the nobler sports, where it prevailed to an unexampled extent, although the parks of this country were never able to vie in magnitude, splendor, and natural beauties with their English originals.

In these places of refuge and of breed for the forest-game in the course of time cultivation was introduced. Horticulture forced its way into the hunting park; it laid out paths, planted flowers, constrained the grouped trees to arrange themselves in form and color, according to artistic rules, and compelled Nature, at each turn in the path, at each resting place, to reveal to the saunterer a new prospect, or a startling view. With the French revolution, with the ideas of freedom which it propagated, the sense of natural beauties, which had become dwarfed and shackled in Germany, threw of its bands, and acquired strength and vigor. The free, English style of gardening was introduced, and the stiff French mode banished. Revolutionary taste discarded every thing, which, until now, had distorted Nature, after French and Dutch patterns. Where Le Notre made leaping fountains, and clipped the trees into grotesque shapes, water-falls were formed, and the oak suffered to unfold itself in all its glory; where the Dutch planted tulips, the wild rose was permitted to luxuriate, and where statues stood, sprang the roe or grazed the stag. The flowers greeted the eye, where they pleased it best. They had again become the merry, lovely children of Nature, scattered amid the scenery, now, as if by accident, now, as if at the beck of beauty; they were no longer Dutch soldiers in rank and file, with shield and inscription.

Thus then, in the midst of unrelenting nature, man has again built his garden of peace, his paradise, to which he hastens, when he would repose from the toils and trouble, which beset him beyond its enclosure.

But is this true? Alas, for the few only, and scarcely indeed for these. The majority bring their sorrows with them into this paradise, and meet the serpent repining there, and others find the cherub with the flaming sword: envy. He it is that daily expels thousands from the Eden of contentment and frugality, and keeps, locked up from millions, the secret of rejoicing in small things, and finding happiness in the possession of the little.

Richmond-Park, a demesne of the British crown, lies in the valley of the Thames, about eight miles above London, and its grounds surpass in extent and beauty the parks of all England. It is more than four leagues in circumference (its area measures 3000 acres) and it contains, in the most delightful variety, all the attractions that nature and art can combine in such a space: hills and dales, woods and meadows, rocks and water-falls, chasms and pleasant vallies, lakes and brooks, villages and farms, castles and cottages, ruins and chapels, pastures and enclosures for game — and through the whole winds the glorious river, swarming throughout the year with barks, steamers and trading vessels, which exchange the produce of the country for the wares and manufactures of the metropolis. The most attractive spot to visitors is Richmond Hill, with its palace, and its enchanting views of Windsor, Harrow, Hampton-Court, Twickenham, Petersham, and the nearer environs, studded with the countless villas of the wealthy Londoners, and beautified by the most careful culture — while downwards the Thames the eye rests on the vast cloud of black smoke indicating the site of the Babylon of modern times,

City of rarest virtues, blackest crimes,
Home of the happy, haunt of deepest woe,
Abode of wealth and beggary.

Sometimes, when weather and wind are most favorable, the spires of the seven hundred steeples of the capital become visible, towering, like masts, above the sea of vapor, and the cupola of St. Paul's, with its golden cross, gleaming in calm majesty in the ether — a symbol of a higher, spiritual, everlasting existence.

Richmond Castle was, for a long period, the favorite abode of the English kings, down to the time of the third George, who usually passed the season of Lent here, amid the lovely, soft scenery of nature, and gathered around him a circle of the most intellectual men in the kingdom. Thompson, the poet, wrote his „Spring“ and died in Richmond. He slumbers in the church-yard beneath rose-bushes. The great Herschel built there an observatory for the king, who was his docile pupil in the sublimest of all the sciences. Many of the most important astronomical discoveries take their date from this spot, and the king, after having borne the burden of the imperial crown during the day, often, in a starry night served the great master, assiduously, as an assistant. Even in later days, when all the dreams of sovereignty were ended, and the pale asphodil-flower of deep, incurable sorrow, was sprouting in his soul, the remembrance of those nights at Richmond were a solace to the old monarch, and he often spoke of them, as if he would again reanimate the world which lay dead within him. Poor George! I saw him once — that majestic form, regal, like Lear's in his sorrow, with the full white locks, — bent on his crooked stick, slowly walking on the terrace of Windsor Castle, his large, blue eyes fixed steadfastly upon the ground, like a spirit that stalks around in a world to which it has ceased to belong. The burden of crowns and sceptres had bewildered his senses, and in a madness of nearly twenty years, he had given up his noble soul, in atonement for that guilt, which roots in the origin of all monarchy. —

The avenging angel, which drove Louis Philippe out of France, made of the fugitive king an inhabitant of Richmond in the summer-months during his last stay in England. Air and water agreed with him better than in Claremont, which his son-in-law Leopold, king of Belgium, had prepared for him, as his last asylum. — Stream of History, how wonderful are thy windings! For the Bourbons' sake England chained the Corsican Titan to the Ocean's rock; then, she affords refuge to the Bonaparte's again; to these follow the elder Bourbons, to these the Orleans, and after them we see the heads of the republic and its factions, from Ledru Rollin down to vile Girardin and the intriguing Thiers, seeking shelter in England while the most infamous of all, Mock-Napoleon usurps the Government of France, of that France which, rent by conflicting parties, convulsed by the wild uproar of demoniac powers, a prey to the worst set of adventurers and swindlers, cannot find repose, and waits but for the signal, to let loose a Typhoon over the continent, which now indeed lies fettered in an abyss, but when the spell is taken off and the hour of judgement has struck, will execute the dreadful verdict against the old society for the sins of the rulers and the ruled. Woe to all that see that hour; for the flood will roll up the bones of the slaughtered mountain high, and the heavy, gigantic, terrific dreams, which now trouble many who sleep, will become reality! — And the end? Have we no right to hope that, as the deluge of old, which once purified the earth from corrupted mankind, passed away — so the deluge to come in Europe will find also its ark and its Ararat, and when the waters have subsided, and the dove has brought the olive-branch, freed and bettered nations will build altars and their thankofferings will ascend to heaven? Or is our guilt so enormous, that no atonement will suffice, and that we dare not hope?

BAALBEC.

From East to West moves the sun, our planet's source of light and fecundity, on a yet unmeasured path through the universe; from East to West runs the life, the spirit, and the glory of nations the course of destiny; from Orient to Occident wandered the sway of empire; the march of pomp and power was from the rising to the setting sun. When the pride of India, Saba, Egypt, Phœnicia, Palestine, Babylon and Persia had passed away, when the diadem had fallen from the brow of Greece, it was transferred to the City of the Seven Hills, where the untamed energy of a youthful people struck deep root into the scarcely upturned soil. Rome, which, like Hercules, had in its cradle done battle with the serpents, became the seat of civilization and dominion. In the East and in the West the powers of the Earth retreated before her; crowns dissolved under her foot and nations bowed their necks to the claws of the irresistible Eagle. In the distant West, Rome rooted up the forests that gave shelter to barbarism and darkness, and in the track of the invader the seeds of civilisation were strewn in the virgin ground. In the East, Rome cleared away the rubbish of decayed and mouldering kingdoms, and introduced order into the Chaos of desolation and depravity. Roman life infused fresh youth into nations worn by old age and debility.

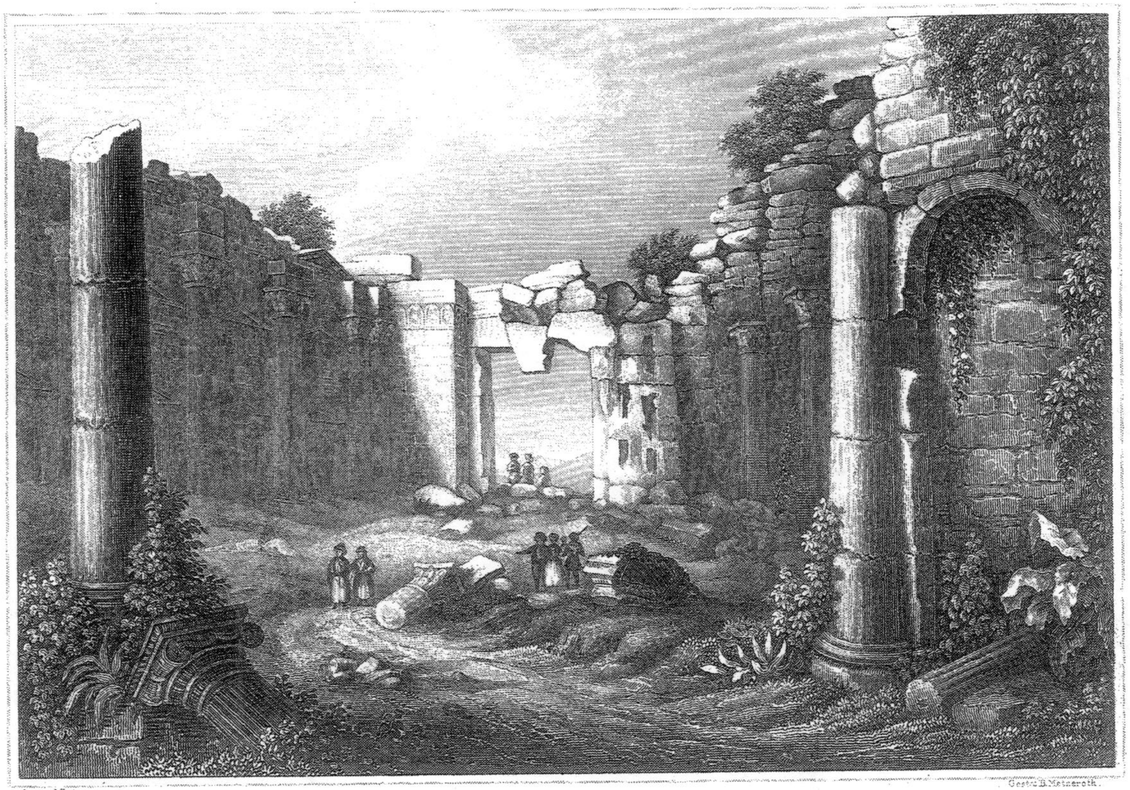

Gez. v. L. Reiss — Gest. v. B. Metzeroth.

THE TEMPLE OF THE SUN AT BALBEC

Published by HERRMANN J. MEYER 164 William Street NEW YORK.

Time rolled on, till after the lapse of many centuries the temple of Jupiter Capitolinus was closed, the games of the ancient gods were played out, and the empty sensualism of heathen worship was exhibited in all its barrenness. From the pastoral vales of Palestine, a new and imperishable Light began to cast its rays into the obscurity of the Roman world and accelerated its decay. The seven-hilled City was summoned to yield up the sceptre to the Teutonic race. From that moment, gone was her pomp and splendor, the Roman towns lost their populations, the roads were deserted; palaces, forum, academies and temples sunk into dust; the ancient world became a ruin-covered cemetery.

Among the fallen cities of the Roman world in the East, Baalbec, the city of the Syrian Province, was among the first in dignity, splendor and wealth. Baalbec was renowned for its luxury, and after the overthrow of the empire, as if struck by the retributive curse of Heaven, became, together with the surrounding country, waste and desolate. Pleasantly situated between the wealthy Damascus and the port of Tripoli in a valley of the Libanon range, its environs were naturally fertile and well-watered, opening towards the Mediterranean; but under the scourge of anarchy and despotism even paradise will turn a desert. — At the commencement of the preceding century, a colony of Turks settled among the ruins of Baalbec, and a small town arose numbering 4 to 5000 inhabitants. Its life was short. It vanished again in consequence of the invasions of plundering Arab tribes, and at present but a cluster of miserable hovels are remaining, half hidden by the huge fragments of the majestic structures of old, the shelter of predatory Bedouins, who pasture their flocks in the sanctuaries of the temples, and make the neighbourhood a horror to the tourists. — Ancient authors mention Baalbec comparatively but seldom. Macrobius speaks of it as the Heliopolis in Coelesyria. „City of the Sun," — this term corresponds in a great measure with Baalbec, the vale of Baal; for Baal is the name of the Assyrian God of the Sun. A doubtful tradition cites Solomon as the founder; a historical fact is, that it attained the zenith of its prosperity under the Emperors of Rome, and to this period we must refer those edifices, the ruins of wich are now the admiration of travellers.

In the Syrian province Roman life was grafted on both the Phoenician aud Grecian trunks and its most splendid blossoms were the Cities of Palmyra aud of Baalbec, both seats of a fabulous magnificence. The vestiges of the latter do not consist, as those of Palmyra, of a mass of masonry and columns covering a large extent of ground, but are confined to three groups of ruins, situated in the valley, not far from each other. They stand on an elevated platform, in itself the most gigantic work ever produced by human hands; for this huge terrace, which is nearly two miles in circumference, is composed of regularly-hewn blocks of stone, the smallest of which is 31 feet, the largest 54 feet in length, 18 in height and 10 feet in breadth. These stupendous masses are so accurately and firmly joined that, after almost two thousand years, it is not possible to introduce the blade of a pen-knife betwen the united blocks. One of the largest stones would, if hewn into cubes of the usual size, suffice for the construction of a palace in which a king might reside! They were brought from a quarry about 2 leagues distant, where stones of a magnitude similar to those described are still to be seen. Some of these are finished and lie at the edge of the quarry, in readiness for conveyance; others repose at the bottom of the pit, in a rough state. From these preparations it is evident that there was a design to carry out other works on a similarly gigantic scale; it is probable that the tempests of destruction and desolation broke so suddenly over Baalbec, that it was all at once swept into irretrievable obscurity. Later attempts at re-colonisation do not, in all likelihood, remount to a higher date than the period of the Moslim dominion, and they failed. — To all appearance the grandest days of Baalbec were during the reigns of the Antonines. The coins which have frequently been discovered in the ruins, mostly bear the stamp of this period, aud that the gorgous remains of the temples, still extant, are to be referred to the same era, has been sufficiently proved by antiquarian research. Subsequent additions are attributable to Saracenic origin and date from the times of the Crusades, when the principal ruins were turned into a fortress, and surrounded with walls aud bastions. These, however, have long since fallen, and are at present but a heap of rubbish. —

The platform, mentioned above, was reached by a majestic flight of marble steps, up which the Pilgrim-crowds were wont to make their way to the sacred halls of the Sun, and they were trodden by the trains of the decorated human victims, preceded by the priests of Baal, who not feared to sully their hands with the blood of their fellow beings. — The remnants of this staircase are to be seen peeping out from bush and weed. Immense fragments of sculptured blocks of marble and the beautiful capitals of columns have rolled down the declivity, and are strewed about in all directions. Between these ruins a narrow path winds upwards to the level of the platform. Here it is, that the imposing mass of the great Temple of the Sun strikes the soul with its gigantic grandeur. — The entrance is from the East, through a portico of 12 columns of granite. It leads into the first compartment of the temple, an hexagonal vestibule of 180 feet in diameter. This is encircled by a series of smaller halls, each in the most beautiful proportions and decorated with the richest profusion. Farther on we come to the Propylaeon or fore-court of the temple. It is of a square form, measures 574 ft. in length and 368 ft. in breadth, and is overgrown with grass and shrubs, here and there over-topped by a broken shaft, or a huge fragment of sculpture. An extensive range of colonnades adjoins this portion of the ruin. It is the Cella, or inner temple. Nine of the pillars, all of colossal dimensions, are standing upright. 56 of these columns supported once the roof of the Cella, which was 350 ft. long, 160 broad, and 90 ft. high. Anything more imposing and grand than this edifice previous to its destruction cannot be conceived by human imagination.

To the left of this largest of all the temples, stands a second and smaller shrine, in a somewhat better state of preservation. Of the 50 pillars it formerly possessed, 20 are erect. Eleven of these Columns support a richly sculptured piece of the vaulted roof that formerly covered the portion of the building between the inner and the external wall. The ceiling is in cassetoni, and each compartment represents a mythological subject in the finest basso-relievo. Contiguous to this structure we see a long row of chambers or cells, in a ruinous condition, in all probability once the dwellings of the priests. Here many admirable works of the sculptor's art struck the eye, but barbarous hands broke the pillars, removed the images from the niches, and struck off the ornaments or defaced them.

The third temple is the least considerable in point of size; the Cella, of circular form, is only 32 feet in diameter; yet it is the most beautiful remnant of antiquity to be found in all Syria. The edifice is constructed entirely of marble, and the decorations are executed with a delicacy that might rival the most exquisite work of the engraver. —

At the northern extremity of the terrace a second elevation composed of enormous blocks of marble may be perceived; here, there must formerly have been a fourth temple of rather small dimensions; but of this nothing is left, except two shafts of red Egyptian granite, and a few isolated capitals of pillars, which, together with some highly sculptured fragments of the entablature, lie scattered about the ground in the vicinity. —

The Ruins of Baalbec, splendid though they be, are yet vastly inferior to those of Athens, and bear evident testimony, that the period at which the buildings were erected, was not one of those epochs that inspire the soul of the artist with ennobling ideas. It was not the age of a Pericles. There is a certain tameness and monotony in these highly-finished friezes, entablatures, and cornices; there is endless repetition in the ornaments and often a want of congruity in design and concection. Technical skill preponderates every where over true art. We find festoons of grapes and wine-leaves suspended from the heads of goats and horses. Poverty of idea is every where manifest, and however much the technical skill may command our admiration, it cannot compensate for intellectual barrenness. In these fragments we see the work of slaves; the Roman Empire, where Despotism was deified, could not be the abode of free creative Art. —

If we seek the veritable inspiration of Art in her works, we must look either backwards or forwards: — backwards to those temple-caverns, excavated in the bowels of the mountain and breaking into the night of Creation, to the ruins watered by the Nile, where hieroglyphs falter forth the mysteries of by-gone ages, and sacred obelisks tower to the Sun; to the temple-crowned heights and Cyclopean remains of Greece; or forwards to the Minsters of the middle ages, whose masses seem to be piled by giants, and whose details appear to have been traced by the cunning hands of dwarfs; to the grand works of the old painters that gaze at us from their walls, and to those airy shapes, that glow in hues of fire on the praying crowd from the arched windows of stained glass. In these works of true art freedom of creation is expressed; but where the artist acts in obedience to extraneous influences, his endeavors will always confine themselves to prescribed formulas, and, as he loses the power of animating the inert material with the visions of his soul, his mastership shrinks into technical skill and his relative facility of imitation will constitute his pride and excellence.

CONSTANTINOPLE.

Stamboul, I ask thee; what hast thou been, what art thou now, and what wilt thou be? And thou repliest: „Man, read my answer in the history of Babylon and Persepolis!“ Yet if there were their history unwritten, if Stamboul were the first city founded upon the earth, there would be no difficulty of reply; for an answer would be given by the mole-heaps upon the field. They raise themselves out of the soil, they multiply, they cover the face of the plain; — but so soon as the industrious being, which dwells within, emigrates, the wind and tempest scatters them abroad, and their places are overgrown with grass and moss, unless a wandering emmet-tribe occupies the forsaken heap, builds there its cells, and introduces a new life.

Birth, growth and decay are the axioms of all created things. All the germinating powers in the organism of the universe are subservient to this triad in God's unbounded kingdom, and their alternate operation transforms time itself into eternity.

Slowly, like every thing great, did Constantinople run through the phases of her existence. An oracle gave her life, Hellas and Asia Minor suckled her, imperial Rome became her foster-mother, and brought her up to maturity. A favorite of destiny, Constantinople rapidly outstripped her coevals and contemporaries, and when she had reached the age of manhood, the genius of commerce conceived the importance of her position on the bridge of two continents,

STREET-SCENERY in CONSTANTINOPEL

and made her his residence and capital. In Constantinople the treasures of the world were piled up. Arts and Sciences sought the lap of opulence and when the empire of Western Rome was narrowed, and urged to its decline by the invading nations of the North, still for many centuries the halo of renown shone about her battlements; for, at a time, when everywhere else upon the earth, barbarism exercised unbounded sway, Byzantium was the preserver of the sacred fire, wherewith to re-light the torch of civilization. In steadfast array against foreign assault the Eastern Empire did, for a long time, held up her proud head amid storms and battles and victories, while the Roman world of the West received laws from barbarians and bore the servile yoke. At last Corruption led Byzantium to her decline, and Despotism caused her final ruin. Her night had already drawn near and still she wore the imperial diadem; but she wore it not like a venerable matron. Frivolity was the shame of her old age, and, harlot-like, she changed her favorites as occasion demanded or wooed for passing favors. Thus, for more than a thousand years, had Constantinople vainly attempted to hold fast her fleeting beauty, while, with unsparing hand, time washed the paint from her faded charms. Though Constantinople once more rose to political power under the Turks it never regained wealth and happiness. The crescent is a declining luminary, and as long as it is shining on the dome of San Sophia, Constantinople cannot revive. The restitution of her greatness depends upon the ruin of the Ottoman empire. Her motto is: sub cruce salus.

The cities of the East have many advantages over those of the Western world. Their sites excel with few exceptions in picturesque beauty and antiquity, and historic lore throws on them peculiar charms. The West made it a rule to build cities where material advantages were most likely to be acquired; on the sandy shore of the ocean, on the banks of broad, navigable rivers, or in the plain, where no mountains inpede traffic. — The imaginative Oriental is, on the contrary, lured by those luxurious, dazzling charms, of which nature is so lavish in the East, to spots, where he can surrender himself undisturbed to sensual pleasures and voluptous reveries.

The Capital of the Turkish empire possesses in a high degree the advantages common to the oriental cities. On approaching it from the sea of Marmora, an archipelago of charming islands swims before the enraptured eye, as they shine in the varied green of groves and gardens. From every height looks down an old fortress, or a gray cloister, or a ruin of Christian or Grecian antiquity, mirrored in the calm, clear waters.

Far to the right, Mount Olympus lifts his head, brightly and proudly, to heaven.

In the fore-ground, the shore of Asia Minor sweeps toward the mouth of the Bosphorus, and the eye roams among the innumerable bosquets of Cypresses, under which the generations of two milleniums repose. This largest of all cemetries in the world covers the shore for the length of a league and a half, overtopped by the houses and mosques of Scutari.

On the opposite side, upon two promontories, which project far into the sea, Stamboul itself is seen stretching out in indolent repose over several hills, crowned with palaces and edifices of many styles and ages, like the pearls and precious stones upon an old and filthy garment. An arm of the sea reaches deeply into the mass of the houses. It forms the harbor. Gigantic and motionless the war-ships of the Porte, with their enormous guns, their clumsy masts, and the threatening lion at the prow, lie anchored beside the agile frigates of France, England and America. Barks, gondolas, caiques, galleys fully manned, Greek and Turkish merchant-vessels throng together, affording a picture, as motley and fantastic as the crews, which crowd their decks, from the handsome, noble Caucasian down to the industrious Negro, through all the types of the human race. On the right of Stamboul many crooked Streets are seen ascending a hill. It is old Galata, the Genoese colony, now a suburb of Constantinople and further on Pera, the quarter of the Franks crowned by the Russian ambassadors proud residence, more resembling a citadel, than a palace. From the terrace of the latter may be enjoyed the most fascinating view of Constantinople and her environs. The enraptured eye roams with delight over Pera, the garden-girded city, and over the harbor at her feet, while the hills of Stambul display their soft and wavy outlines, from which the Imperial mosques, with their shining metal-roofs, slender, sparkling minarets, and flashing crescents, look down, like the characteristic features of an expressive face. The artless heart glows with joy over the beauty with which kind Nature enwraps this weak and aged body.

So much the greater is the disappointment of the European traveller, on entering the gates of the Turkish Capital. Constantinople has not, like London, its Cheapside, nor, like Paris, its Boulevards, which course, like veins, through and round the city, and in which its life moves back and forth in a constant tide. Here are no elegant, straight streets, no clean side-walks, with a throng of foot-passengers, humming in all the tongues of the globe, with the din of carriages continually crossing and barring each other's way; no houses with graceful or magnificent fronts line broad avenues; no signs on the corners with the names of the streets, to help the stranger find his way; no placards stare him in the face, with their gigantic characters; no ringing of bells proclaims the festival; no clock tells the hour; no lamps light the streets by night — nothing of all this; numberless narrow, crooked, dirty alleys with a wretched, uneven pavement, show you labyrinthian ways, trodden in general by a shabby and mean-looking population.

That most common feature of every great city of Western Europe — the dashing carriage with its pair of horses — is wanting in the city of the Turks. In their place we see the Oroba, a cumbrous caleche drawn by oxen. The Turkish Ladies use these vehicles, and oftentimes they are attended by an escort of armed eunuchs. The houses are, for the most part, poor fabrics. They rise in the form of a quadrangle, with walls of bricks or clay, and upon this rests a wooden structure of two stories, loosely put together, the upper of which projects over the lower one far into the street. Carved work, in miserable taste, decorates the façades, and a coat of red, white, or yellow paint completes their outward ornament. Owing to this slight and wretched mode of construction, conflagrations are so frequent and so destructive. It is computed that the city is generally rebuilt every hundred years. The Turk occupies with his family generally a house by himself, as the mysteries of the harem do not permit the reception of lodgers. It is divided into the portion inhabited by the master of the house, and that destined exclusively for the ladies. The former contains seldom more than two rooms, and no furniture except carpets and divans of more or less costly material. The richer household furniture is devoted to the apartments of the women, and consequently is withdrawn from the eyes of strangers.

With reading rooms, clubs, banquets, concerts, theatres, balls, and whatever else in the West turns the night into day, the Turk is entirely unacquainted. He shrinks from all noisy and violent agitation of the senses and feelings, and when evening comes, he is desirous of nothing but repose. It is in the day-time, and then only in the harbor and bazaars, upon the market places, in the coffee-houses, in the baths, in and about the principal mosques, and in the khans and caravanserais, that the popular life of the Ottoman capital stirs in a quicker, livelier round, affording a glimpse of its characteristic features.

Almost all the mosques in Constantinople bear the names of their founders. They are, for the most part, expiatory offerings of Sultans for slaughtered nations, or for murdered subjects, and for horrible crimes committed against their own family or offspring. In short they have arisen, as the St. Peter's, the Escurials, the cloisters and abbeys of the west, which to the shame and mockery of the age, are now rebuilding at the command of kings and priests.

No rule so bad as to be without honorable exceptions! True and genuine faith in God has erected many a mosque, as well as many a church, and whether the crescent or the cross proclaims its sway, there is ONE who, doubtless, recognizes true piety under the turban as well as under the cowl. — All the principal mosques are surmounted with a vast, semi-spherical dome, which, covered with metal, and with the slender gold-tipped minarets at their side, appear in the rays of the setting sun like glowing canopies, supported by golden columns. The smaller mosques have but one turret of the kind, the larger ones usually four. From its uppermost gallery, the muezzin calls five times a day to the people below: „There is but one God, and Mahomet is his prophet: assemble to prayer!“ And when this call resounds from all the minarets, pronounced by more than two thousand human voices, it produces a solemn, unearthly impression. This summons to prayer at fixed hours compensates for the want of clock and bell. — The markets (here, as in all the East, called Bazaars) are most numerous in the neighborhood of the great mosques; they often stretch undisturbed into their front-courts, as, for example, the great Rasesta, near Soliman's mosque. They represent wide, vaulted galleries, with strong, massive walls, in which the luxury of Oriental life lies spread out in array, and Turks, Franks and Rayahs of all ranks and conditions are constantly seen walking to and fro in motley confusion.

The inclination to social pleasures is but weak with the Ottoman. The entertainment, he does not find in the Bazaar, he seeks in the coffee-houses, upon which he lavishes all imaginable elegance and ornament in his peculiar taste. Sumptuously decorated on the front, which faces the street, every coffee-house has, for its entrance, an open portico, sustained by pillars. The rooms in which the guests assemble, are also decorated with pillars, and furnished with cushions and divans, upon which the visitors sit cross-legged. In silence and grave repose they listen to the music of a mandoline or tamburine, with which Greek slaves accompany their simple songs.

Smoking his pipe and drinking his coffee, the Turk dreams the hours away in silence; he never desires the pleasures of conversation. He prefers to listen to the tale of a wandering story-teller, one or more of whom may be met with in every Turkish coffee-house.

The use of the bath is indispensable to the Turk, and the public baths range among the most spacious buildings of the metrepolis. To the Mahometan, cleanliness of the body should be a symbol of cleanliness of the soul, and the Prophet has commanded this most strictly. He did it for the same wise reason that he forbade them the use of wine. Mahomet wished, by cleanliness and temperance, to preserve the corporeal and mental health of his people; for the robust and strong alone can conquer the world, and permanently maintain his rule over subjugated nations. But how greatly has the Turk perverted the intention of his prophet! Instead of wine he indulges in the enervating, stupefying opium, and of the prescribed cleanliness he has made a screen for the most inordinate voluptuousness. In the saloon of an Oriental bath is found every thing that can effeminate and blunt the senses. The warm bath, if habitually used, is always detrimental to a healthy constitution; for it relaxes and enervates instead of strengthening. The Turkish population of Constantinople are a proof of this upon a large scale. It is, in fact the speaking, appalling picture of the disease and decay of a nation! These Musselmen, who poured forth, like a tempest, from their deserts, through the gates of Africa and Europe, who subjected millions to their sword and their faith, and caused two continents to tremble to their very centre — without sympathy for all political emergencies, incapable of any intellectual elevation, physically and morally benumbed, now creep over the conquered land, wasting and withering in the luxury of their harems, and their fancies creating nothing but the extravagant visions of sensuality. Though good-natured, and sometimes even generous, the imbecile Sultan follows the train of despotism and cruelty; while the nation herself is sinking in the mire of enervation and degeneracy defenceless against the sharp weapons, with which time, more merciless than the great powers of Europe beats against the old, crumbling structure, which already totters to its fall.

Constantinople has passed through three transformations. To Greek life followed Roman sway, and over the ruins of the Eastern empire, the Turks marched into the ancient city of Byzantium. The people of the north will renovate it for the fourth time. But when the circle of its metamorphoses is closed, it will pass away, like all temporal things; — her place will become a waste and a desert, and after a few thousand years the wanderer will, perhaps, inquire in vain for its last ruins.

THE CATHEDRAL AT STRASBURGH

Published by HERRMANN J. MEYER 164. William-Street NEWYORK.

THE CATHEDRAL OF STRASBURG.

Meyer's UNIVERSUM is something more than a picture-book. Its chief aim is not to please the eye of the amateur, to amuse the idle, or to satiate the inquisitive with geographical, ethnographical, statistical and historical notices. In effecting these objects, hundreds of pens, pencils and presses are continually busy. We rejoice at their activity, for „knowledge is power“.

The leaves of the „Universum“ belong to another tree. We will elevate the mind to the contemplation of God's wisdom in his creation and propagate Truth that stirs the soul of man. Truth! if it lies in the abyss of ocean we dragg it forth; if it be concealed in the infinitude of space, we find it out! God's works are spread out before us, and we contemplate them with a heart open to every emotion, which the view calls forth. We sport with the verdure of the meadow, pause over the enamelled fields of the quiet landscape, soar with the Alps to the clouds, follow the stream and river toward the unbounded ocean, and tremble in reverence before the omnipotence of the Creator, which speaks in the yawning volcano, and the thundering waters of the cataract. We know nothing of a dead nature. We seek and find life every where. And for that very reason our thoughts by preference hold fast to man — to man, the highest developem ent of created life.

Man's great works are consequently among our favorite pictures. If, before the overwhelming, gigantic masses of the Creation, and their immensurable powers of Nature, man stands silent and trembling, if his senses reel at the sight of the ladder, which should lead him up to the full recognition of the master-builder and his plan of creation, in the great works of human genius he finds a convenient and safe bridge to the recognition of the Allpowerful, und he trusts himself to it with confidence. Such works may be either the words of the poet, or the reasonings of the philosopher, the writings of the scholar, the tones of the musician, the productions of painting, sculpture and architecture. In viewing a great edifice, for instance, we imagine to see thousands of human powers at work, who for the benefit of living and future generations copy in stone the images that arose in the mind the artist. As the thoughts of God are represented in the Universe, we see man's thought represented in the grand works of architecture; and though such copy in brass and stone perishes in the storm of time, its effects on the minds of generations is not lost or perishable.

Therefore on our wanderings through the world we gaze with ever-renewed delight at those beautiful and mighty forms, which the ant-like industry of men has, in the course of many centuries, called into exitence. The thought of human helplessness and frailty, of the many workmen, who have graved and carved, for many years, upon the pinnacles and pillars, blocks of stone and piers, and on the multifarious sculpture, and who now lie all buried and forgotten, has nothing discouraging in it; for our bosom heaves, and our head is raised aloft at the consciousness that such a work has arisen in the mind of a single man, upon whom God deigned to cast a glance of favor. Such works alone are able to enchain the admiration of ages. Each century has its own taste, and man changes the forms of his productions accordingly. The taste of the age, that unstable child of the hour, dictates its laws from generation to generation like an absolute monarch; but its influence is powerless upon those mightiest of human works; they stand, through thousands of years, as unchangeable symbols of beauty and as objects of universal admiration.

A structure of this kind is that giant of German architecture, that towers aloft upon the cathedral-square in Strasburg. We have a correct view of it in the accompanying engraving, and our descriptive pen might stop here, if we had come as an architect, as an amateur or antiquary. But no! we will ascend Erwin's tower, to look at more stirring scenes than the assembled wonders of German art in the church below.

We have ascended. — A joyous din resounds from the streets of the ancient city of Alsatia. Look down! the market places and squares are thronged, the houses arrayed in festive green, the tricolored flag flutters from gable and tower, crowds of men, in variegated attire, march behind bands of music. Gaily dressed groups pour in through all the gates, and the cannon thunder forth their greeting, amid the rising hum and bustle of the throng. What can this mean? Some grand national festival, you guess! — Every people has times and days in its life, which stand printed in red letters in its almanacs, proclaiming joy to the Land and its citizens. Such holy-days appear like Alpine peaks, and glow long in the light of a proud and happy remembrance; they are the days on which the people, as it were, cuts a score on the tally of Eternity, and on which it pledges itself in the cup of joy, filled to the very brim. And it is probably such a day that the people of Alsatia are celebrating; a day which mounts the ladder of time from century to century; a day, which rooted in ages long gone by, entwines the people's heart with the national evergreen; a day on which German life puts forth new shoots.

And for the confirmation of your guess you ask your guiding friend: „Good Sir! what does this festivity below mean?" — „„Alsatia celebrates to day the two hundreth anniversary of her union with France!"" is the answer.

You stand amazed. „„And the Alsatians are not the worse for that, I think,““ continues your companion after a pause. — The blood paints your face with the color of indignation. „No Sir“ — you retort with elevated voice. — „I would not partake in your judgment! Celebrates the separation from her native Land? In the game of war, a portion of a nation may be lost to a foreign winner; of this History gives thousand instances; that such portion of the people, torn from the common country by a foreign conqueror and subjected to his sway, has never, during more than two centuries, made the slightest attempt to shake off the yoke, and join itself again to its native land, is humiliating in the eyes of all nations; but that such people should even celebrate its separation from its native country with a jubilee — this stands as an instance of complete national degradation.“

„Allow we some remarks to rectify your severe judgement dear Sir;“ said the Alsatian with composure. „The fault is not on our side of the Rhine. After the German princes, by continual rebellion, had broken the strength of the Empire, after they had raised the standard of Despotism, and had cast upon the Germans the yoke of slavery, after they had robbed the domains of the church, and oppressed and swallowed up the weaker princes of the empire, they directed all their efforts to root out the popular rights, manners and customs, and to effect the destruction of all freedom, for the sole advantage of their family-sway, and to satisfy their thirst for despotism. In the lands under their dominion they saw mere court fiefs; in German citizens, mere serfs. They had transformed the empire into a pestilential march, and rendered the imperial sceptre a mockery to the whole world. To be called a German became a public insult. There was a time when they even garnished the language with foreign words, that no one might recognize it, yea, a time was, when the princes and their courts were ashamed to speak their mother-tongue! Were the Alsatians then to be blamed if they esteemed themselves fortunate in being loosed from a tie, which was but a chain of slavery, and which was branded with the universal scorn? Even on a comparison between the wild misrule in the German empire, and that of the most licentious French kings in the seventeenth and eighteenth centuries, — the question: „Which way to turn?“ could excite no hesitation in the people of Alsatia. All the baseness and meanness of the French government was surpassed in Germany, and corruption united with feebleness and disgrace filled every heart with loathing. This state lasted until the French revolution broke out. The revolution made Alsatia free, though her freedom lay in a sea of blood. The great Corsican defrauded the revolution; he gave the French *glory* instead of *liberty*; the *eagle* flew from battle to battle, and from victory to victory over the continent. Alsatia shared in the intoxication and kneeled before her idol in the imperial mantle. It was an idol; true! yet it was one of *their own* making. The German princes however, in union with their degraded people, bowed like cowards to the *foreign* master and kissed the fetters which they received from his hands. No sooner, than when the irons had become intolerable, were they thrown off; and then — the cheated nation exchanged chains for chains. What oppression was heavier than that following the downfall of Napoleon? And what, during this period of bondage, could have lured the Alsatians to sympathize with their fatherland of Old? It was a night of despotism, which Metternich and his comrades guarded as carefully as Cerberus the gates of Hell.

For the crowned heads of Germany *that* was a golden era. Their faithful house-dogs watched; the people, closely penned, slept; the press was deaf and dumb. The princes felt secure. They went travelling. Like the gnats in the sunbeams of a summer-evening, uncles, aunts, nephews, cousins swarmed around in Asia, America and Europe, revelling in the good things of life, and the forcing-pumps which stood in the marrow of the German people, were kept, the while, merrily at work, and the millions which these travels cost, did not cease to flow. That, you conceive, dear Sir, was no time either for the Alsatians to sympathize with the old fatherland. Nor is such a time come at present. For you will allow, that no word is able to express the disgrace of Germany and the baseness of her condition at the hour in which we are speaking.

And taking me by the hand and leading me to the other side of the gallery of the tower, he exclaimed: „Look around! —“

„Yonder lies the lovely land, nestling closely about the old city and her gigantic Cathedral. Westward, the Vosges-mountains bar to the eye the gates of France; east-ward the beautiful plains unfold themselves, as if spreading out their arms in welcome. And can that be called a boundary-line? The Rhine divides nothing, it but adorns, as a silver girdle, the green, rich robe of the fairest German land.“

„Yes, Sir“ — my friend continued with emotion — „a day will come for re-uniting this paradise to the old fatherland? The union-ties will be perfect freedom and national honor. But not until the nation has stripped off its old superstition to the last shred, not until the belief has become a living one, that she possesses „by God's grace“ the right of selfgovernment and that no other right of domination exists besides; not until she proudly feels her power, and knows that not another on earth should be greater than hers; not until she will no longer doubt that all Germany should belong to her alone, and that she may not concede the smallest portion of it to other kingdoms and to foreign kings; in fine, not until the knowledge of her strength and of her rights has penetrated the nation's bone and marrow; not until all the liveries of Dynasties have faded, and instead of many crowns a single civic cap covers the head, by which the nation is governed according to laws, which, by virtue of her eternal rights, she has given to herself; not until Germany has found her Washington and built her Capitol: not sooner! —

Though distant far the day, and hid in gloom,
This do we know: — the time will surely come!

As a work of Architecture, the Strasburg cathedral takes its place among the grandest and most sublime monuments of the middle Ages. Neither pen nor pencil is able to depict, with due force, the impression which the sight of this temple produces upon the beholder.

When we have grasped the effect of it as a whole, and then proceed to examine the single parts of the gigantic edifice, we know not to which to give the preference: whether to the proud and lofty tower, planned with the most profound knowledge of the equipoise of masses, and decorated with the utmost beauty, or to the glorious construction of the oblong building, of the transept and of the choir, with their harmonious and admirably arranged ornaments, or to the lofty middle nave, with its forest of pillars, and colossal windows, filled with stained glass, or to the admirable pulpit, adorned with the richest sculpture, or to the side-chapels, with their elaborately decorated vaults, and grave sepulchral monuments, or to the three front-portals sumptuously adorned with statues and carved work in stone, or to the lofty and slender clustered columns, which separate chapels and naves, or to the outer halls with their innumerable ornaments, whether to the grand arrangement of the exterior or of the interior, whether to the massive construction of the architectural pile, intended to endure for milleniums, or to the art which has decorated it. Even the coldest mind feels the fire of enthusiasm, and scepticism itself can find no fault; no one leaves the marvellous edifice without the thought: „Its like I shall not see on earth again!“

The material of which the cathedral is constructed, is a pale red sand-stone. The dimensions of the structure are most colossal. The length is three hundred and forty three feet; the oblong building which is divided into three naves is a hundred and fourteen feet wide; the length of the transept measures a hundred and seventy three feet. Its area, forty eight thousand and fifty two square feet, bears a proportion to that of the largest Churches in the United States as four to one. The lofty pillars of the middle nave support two rows of arches, and through these the light enters from fourteen immense, pointed-arched windows, which, as well as the windows of several side-chapels, are decorated with exquisite glass-paintings. A circular window, of the most wonderful workmanship, and of a size without parallel on earth, is pierced above the middle doorway; and others placed over the two side-portals at the ends of the transept, and in the choir, complete the effects of light a shade. Beneath the choir is built a subterraneous temple in the purest gothic style, a kind of crypt, commonly called the chapel of the sacred grave, and under this, forty feet under ground, is the treasury, in which are preserved the sacred objects and relics belonging to the cathedral. The treasury receives its light through two windows in the ceiling, which communicate with the transept.

Before leaving our object we cast a glance on the architectural beauties of the towers. The front is pierced by three vast doorways, deeply recessed, in the German style, which are decorated with rich pediments and a profusion of sculpture. The proportions are so colossal that men standing in the middle archway appear like emmets. It is twenty four feet wide, by a height of nearly thirty eight feet. The side of the doorway-walls, are divided, by a succession of shafts, into five deep hollows; the latter are adorned with not less than seventy statues of saints, and a profusion of the works of sculpture. Before the middle-shaft, which divides the inner door, stands a colossal statue of the Virgin, with the infant Jesus, playing with a globe. The fine, dark sand-stone, of which all these images are carved, is of a peculiar color; they seem as if cast in bronze. Many have undergone repairs, several indeed are entirely new; for the Vandals of war and revolution have not spared the church in their devastations. The celebrated tables of bronze that adorned the portals, representations of biblical subjects, — in consequence of a decree of the Parisian Convent of 1792 — were coined into cents! The noble carved work in stone over the middle entrance was more fortunate; it is in a state of perfect preservation. It represents the Lord's Supper, Jesus taken prisoner, the Crucifixion, the Resurrection, and the Ascension of Christ. The side door-ways are ornamented in a similar manner, with statues and bas-reliefs. Ornaments in the arabesque style of the middle-ages twine and shoot up along the façade of the tower, forming and enclosing niches, in which stand the stone-figures of the heroes, high-priests, and prophets of the old testament, of the christian apostles and saints, and of the palatines and emperors of the German empire holding their swords and globes. The colossal equestrian statues of the kings of Franconia, Clodowig and Dagobert, and of the emperor Rudolph of Habsburg, were of unrivalled beauty; they were hurled from their pedestals by the Vandal-apostles of equality. Those which now supply their places scarcely give the bare idea of the excellence of the originals. A masterpiece of the architect, a winding staircase of stone, numbering three hundred and twenty nine steps, leads to the platform of the tower, where the watchman has his lodge. From this platform, one of the two spires originally projected, rises to the clouds. The pinnacle, shooting up in the form of an octagon, and diminishing by graduated steps, is a perfect model of elegance and lightness. It terminates in a colossal cross, once crowned with a golden statue of the virgin Mary.

Goethe, the celebrated poet, judges of the wonderful structure in the following terms. „The architect had made it his task to combine contradictory principles. He has blended the colossal with lightness and grace, and although pierced in a thousand places like lacework, he gave to the heaven-aspiring walls the idea of immoveable firmness. The solution of this problem was most difficult. It belonged to the highest realm of the art, and the architect, in conquering the difficulty, has shown his mastership. The carved network in the walls, their solid masses, the gigantic pillars, have each their peculiar character, arising out of their particular destination. Hence, all the decorations are appropriate. The great as well as the minute are found in their proper places, where they are easily comprehended. Beauty is thus harmoniously combined with Grandeur. Proof of this is afforded in every part of the structure. At the very doorways you are struck with their perspective, and their massiveness is combined with the most elaborate ornaments; looking up at the window above, which, from its circular shape, and beautiful carving, forms an artificial rose, admiration seizes your soul. If you were standing in this doorway for a whole day, your imagination would be continually busy. You might fancy the pillars retreating, accompanied by the slender-shafted, pointed-roofed niches, shooting aloft, destined, as canopies, for the protection of the statues of the saints, and, at last, each rib, each boss will show you a flower, or row of foliage, or some object of animated nature moulded in stone.“

The history of the erection of the celebrated cathedral stretches back to the early time of the first propagation of Christianity in the Roman cities upon the Rhine. On the site of a famous temple of Mars, king Clodowig (between the years 504 — 510) built a christian Basilica. The main part of his church was preserved, when Pipin undertook to rear the cathedral, which Charlemagne completed. This oblong building, in the Byzantine style, with its arches of light tuffa, has, in spite of all the metamorphoses effected by later alterations, by conflagration, war, and the devastations of fourteen centuries, been preserved to the present day. After the storming of Strasburg by Herrmann, duke of Alsatia, on the 4. April 1002, during which the greater part of the city fell a prey to the flames, the Cathedral was destroyed, with the exception of the above mentioned erection of Clodowig, which proved indestructible. Bishop Wernher undertook the rebuiling of the church; but scarcely was it completed, when the lightning struck the roof of the tower, and the glorious temple was again burnt to the ground. Then a saying went through the German lands that Satan himself had fired it; and that in his joy he had promised to feast Hell as long as the God'shouse in Strasburg were lying waste. Now, to shorten the devils' festival, a hundred priests went wandering through all Germany, summoning the people to contribute offerings for the speedy rebuilding of the temple. So freely, in consequence, flowed the golden stream toward Strasburg, that Bishop Wernher was enabled to plan the re-construction of the edifice upon a much more magnificent scale than originally intended. Wernher began the work, but died long before its completion in the year 1028.

Thirty years after, the lateral naves were over-arched. The building of the chapels occupied the workmen down to the thirteenth century. In the year 1269 the church itself was completed. Decorated by art within and without, it stood, the great speaking deed of religious enthusiasm. Yet the crown was still wanting to this gigantic work; it had no tower. This was the object of the third attempt to rouse the religious fire. The undertaking was the most difficult, and its execution occupied the longest period. — The greatest German architect of all times, Erwin von Steinbach, sketched the plan at the command of Bishop Conrad von Lichtenberg and the solemnity of laying the first stone took place on the 25. May 1277.

With the Pope's consent, Bishop Conrad proclaimed an indulgence. All believers in the Christian faith, who contributed to the construction of the tower, whether in money, in building-material, or in labor, were promised forgiveness of all sins, as well of those already committed, as of future ones, for 40,000 years! Parchment now became dear in Germany; for each quittance of sin was written upon asses' skin. Money poured in from all quarters and the flood, continually nourished by the sale of indulgences, did not subside for a long time. With the offerings of credulous stupidity were mixed those of national pride. Year after year thousands of workmen came to Strasburg from all the districts of Germany to offer their hands and skill without reward or hire, and large trains of waggons drove on from the most distant borders, even from Austria, charged with iron, stone and timber for the structure. The rich bequeathed on their deathbeds large sums for the prosecution of the work, princes and lords sent artists to decorate the building at their cost, and many cloisters devoted the fourth part of their revenues for a succession of years to further the grand undertaking. A violent earthquake, which, towards the end of the thirteenth century spread a panic through all Alsatia, put the strength of the structure to a rude test; houses and palaces tumbled down in Strasburg, but not a stone in the Cathedral was loosened from its place. A terrible conflagration, which, in 1289, laid all the city around in ashes, could only consume the wooden portion of the roof, and the scaffolding for the steeple then building.

Erwin, the grand architect, died, after having reared the tower to a level with the roof of the church and his son John was chosen in the father's place. The latter continued the gigantic work up to the platform. He died in 1339. John Erwin was succeeded by John Hulz, whose grandson completed the spire. In the year of our Lord 1339 he erected the colossal cross, and placed upon its top the statue of the virgin Mary. From the laying of the corner-stone in 1277, more than a century and a half had passed away, and during this long period, which had consumed five generations, the labors of the workmen had not been interrupted for a single day.

Since then, embracing a period of four centuries, rain, storm and thunderbolts have beaten against the wondrous structure; but only to display their impotence. More than sixty times has the lightning struck the cathedral-tower, without doing any material damage, and five earthquakes have in vain shaken its firm foundations. What the elements have been unable to accomplish, has been attempted by human folly. In the seventeenth century, when the degeneration of taste broke in, like a flood, at all the temple-doors, the altars and chapels of Erwin's time, with their inestimable monuments of art, were torn down and removed, to make room for the abominable, senseless decorations of that disgusting roccoco-period, which is known as the age of Louis XIV. The French revolution made an end to this period and relieved the social world from the disgusting spectacle of a thoroughly-rotten monarchy; but she appeared as a destroying angel in the cathedral of Strasburg. Fancying, that the glorious grandeur of the building stood in opposition to the principle of equality, it was proposed by the common council to take down the spire and to deprive the church of all artistical decorations. The mad proposal of the fanatics met with the applause of the Paris Convent. The scaffolding towered up and the levellers went to work. They destroyed fifteen of the noblest statues in the great doorway, seventy of the most beautiful groups of sculpture, placed in the recesses of the walls, were thrown down and broken in pieces; eighty statues were cast from their niches, the angels hurled from their basements, the colossal statues of the Apostles, wonders of art, destroyed, three of the admirable equestrian statues blown up with powder, and the countless ornaments of the walls, windows and altars broken off, or mutilated. Inumerable works of art perished under the axes and hammers of the fierce, ignorant rabble of liberty. When at last, reason had resumed her sway, shame and repentance stepped in; alas! too late. The French government and the ecclesiastical authorities did all they could to conceal, by skilful repairs, the disgraceful mutilation of the grandest work of German architecture; yet what modern art has placed in the room of the destroyed works, can no more compensate for the irretrievable loss than a clever copy for one of Raphael's originals. It is but too often that incapacity speaks out of these imitated forms; the higher inspiration is wanting, they are not works of creative genius.

A last fare-well to the grand work of Erwin! Bitterly and angrily does the cross of the spire look down upon Alsatia, the German land in a foreign hand. There is no hope of a voluntary restitution. But the time will come, when Germany's claims will be vindicated, not by the lips of treacherous princes and diplomates, but by the sword and arms of a selfgoverned people.

TELL'S CHAPEL NEAR KUSSNACHT IN SWITZERLAND.

In the heart of Switzerland, in the bosom of wood-crowned mountains, lies the Lake of Lucerne. Its length, extending from Altdorf to Lucerne is eighteen miles. Its width is very irregular; from Kussnacht to Stantz, where it throws out arms somewhat in the shape of a cross, it measures twelve miles. The lake narrows in many places to an english mile and in most it is hardly broader than two. Lucerne-lake is inferior to none of the Alpine basins in variety of beauty. At each turn new scenery presents itself, and the surrounding landscape is clad with new charms. At its northern extremity, where the Reuss pours forth its waters, the prevailing character is that of the picturesque and graceful. Low hills, clothed with vineyards, clumps of trees, and isolated groups of rocks, form, as it were, a Propylaeon to the awful splendors of the Alpine world, which an excursion on the lake discloses to the traveller. As you proceed, the shores rise, the separate groups of rocks draw closer together, forming perpendicular bluffs; the dwellings of men no longer find room on the margin of the lake and at last, entirely disappear. On either side, the mountains tower their steep and rocky walls towards heaven, the tops girdled with woods and till late in summer capped with

TELL'S CHAPEL NEAR KUSSNACHT

(SWITZERLAND)

Published for HERRMANN J. MEYER. 164, William-Street, NEWYORK.

snow. The clouds continually play about their brows. There begins the region of the Alpine pastures, (Alms) sprinkled with the lonely huts of the herdsmen and with grazing cows, and the ear listens to the tinkling bells, or the melodious horn, mingling with the solemn dashing of the waves. Still further up the perpendicular walls of the shore rise higher and higher; often overhanging, often inclining their summits toward each other, as if to hold conversation.

In this region deep chasms abound and the mountain-crests are perfecty bare; not a shrub can strike root, nor a blade of grass or a creeping evergreen find a cleft in which to cling fast. Lonely peaks, which no human foot has ever ascended, pierce the clouds — asylums of the eagle and haunts of the bear. In these regions of eternal ice and snow not a voice is heard but the cataract, which gushes over the precipice; no sound rises from the depths, but the dash of the waterfalls or the thunders of the avalanche, or the cracking of the glaciers or the howling of the storm. For the space of a league not a hut or dwelling is visible, or finds room on the rocky shore. The first human trace that appears again, is a fisherman's hamlet, upon a sloping promontory, and upon the green matten on the heights the eye again perceives the herdsman with his beasts and goats seeking the sprouting herbs. At times, a mountaineer is seen climbing aloft, who, with a net bound about his loins, scrambles onward from rock to rock, and hazarding his life for an arm-full of grass.

In the neighborhood of this lake, nineteen hundred years ago, the remnants of the Cimbri and Teutones sought a refuge from a war of extermination, they fought with the Romans. They occupied the desolate valleys and dales near the shores of the lake, and colonized the adjoining woodlands, that are rich with juicy herbs and nourishing grasses. The descendants of these German tribes, a race of shepherds, spread in the country now known as the cantons of Schwyz, Unterwalden, and Uri. Patriarchal simplicity is still the leading character of these people. They are equally ignorant of the advancement of sciences and of the refined pleasures of social life. German feelings and

German customs are scrupulously preserved among them. Neither Romans, nor Goths, nor Huns, nor Allemanni, nor Burgundians, nor Franks have ever coveted their poor wastes, or desired a contest with this hardy race of men. From ancient times they have pastured their flocks upon the mountains in undisturbed possession of their hereditary freedom and institutions. Even late in the middle ages, neither baronial castle, nor cloister was seen upon these heights, nor a town in these vales. Centuries passed away and they owned but a single church. It stood in the valley of Mutten; thither the inhabitants of Uri, Unterwalden and Schwyz repaired for worship, and as one house of God gathered all these tribes, so also they had but one magistracy in common. After the usage of old, they chose honest men for judges every year, by the voices of the people.

The customs and traditionary laws of a free common-wealth were cherished in purity through many generations. By and by the people had grown more numerous, so that a single church could no longer take them in, and a single tribunal could not adjust and decide all causes. Therefore they divided into three communities, each of which chose its Landammann, common council and court. Schwyz, Uri, and Unterwalden became separate republics. At that time there was no claim of sovereignty over the country, except that of the German Empire and the people were content to enjoy the imperial guaranty of their liberties. The emperor on his part was satisfied with the bare semblance of supremacy, and left to the people even the choice of the imperial Lord chief-judge, who, as the highest court of judicature, decided all differences between the cantons. While, in other parts of Switzerland knights and cloisters attained a great power over the people, the three cantons on the lake of Lucerne were dependent but upon the emperor himself, and when the princes of Germany chose the Swiss Rudolf of the race of Habsburg for their emperor, his first act was the sanction of the self-government of the three cantons bordering the lake of Lucerne.

At Rudolf's death, a different state of things succeeded. Albert, his son and successor, was of ambitious temper, and paid no regard to popular freedom. Then Uri, Schwyz and Unterwalden saw the danger; they convened, and „in expectation of evil times" they solemnly renewed in full assembly of the people their ancient league, and swore a solemn oath to be henceforth „like one body and one soul," and to assist each other with their property and lives against every assailant of their liberties. In consequence they were called confederates by oath (*Eidgenossen*), a name which they have preserved to the present day. Albert, on being informed of this confederation, resolved to put it down. He came at the head a mighty army, which he reinforced with those Swiss knights and their men, who hastened to assist him in the overthrow of the liberties of the three cantons. It is true, Albert did not venture to annul at once the letters-patent, which his father had granted; but he left them his Landvogts or governors, stern men, initiated into his plans, who were to oppress and vex them, until they should lose their stubborn courage, and become accustomed to wear their neck in the yoke. These Landvogts were the haughty Hermann Gessler von Brunegg and the Beringer von Ladenberg. Gessler built a strong castle in the midst of the canton Uri, where he resided. Henceforth there was no justice to be had in the land. Gessler's will was the sole law.

Death seemed preferable to this shameful yoke. The three men, who, upon the matten of the Rütli, on the night of the 17. December 1307, lifted up their hands to the starry heaven, and swore before that Lord, in whose eyes kings and peasants are equal, to wrestle, even unto death for the preservation of their liberties; — these three men knew that their oath would find an echo in the hearts of their fellow-citizens; for the shame was alike to all, and each one shared in their own indignation. Gessler scorned these signs of resistance. He resolved to add mockery to oppression. He had a pole erected before the gate of his castle, close by the high-road, placed upon it his hat, and ordained, that every one who came that way should bow to it. In this manner, he would, as he proclaimed, find out who was for, and who was against Austria.

William Tell, the man of Burglen, in Uri, happened to pass that way, with his crossbow upon his arm, and accompanied by his little son. He looked up at the hat, stopped, and did not bend his head. The soldiers, who guarded the pole, arrested him, and led him before the Landvogt. The tyrant, in the insolence of his power, called the man a traitor and left him the choice between instant death and the attempt to shoot an apple from his own child's head. Tell performed the cruel task miraculously; and to Gessler's question: „Wherefore didst thou take two arrows from thy quiver?“ The dauntless man replied: „The second was meant for thee, tyrant, if I had missed my aim!“ The Landvogt, struck with fear, ordered his soldiers to fetter Tell, and to cast him into his boat, to sail across to Kussnacht, in order to destroy him there far from his home. When on the way, God sent a hurricane, that piled the waters of the lake mountain high, and Gessler, in terror, ordered the chains to be removed from the strong man of Burglen, that he might take the rudder and rescue them. Tell took the rudder and mastered storm and waves; but when near the Axenberg, where the naked, rocky platform extends into the lake, on the very place where the chapel now stands, Tell leaped upon the shore, and thrust the vessel back into the lake. Thus Tell regained his liberty. But whither should he fly to escape the Landvogt's vengeance? What should become of his wife and child, hostages in the tyrant's hand? And could a man like Tell endure the affront inflicted on a free people in his person? An oath bound him; for, (Schiller's words,)

— In that hour,
When, with a trembling hand I drew the string —
When thou with horrible — with devilish joy
Didst force me at my darling's head to aim —
When I, in powerless agony knelt to thee —
Then, in my inmost heart I made a vow,
And sealed it with a solemn oath to God,
That the first mark of my next shot should be
Thy heart. The solemn vow, silently made
In the tremendous anguish of that hour,
It is a sacred debt; — — I'll pay it now.

With this resolve Tell, familiar with thé mountain paths, hastens to the road that leads to Kussnacht. On the spot where the chapel now stands upon the height, he stops; — — —

„He must needs come along this narrow pass.
No other road will lead to Kussnacht. Here
I'll do the deed. — — — — — — — — — —
— — — — — — — — — — — — —
Now Gessler, settle thy account with Heaven!
't is time thou wert gone hence: — the hour has struck."

The Landvogt comes riding up the narrow way. Tell's arrow pierces the tyrant's breast, and Tell's nation throws off the Habsburgh yoke for ever! —

Five centuries have since passed; but Tell's name and deed remain ever-green in the memory of his people, as do the name of those who after him sacrificed their lives fighting for their country's freedom. They have come down to posterity as the standard-bearers of honor and fame. The free sons of Switzerland still pray for them and a thankful highminded people erected altars, and instituted festivals to celebrate their exploits. In a similar way did the nations of antiquity pay honor to their heroes. As Rome and Greece built temples to their great ancestors, so the devout herdsmen of the Alps erected chapels to the founders and defenders of their independence. Pilgrimages to these chaples are kept up by the people as sacred customs. On certain days of the year you may still see processions move to the spots, where the Confederates manured the young seed of freedom with their blood, to the battle-fields of Morgarten, Sempach, Laupen, Morat and Granson. Above all others the „Tell's chapels" are venerated — Tell's, whose dauntless deed first emboldened the nation to exert their strength for throwing off their fetters. The people of Uri erected a chapel at Burglen on the spot, where his house stood, and another upon the cliff near the lake, (Tell's platform), where he fortunately escaped from Gessler and his guards. The people of Schwyz, not less grateful to his memory, dedicated to him a third chapel near the pass between Immersee and Kussnacht, upon the very spot where he stood when he laid the Landvogt low with his arrow. Of this latter edifice our engraving is a faithful representation.

Unchanged as the memory of their hero, have the herdsman of the three Ur-cantons, the people of Uri, Schwyz and Unterwalden, passed down the stream of time; — devout and full of the fear of God, clinging fast to the great inheritance handed down from the days of yore, and above all to their forefather's religion and laws. Both are sacred to them, and, according to their ideas, every change in the latter is an attack upon freedom itself. Reverence and ardent love for the ancient constitution of the land, the offspring of the wisdom of his ancestors, as also for the Catholic church, so closely connected with it, the shepherd imbibes with his mother's milk. The destruction of the one is, in his eyes, the destruction of the other. Hence originates the obstinate resistance of these original cantons to all improvement and all progress in the constitutional life of Switzerland, and their perpetual contention with their innovating confederates. The fact is to be lamented; the motive, however, is praiseworthy and good.

We conclude. The present age, that prides itself so much upon its antitheses and paradoxes, an age that has ventured even to deny and disprove the existence of the most exalted and venerable of mankind — has seen also the foolish attempt to strike Tell's name from the page of history. Tell, who practically taught the national right of self-defence, has ever been an object of abhorrence to the advocates and apostles of tyranny and princely misrule. These knaves now conceived the thought of denying outright the reality of Tell's existence, and to denounce his whole story as a fable, as the invention of idle chroniclers, which had been palmed off upon a stupid people as an historical truth. It is not long ago, that this sly device of the vile tools of despotism terminated before the tribunal of historical research to the utter discomfit and ridicule of its inventors. Since then, the advocates of tyranny have changed tactics. As it will no more do to deny Tell's existence, they dissect Tell's deed with the knife of orthodox morality, and of the hero of Swiss liberty naught is left but a murderer! To them I recall the words of Schiller:

Ay, there's a barrier to the despot's might!
When the oppress'd for justice cries in vain,
When no more can be born oppression's weight,
He lifts his hands, lays hold on heaven itself,
And fetches down his everlasting rights,
That hang on high, all indestructible,
Unalienable as the fixed stars. —
The old primeval state comes round again,
When man contests with man for nature's rights;
As a last refuge, when all others fail,
She puts the sword into her children's hands.

And sustained by these rights, which cannot be denied or disproved, because their code is laid open by God himself in the breast of every man, the „murderer" Tell will pass through time with the halo of a hero about his brow, so long as Clio shall inscribe a page of history.

THE PALACE OF THE LEGION OF HONOR IN PARIS.

That curious galaxy of stars, stars of knightly orders, with which the monarchs of the earth endeavor to dazzle the eyes of „the vile multitude," first shone upon the world in the days of Christian enthusiasm. Pious knights united themselves with the ecclesiastical fraternities, founded institutions of charity and hospitality for men journeying to Palestine, and vowed protection to the pilgrims, and war against the infidels, as the enthusiastic Christian termed all those, whose faith was different from his own. The members of such knightly orders bound themselves by a vow to fraternity, poverty, chastity and obedience; they wore a common garb and a common badge. Time changed these institutions. From their professed poverty the orders rose gradually to great wealth and power. The knights of St. John, the knights Templars, the Teutonic order, possessed immense territories. The vow of poverty became a phrase, their other vows were neglected likewise, and at last, after the bright flame of religious enthusiasm had sunk lower and lower, the very object of the ecclesiastical orders of chivalry was entirely lost sight of. These institutions roused at last the rapacity and jealousy of the princes. They were persecuted, robbed of their estates, or transformed into mere tools of despotism, or into toys to lure the ridiculous vanity of frail mankind. The ruling lords of Europe early recognized in the contemptible thing, which remained of the old, knightly fraternities, namely in their common badge and costume, some means for the increase of their power. They transformed the plain knightly cross into sparkling, and often costly decorations, which entitled the possessor to a higher degree in the scale building is the old Cathedral — a monument of the Lombard times — built on the site of a Roman temple, the sculptures from which were long preserved and afterwards destroyed by a senatorial decree of the fifteenth century. The new cathedral is built of marble. Some others of the numerous churches are splendid buildings, and contain paintings by the best masters, such as Titian, Paolo Veronese, and treasures of Art are to be found in the Council-House (della Loggia) and in the Cosi- and Zecchiferari palaces. The antiquarian admires an antique temple, and among the works of classic art found in the vicinity, is a bronze figure of Victory which is considered one of the best extant.

BIRMINGHAM.

Our age is the birth-day of an eventful futurity. In the active movement, in which society is involved, in the lively interchange of thought and experience between the different nations, in the rapidity of commerce, which, with the wings of electricity and steam, rushes forward on its iron pathways, shortens the passage over the oceans and makes its messages traverse a thousand miles in the twinkling of an eye; in the facility with which intelligence and thoughts penetrate to the most distant points: the life of civilized society has become transparent to the centre. Men's minds are brought into such close contact with each other, that they seem to form an unbroken chain, on which every grand idea, like lightning, darts forth from one end to the other. It is of no use now to veil human proceedings in mystery and darkness. In spite

of monarchical society or to a certain share in the revenues of the order. The new bait was prepared to catch weak souls, and to make them the servants to their Lord's will and projects.

In early times the princes paid some regard to the signification which they themselves attached to their various-shaped crosses and stars. They bestowed them on their servants and vassals as tokens of their favor, as an outwardly visible proof of their personal inclination or esteem. By and by other motives stepped in. The more ardently the princes pursued their plans, to destroy, piece by piece, the rights of their peoples, rights which hemmed in their lust for arbitrary power, so much the more greedily did they catch at every means to separate the wealthy, the strong, the honored from the mass of their subjects and to bind them to their own interests by some tie of vanity or private advantage. A fit tool for this end they found out in a long, and well graduated chain of knightly-court-, house-, military- and civil-orders. The stars and crosses, which dropped henceforth from princely hands like rain-showers, were proclaimed as tokens for honorable service done to Monarchs and Monarchy. And to make the mockery and puppet-show complete, individuals, who suffered themselves to be thus decorated on acount of their actions, or of faithful service, were entitled to rank with the parasites and tinsel-men of the courts, and admitted to the right and honor to make their bows at court in the livery of their gracious masters. A paragraph, common to the statutes of all orders, declared the members of reigning families by birth entitled to the highest degrees of the orders, being a solemn declaration, that it was a merit to come into the world a born prince! But it was less by absurdities of this sort, that the system of orders exercised a corrupting influence upon the popular vitality, than by the division of them into a classified scale. So long as the orders had but one class, the selection of knights was confined to a certain circle in society, and to a smaller number; the life of the middle and lower classes remained untainted by that pestilence of vanity, the mass of the people ranked as equals at least in point of their claim to decoration. But by the division and subdivision of the orders, which now shot up like mushrooms from the ground, a way was found to bind individuals, even of the humblest classes, by the long string of badges; to increase the number of their members at will, and to diffuse the demoralizing air of the courts and their falsified ideas of honor, in the widest circle, and, above all, to force upon the compact middle-classes, to which, until now, it had been a stranger, that sense of nice distinctions of rank in society which could not but destroy the independence of the citizen, and his proud defiance of every usurping power. Moeser, the popular writer for popular rights, remarked long ago on this subject: „In consequence of this order-system, princely governments have acquired a new and mighty power, without any particular expenditure of capital; for if there be any, it is defrayed by the state-treasury. By their tinsels, their shabby medals, their crosses and stars, they are enabled to make vain men by thousands slaves to their interests, or, at least, to weaken and neutralize the spirit of opposition, to reward services performed and promised, and by passing some over, to excite a feeling of mortification in the bosoms even of those, supposed to possess more moral fortitude." In this spirit of corruption has the system of orders been managed to the present hour. Services done to princes and monarchy have always been rewarded with orders, services to the people with the dungeon. To men, who enjoy the people's confidence, the brilliant star of court-favor is displayed, as a bait, so long, till dazzled by its lustre, they have caught the hook and turning their backs to the people, and forsaking long avowed and defended principles, they unite freely in the career of oppression and persecution. The graduation of orders has been in these latter times carried to such an extent, that it appears now downright ridiculous and childish. They have created classes of crosses and medals with the ribbon and without the ribbon, and the distinctions set down in the statutes are so manifold and minute, that a correct knowledge of them assumes the rank of grave science.

The storm, which is gathering over monarchical Europe, will do away with these institutions that mock human reason. Their sentence was pronounced long ago by the deep scorn with which the people everywhere looked upon it, a scorn which considered the decorations, even when viewed in the most favorable light, only as a proof of — vanity. Now-a-days, though despotism triumphs in Europe, it is considered creditable to an honest man, to keep his coat clean from such trash and there are thousands of poor knights, who conceal the worthless gifts of royal grace in a secret drawer, that they might not meet their own eyes and offend their better feelings.

All that has been said of these „orders“ in general is applicable to of the Legion of Honor in France. So long as Napoleon, the founder, was himself grandmaster of the order, its badge stood foremost among all; it had some rational meaning and some claims to the popular esteem. The great emperor's star of glory cast its beams upon it. The restored Bourbons made it their particular aim, to bring it into disrepute. Under king Charles X., the popular wit called it „the shoe-black's badge“. It became utterly contemptible under the crafty Louis Philippe; and under the present government, which has degraded the „*grande nation*“ to the laughing-stock of the world, and transformed France into the tomb of liberty, no man can wear the cross without creating a suspicion of belonging to the set of men, that are now busy in timbering the imperial throne for their captain. While the uncle in instituting the legion confined its number to sixteen cohorts, and to each cohort gave seven grand officers, and three hundred and fifty legionaries, the order, under the nephew, counts a hundred thousand knights.

In the engraving we behold the palace of the order, so called as the dwelling of its high chancellor. This splendid structure is the principal ornament of the Rue de Lille in Paris. The inscription: „Honneur et Patrie“ which adorns the portico in golden letters, has, long before a scoundrel lavished the cross upon the thousands of his accomplices, become — a lie.

THE RUINS OF ETAWAH IN BENGAL.

High over Jumna's stream, tho lofty walls
Proclaim thy name, but towers, and banquet halls,
And city, seat of royalty, are lying
As dust within a tomb, where all around is dying.

The history of India is written in colossal hieroglyphics. There cities and empires rise, grow, decline, and perish with the ruling dynasties. In the midst of a closely crowded population, India is covered with ruins, which, like the torn leaves of a book, lie mingled in confusion, perplexing all who would decipher them.

Etawah, on the Jumna, was the ancient metropolis of the country, before Akbar, two centuries ago, founded the dynasty of the Moguls, and built Agra for the capital of his new kingdom. Agra herself has since become a ruin, and the heiress of her magnificence, proud Delhi, where the Mogul race is still stalking about like a ghost, is in her speedy decay but an instance more of the fact, that nothing created at the mere command of despotism can live long, and that all things truly great want a free, organic development in accordance with Nature's eternal laws. St. Petersburg would undergo the fate of Delhi, it would be depopulated in fifty years, and herds of cattle would pasture in its streets, were it left to its own resources. On the contrary in the United-States of North-America half a century has sufficed, without assistance or interference of government, to raise cities, larger and more splendid than the proud capitals of continental Europe. When the antiquary shall

RUINS of ETTAIA
(India)

be wandering in the ruins of St. Petersburg, Berlin, and Vienna, millions of men will throng the streets of New-York, Philadelphia, Cincinnati, St. Louis, and St. Francisco, — millions of happy citizens, as the Lords of their empires, not as the slaves of self-styled Majesties „by the Grace of God“ and not „humble subjects“ whom, at any hour, a gracious master with his knout, his pretorians and executioners, — the Jellachiches, the Wrangels or Haynaus — may destroy in a single day, what industry, skill and perseverance have reared and earned in many centuries.

Now that steamboats ply from Calcutta up the Ganges and the Jumna as far as Delhi, the last mentioned river presents an aspect of great life and animation, and its romantic shores, which much resemble in point of picturesque beauty those of the Hudson, have become a fashionable resort of the Indo-British tourist. Etawah is the chief attraction of the journey. Nowhere are the banks of the grand river more charming, and the accessory features peculiar to them, the ruins upon every rocky peak, the temples upon the heights, the sepulchral monuments in the dales — are not surpassed in magnificence at any other part of the landscape. The steamers stop near the temple, which is erected in the very midst of the ruins of the lower citadel. The stay is long enough to give travellers an opportunity of seeing every thing worthy of notice. Some Bramin acts as guide, and it is their habit to relate the history of the place.

Europe has no monument of the ages of feudal splendor, that is worthy, either in extent or in magnificence, to be compared with this double royal citadel of Etawah. It is divided into the upper and lower castles. The former stands upon the top of a lofty, colossal rock, which rises, almost perpendicularly, to the clouds.

This upper castle, with the exception of a small temple, now inhabited by an aged Bramin, has fallen to ruins. It consists of several terraces, rising one above the other, formerly connected by stairs which now lie buried under the rubbish. Vestiges of its original splendor, however, are visible every where. Sculptured works and costly building material, large blocks of the finest marble, lie scattered about. The lower castle is in a somewhat better state of preservation, and neither engraving nor description can give an adequate idea of the beauty of the architecture, both internal and external. Several halls are supported by pillared arcades, and the floors consist of fine mosaic work of varicolored stones. Destruction is making rapid progress in the parts preserved entire. At every violent shower of rain the water finds its way through the roofs and arches. Some poor Hindoo families have established themselves in the grand banqueting-hall, and on the steps of the royal throne, which, if the legend speaks truth, were once inlaid with gold-plates, and upon which the grandees of the empire cast themselves down in reverence before a despot, — the Pariah is now cooking his rice.

Etawah — the wind is fast scattering thy dust! What were thy deeds? Thou hast eaten and drunk, thou hast flattered and obeyed thy kings on the golden throne, and these kings have revelled, and oppressed, and enslaved, and slaughtered from generation to generation, until a stronger than they came and did unto them as they had done unto thousands. Not a penny's worth hast thou contributed to the sacred temple of humanity, not a grain of sand hast thou added to the treasures of human knowledge, not one fruit-bearing idea hast thou left as an inheritance to man! Mushroom of Despotism, thou didst shoot up in the stench of rottenness, and in rottenness hast thou perished! Had the human race had but one neck, thy despots would have struck it off, and had civilisation been in the reach of their arm, they would have murdered it. — Thy ruins have no claim to immortality; they are not sacred to the Genius of Humanity like the ruins of Greece and Rome. One or two centuris more — and thy last pillar will be buried in the silence of the wilderness and forgotten will be thy very name. —

C. Reiss del.

NOTRE DAME - CATHEDRAL

in Paris.

Published by Hermann J. Meyer 164, William Street, NEW YORK.

THE CATHEDRAL OF NOTRE DAME IN PARIS.

I gaze with silent joy on the fair image of this Colossus and read with surprise the inscription underneath,

„NOTRE DAME IN PARIS.“

Who was that „Notre Dame“? „The mother of God“ answers the tonsured priest.

Blushing I hide my face, and struck with indignation I exclaim: Who shall dare to mock the Almighty?

Temple! The day cometh which shall witness thy fall, and the night steals on, whose pale moon will spread her funeral pall over thy mouldering relics. Thou shalt be painted as ghosts are painted, who wander among graves. For Man will not always be blind to the true light, nor his heart be closed to the inspirations of Reason and Truth. The hour which is to raise from his eyes the thick, black veil of delusion, cannot be distant for ever, and the dust of these walls, which are the witnesses of a thousand years of error, will give fresh proof that nought can last save Truth alone. Were God as the God of Israel, threatening vengeance upon the children even to the third and the fourth generation, He would summon Earth and Heaven to be the instruments of his wrath on those beings, who scorning His nature and disclaiming His power, set forth a puppet, as worthy of devotion, in place of the Creator's infinite Majesty.

Wail not over a faith, which leads Man's Soul astray — say not that it is the foster-mother of religious error! No! The darkness in which Reason wanders, is not a darkness from God. The fountain of superstition flows not from Heaven, but lies deep in Man himself, and the soil from which it leaps, is his own heart. Yet be consoled. So certain as the sun follows his appointed course, even so surely will wisdom gain the victory over folly, and knowledge be proclaimed triumphant over priestly deception.

First Soul of the Universe, Father and Ruler! Greatest, Best, Almighty and All-loving! Thou whom mortals worship under many names, yet without knowing Thee—everlasting, uncreated God, that in the Universe of Heaven dost order the course of worlds in the endless Abyss of space, that peoplest Immensity with numberless suns,— reveal to us, to what tend all these religious systems of men on this little earth, who before Thine eyes, in hatred and scorn strive the one against the other? What are the opinions of a handful of children, in Thy infinite world of spirits, to Thee, at whose command the starry spheres of Heaven, in silence and order, fulfil their destiny? What are to Thee the subtilities of their teachers, and the quarrels of their creeds? Canst Thou find pleasure in this endless dispute, this self-torture of Folly? Ah! that men, instead of forming a hundred different religious sects and faiths, which have naught in common save hatred and error, did stimulate their soul to find in disconnected systems the clue to harmony with the unchangeable laws of Reason and Morals, and would seek the revelation of God in Nature — where all and every thing is the manifestation of God, where Truth rays forth the fullest conviction, where we see the open code of eternal justice and the wisdom of a father of infinite goodness, who with equal love embraces all his creatures, who in giving rain to a land asks not what prophets it have, who bids the sun shine on men of every faith, on the white as on the black, on the Mussulman as on the Heathen, on the Catholic as on the Protestant, who permits the seed to florish where it is sown by careful hands and watched with love; who increases every nation and prospers every family in which honesty, industry and order bear the sway; who causes every land to flourish in which justice is enforced and makes man happy, where the mighty are bound and the poor are protected by laws; who gives to the nations strength, where the weak live in safety, and where their share in the enjoyment of social right is undisturbed and undiminished by the strong. I say that if people would hear the voice of the Lord in the green temple as they now listen to it in the house of stone, then the simple and unchangeable principles of true religion would not be a hieroglyph, comprehended only by a few among the thousands. All would understand them, and Christ's doctrines, the wisest and best ever revealed to man, now buried in the dust of dogmatical errors, would no longer serve in the hands of crafty priests as the footstool of superstition. —

On the site of this church, into which I conduct my readers, other deities have had their temples before the „Mother of God!" stepped in. Everlasting duration was also proclaimed by the priests who performed the rites of their Idols, and the people believed in them as they do in the divinity now worshipped. On the very spot where the anointed priest now sips the blood of the crucified One from golden goblets and divides his consecrated body among the worshippers — the ancient Gauls once offered to their deities Isur and Cornunnus human sacrifices. When the conquering Romans came, they overthrew their altars and Jupiter entered the palace of columns built on their site. Four centuries later the eagles of Rome fled with the Capitolinian gods. Then the Divinity of the Christians, with the innumerable throng of saints, took possession of the deserted site, and from the foundation of the temple of columns, and during the long course of centuries arose that Church, which Christianity counts among its most venerable. In this early history of Notre Dame is there not hidden an overwhelming proof of a truth whose tendency is to strike terror into many a superstitious soul? Yes, thou tremblest, wanderer in the path of error! and thy reflecting mind is torn by thoughts which thou darest not reveal! Thy understanding comprehends their character; but the wonted veneration for error holds thy soul in thrall. Know then, that only Ignorance and Folly believe without evidences, and the attempt to make a doctrine inassailable by the mere command of authority, or to withdraw from it all test and examination, is the doctrine of Tyranny and Falsehood, which betrays its own weakness. A religious dogma which places in the fore-ground a prohibition against all critical research; which requires the renunciation of our own judgment; a creed which at every trifling doubt summons with gleaming sword the consciences of weak minds to a bloody expiation; a creed which trembles at every scruple, calls on heaven for aid, and directly condemns as blasphemy all criticism, has, though a seven-fold halo of sanctity surround its head, nothing in it worthy of honor, and it has no chance of eternal duration. It can have none; for the deluded man who embraces such a creed fetters with his own hands his noblest faculties, and must become for ever the resistless slave of his ignorance, and the puppet of priestly craft and cunning. This is not God's will and intention. Movement and action constitute the principles of God's own existence; not torpor or inactivity. All that belongs to God's creation is subordinate to this principle, and therefore no immoveability can be presumed even in religious conceptions. The doctrines of so many different faiths — all proclaimed in their time unchangeable and holy truths — have vanished with their times, the children of which they were. This is an additional proof, if any more were wanted, that Religion cannot exclude man's capacity for progress unpunished, and in this fact Mankind possess the surest pledge for their future advance to happier conditions.

Before we enter the Cathedral of Paris, let us cast a glimpse upon its history. I will not weary my reader; a few lines shall suffice.

Christian Faith built on this spot the first church under king Childebert in 522. The Normans who in 875 conquered Paris, destroyed it. The construction of the present Cathedral, begun in 1010, consumed three centuries. From 1300 to 1331 Art was busy in ornamenting the choir. The temple remained untouched until the time of Louis the Fourteenth. Notre Dame shared then the fate of the dome of Strasburg. Under the pretext of a restoration many treasures of ancient Art dissappeared, and in their place the king introduced worthless sculptures and showy trellis-work of gilt bronze — disfigurations which at a later day were removed to make way for alterations still worse. Even the exterior could not resist the barbarous mania for architectural improvement which characterised the seventeenth and eighteenth centuries. To the grand portal, which was used as a royal entrance, a sort of triumphal arch was appended, as if something were yet wanting to testify the utter degeneration of taste.

In size Notre Dame is the sixteenth church of Christendom. Its external length is four hundred and twelve feet, its breadth one hundred and fifty six, and it covers nearly sixty thousand square feet. The cubic contents of its masonry are computed to be nearly two million feet.

The most imposing view of the Cathedral is its front with the towers. These are left unfinished. After the original design they were to receive an elevation of 500 feet. Their present height is two hundred and twenty five. From their summits, that are crowned with balustrades, we have a birds-eye-view of the city, whose centre is the Cathedral itself.

Notre Dame is never closed. Night and day a mass-reading priest is ready to administer divine service. Those who do not go to pray, do well to choose an hour late in the afternoon when the pious crowd is not numerous, when the day casts its last golden gleams through the varied and glowing stained glass of the windows, and the slowly coming twilight inspires the soul with unearthly feelings, while it closes from our eyes all outer vision. Let us enter on the façade of the Cathedral, through the centre-door between the towers, which leads directly to the grand altar, above which the choir rises with slender columns to a cupola. Truly the view is glorious! Even the modern additions disappear in the splendor of the whole, and pure and inviolate the colossal, simple edifice displays itself to the spiritual and bodily eye. All is awe and stillness. The church appears deserted. Through the majestic nave, and between the rows of mighty fasciculated columns, measuring more than a hundred feet — our eye seeks the end of the beautiful perspective, where it meets the grand altar around which a dim light gleams from four immense tapers on silver candelabers. We proceed, to the right and left admiring the transepts which extend out between rows of columns, like avenues in a pine-forest. The columns support magnificent arcades, which embrace the beautiful windows decorated with lacework of stone, through which the many-hued and broken twilight casts a magic gleam on the carvings, monuments, statues, and groups of saints, which occupy every portion of the walls. Carved pulpits, dark-brown colored by time, are scatterd here and there. Numbers of empty chairs stand, or lie overthrown around. We ask the guide their meaning; and with a smile he points to a man who sweeps a mass of sou-pieces from the balustrade of an altar — the harvest which the chair-owner has reaped from the last pious assembly. For in Paris a seat in the church is *sold*, as they sell a seat in the comic opera, and the bargain is made in the one as in the other case, *for but a single performance*. In Paris nothing is given gratis, neither life nor death, neither joy nor sorrow, not the acting of the mimic on a worldly stage, not that of the priest on the pulpit. Every thing must be paid for with francs or sous. To the lighthearted people of Paris all is theatrical, be it on the cothurnus or under the cowl, whether with red heels or with red caps, in parliament or in the dancing saloon, in the halls of justice or in the market, in the café or in the confessional chair. Lightly they swim over the surface of time, hating and even despising all that is serious and profound. And yet this race holds, or fancies to hold, the reins of the world and directs it, as well as it can, at its own pleasure.

We step back to admire once more the stained glass windows of the choir gleaming in the fire of the western heavens. Lo! the full moon has risen in the East, and its pale light falls on the capitals of the columns, animated with strange figures, and on the twining ribs of the ceiling. The variegated light grows dim, and the trembling many-hued reflection on objects around is vanishing. In the pale moonlight all is pale and even the nankeen-colored wash of the temple is changed to a calm white. All becomes mute and solemn as before some great festival. Suddenly a stir is heard in the distance. We listen — there it is, below, near the high altar. Lights wander here and there — torches appear, first two, then four — six — twenty — a long array. It is a procession. The lights pause before the steps of the altar and form a circle. And now the gleam of the torches has driven away the moonlight, only here and there in the most distant corners, or in the transept the pale radiance still maintains its sway and gray darkness covers the portal in the back ground with its veil. But before us all flashes in the lordly light of the High Mass. Priests and attendants take their places on the velvet-covered steps, bells and censers are moving, while the devotees form groups either sitting, standing or kneeling. With slow pace we approach nearer the scene. What disappointement! how quickly disappear the forms of devotion! The spirit is gone, but the show remains. On one side stands a group of young people chattering and tittering, here a gentleman balances himself on his chair as much at ease as if in the gardens of the Champs Elysées, while there another, leaning on his cane, eyes the female figures through his lorgnon, and surely entertains not very heavenly thoughts. Chattering aloud a party comes from one wing of the transept, and many a suspicious-looking couple glide between the columns and are lost in the temple's darkest space. It strikes us that the greater part of the audience are idle spectators like ourselves, seeking distraction or amusement, — people, who go to the Lord's temple as they would to the Theatre, or the Masquerade. Meantime the mass is at an end, the solemn tones of the organ peal forth, — grow fainter — are silent, the priests and choristers depart, the chairs are vacant, the rustling of the multitude moves towards the door, the tapers are extinguished one after another, solitary whispers and slight footsteps are heard until even they are silent. Empty is the church, empty are the chairs and only the moonlight animates the solemn space with its dim shadows, until after an hour or two the same drama, the same scenes are played over again.

THE SCHOOL OF PLATO.

Plato's sentence: „Education makes the man and the citizen, and the school either spoils or enobles the nations!" will hold good through all time. All end and aim of eduction is assuredly no other than to awaken and guide the slumbering powers of men, so that they may be enabled worthily to discharge the duties of humanity. To this object should be directed all public instruction. It should give the first place to the Good and Noble in sentiment and exertion, and to the strengthening of the Will for purposes of generous action. — Not a one-sided discipline of the understanding or the memory, but the culture of the higher and nobler faculties of the soul to a harmonious character is it, that renders a man amiable, elevates his mind, and augments his personal dignity. When seconded by a cultivated understanding, to assist the moral sentiment in sharpening the judgment, the errors of overstrained feelings will be avoided, and the dangers that continually threaten the too sensitive persons in practical life will be avoided.

A school-discipline tending to this aim, is not only desirable for the individual, but necessary for society at large. No man exists merely for himself; he constitutes a link in the great chain of

PLATO'S SCHOOL

in Bithynia.

Published for HERRMANN J. MEYER, 164, William Str. NEW YORK.

mankind. He has the duties of his station to perform, and these demand not only the development of his intellectual powers, but also a mass of special acquirements; above all a correct idea of the structure of society, as it ought to be according to the laws of equity and morality. Not till he be endowed with this knowledge, will he be able to co-operate in the foundation and establishment of the empire of Truth, Virtue, and Happiness among his fellow-men, and thus to fulfil the sublimest destiny of human exertions. All educational establishments ought to be thoroughly impressed with this principle, and all their arrangements ought to be directed to carrying it out in practical results suited to the especial wants of the respective times and countries.

Thus it was with the most cultivated nations of the classical world. With the Greeks the main object of instruction was the formation of a generous character founded on a true knowledge of the duties of man in accordance with the destination of mankind. It was in this spirit that Socrates and Plato acted as teachers and formers of their people, and in this same spirit they act on the modern world through the writings they left behind. Of course not with equal success. The construction of the state in ancient Greece was more favourable to a rational system of public education, than is the case with us. Ancient society had a conception of a citizen's life and duties very different from that which the moderns entertain. In the ancient states, private life was merged in public life. The Individual lived not only in the State but chiefly for the state. His greatest prosperity was the prosperity of the republic; his highest honour, his chief glory, were the glory and honour of his country.

This has changed. We allow extensive privileges to the family and the individual, in contra-position to the state. The ideal of the republic of modern times respects all men as free. We acknowledge the dignity of Woman in the family, we place her on an equal footing with Man; and we consider the noblest development of the individual as the highest and most important in the moral world. We make it the principal aim and duty of government and legislature, to promote this development. Hence the general cry even in monarchical Europe for reform in the education of the people, for the reform of the schools. The watch-word is every where „schools for practical life.“ None but such can content the popular demands, none other are rational or adapted to still the wants of civilisation. Simple as this may be, there is much party-controverse on the subject. One defends the classical schools, another will do away with them. The first considers their abolition a death-blow to all liberal knowledge; the second sees in the study of the dead languages and of the classics the chief obstacle to a national education, and accuses it of rendering the scholar unfit for the duties of practical life. Both are in error. It borders on folly to depreciate the value of classical studies as a means of enlarging the intellect; but a line is to be drawn between this and allowing the whole period of youth to be swallowed up by the acquirement of dead languages. Let school-instruction in the Grecian and Roman literature rather aim at inciting to a fruitful application of that which is grand, noble, and beautiful in the works of the ancients, and at the same time serviceable to the purposes of the present.

Whatever lies beyond this limit, repays neither the time nor the trouble of learning it. Of what practical use can it be to torture youth during eight or ten years with acquiring the dead languages as a key to that classical knowledge, which, the moment they leave school, is no more thought of; a key, with which, in nine cases out of ten, the shrine enclosing the sacred treasures is never opened. Pedantic drudgery takes away their appetites before they come to the feast. And what have boys of 10—14 years of age to do with Cicero, Tacitus, Virgil and Homer, or with Plato and Thucydides? Is not a riper age, a more mature and cultivated understanding necessary in order to comprehend such authors, and is it not an absurdity to set before children that intellectual food, which requires a full development, physical and moral, to be able to digest it? Is it rational, to lead such unfledged youngsters into the battle-fields of Ilium, to introduce them into the chamber of Penelope, to explain to them the mysteries of the pagan rites, to make them trace on the map the wanderings of Ulysses, or debate on the institutions of a Solon or a Lycurgus, or to initiate them into the artifices of Roman diplomacy? By the time their beards are grown, they are, indeed, perfectly able to detail the functions of a Roman or Grecian civil or military officer, but if you question them about the constitution, law, and government of their own country; — their answers will betray their ignorance. They know by heart the bill of fare at the Olympic feasts; but they are not able to distinguish barley from wheat, the elm from the ash. They will with profound learning criticise the Codes of Lycurgus, Thales and Solon, while the duties of the citizen, magistrates, the parliaments and judges of their own country are unknown to them. They will patch up Latin hexameters and scribble sheetsful about a Greek accent, while the classics of their own nation are to them sealed books. —

Continental Europe has fostered and overrated dead learning of this kind for many centuries and dearly has society paid for the error. Above all poor, enslaved, downtrodden Germany. Have we not seen them in the Council of the Nation, our celebrated professors of Greek and Sanscrit, they, who knew by rote the 12 Tables and paragraphs of the constitutions of the ancient world; they, who knew every-thing, except all that was so urgently needed by their fellow-citizens? These sages sat on the benches of the parliament full of wisdom and rich in good intentions, but more barren of counsel than a simple farmer. They looked on the struggling nation, as on an audience in their college-room, and dreamt the dreams of their closets over again in the halls of St. Paul. While disputing about the form, they lost the substance; while wrangling about the binding, they lost the book — that glorious code of freedom and self-government, which the Nation had written in the days of March with their hearts' blood. — Germany was praying to God day and night: „look down upon us in mercy and help the wisest of our men to common sense;“ — Alas! Her prayer was in vain!

„Let us have schools for practical life!“ — cry the cheated, refettered nations and though this cry is answered by the tyrants with the delivery of the public instruction to the Jesuits, yet it will not for ever be scorned. — Mean-while let us listen, to what Plato, the pedagogue of old, says on the subject. — „The Greeks, as soon as their children had learnt to read, put into their hands the works of the illustrious poets of the land. Their writings glowed with enthusiastic admiration and praise of the great men of the country. Their lecture inspired the boy with the fire of emulation. The resolve to go and do like their great forefathers was indelibly imprinted on the young hearts. — „The Poets,“ concludes Plato, „are our fathers and guides in wisdom.“ In their schools, the reading of Homer constituted the chief study. Every Grecian youth learnt him by heart. He was the chief medium of education; he was the enchanter, that elevated the Greeks to the most poetical, the noblest, the most cultivated nation that ever earth has known. In Achilles the youthful young Greek saw the Ideal of Heroism. Ajax, Hector, Agamemnon, Patroclus — men approaching the eternal Gods in nature, — filled his soul with illustrious models worthy of imitation. At the public examinations, passages recited from Homer played the prominent part. The Greek always found the ornaments of the human race among his own people; with such, in his idea, no foreign hero could compare in honor or in virtue; an advantage not not to be under-rated! Thence sprang that majestic pride which exalted the Greeks above the other nations of the earth, made them ripe for every grand deed, ready for every hazard; which covered the world with her glory, her victories, her colonies; and through thousands of years diffused Hellenic culture over the world. —

The system carried out in the Grecian schools corresponded exactly with the natural course of youthful development. Every one knows, that in childhood the power of intuition, the feelings and the fancy are strongest, and that hence arises the lively interest taken in works of fiction. Why do we not pursue the same path? If on the old hackneyed road, we infuse disgust of the classic poets into the minds of our youth, is it not natural that they should acquire a hatred for poetry altogether, and discover nothing in it but preposterous sentiment or the ravings of an enthusiast? How many thousands who boast of their „*classical learning*“ have, in the tortuous paths by which they had been conducted, for ever been incapacitated from really enjoying the fruits of poetry, and have been rendered insensible to those beauties which enrapture and inspire every enlightened mind. How many are there on whom an acquaintance with the classics has had no other effect, than to make them, at the expense of good taste, ape the style of a Virgil, a Horace, or a Cicero, in the transaction of their ordinary affairs! They shut their eyes to the present in pedantically trifling with the past; if they allude to God, they prate of the immortals on Olympus; if they speak of offices and dignities of their own state and time, they fetch their nomenclature from Hellas and Rome. —

Let us have schools as Plato describes and recommends them, *schools for practical* Life! Not that classical literature is to be thrown overboard; but let it be confined within proper limits and to proper time. Neither would we have education divided into technical and classical Schools. That system of instruction which turns out mere men of business, creatures, who descry honour or shame, salvation or perdition in the rise and fall of the price of stocks or cotton, is not to be lauded; but on the other hand let not the study of the ancient languages be the main object; let not the mastering of dead syntactical forms and contractions be held up as the pride of knowledge. Make the *living spirit*, which breathes in the works of all truly classical writings, help to form the ductile mind of youth, and, for this purpose, employ not the Greek and Roman authors *exclusively* but the best Classics of *every* time and *every* nation! —

And while the School is forming Men, let it at the same time make *Citizens*. Man and citizen, — in these two words is contained the vocation that is common to us all. Never let the spirit of *caste* and exclusiveness be allowed to enter the realms of knowledge! *One national* school-system should embrace the whole community, a system such as the Greeks adopted, in which all members of the state, without distinction, are included; in which all may mount from step to step, as inclination or circumstances may dictate. What results are to be expected, when boys of 10 years old are already divided and sent into schools of a different rank; when he who is able to conjugate a Greek verb is to look down with contempt upon his former play-fellow, and assumes, by anticipation, all the airs of the Doctor or Senator? Is there not enough separation, enough pulling in different directions, enough egoistical living for one's self already, — yea, more than enough, to stifle every development of public spirit? Must the germs of exclusiveness be sown in the tender hearts of youth even in the school! — Despotism ordains it so; for „*divide et impera*“ is its motto: — but let nations never forget that „Discord is the death of Freedom.“

„The School (Temple) of Plato“, is the name given to a grotto at the foot of mount Olympus (near Brussa in Natolia, in ancient Bithynia) which was devoted to purposes of instruction and public assemblies in Homer's time. — The remains of seats, amphitheatrically arranged, may still be seen in the interior, and the walls display vestiges of sculpture, which are to be referred to the dawn of Grecian art. The tradition, that Plato himself taught here wants the confirmation of the antiquarian and scholar. At the present time, this grotto is used as the church of an Armenien convent.

VIEW of the HUDSON RIVER

NEAR NEWBURG

Published for HERRMANN J. MEYER 8 North William-Street NEWYORK.

THE HUDSON RIVER NEAR NEWBURGH.

The Hudson is, by association, the most romantic of American rivers. The dreamy legend of the Catskill mountains, and of sleepy Hollow, — the quaint pageantry of Knickerbocker's History and the sterner array of men fighting for their independence and freedom, accumulate along its shores a variety of real and unreal interest which no other American river can boast. It is associated with some of the most important and romantic events of the Revolution: the treachery of Arnold, the fate of André, the residence of Washington at Newburgh, and the disbanding of the Continental army at that place on the 23. Juni 1783. Upon the green hillsides of West Point glistens the marble memorial of Kosciusco, thus uniting a strain of European heroism with the mighty remembrance of American valor. — The Hudson has a stately breadth surpassed by few rivers of the world and sweeps with an inspiring sense of freedom by the Catskill and through the Highlands and under the Palisades, bearing to New-York, at whose feet it mingles with the eastern waters, the golden abundance of the Western harvests.

With American travellers an excursion up the Hudson enjoys the same kind of preeminence, as the ascent of the Rhine with the Germans. To see the „North River“ as it is familiarly termed, is the ardent hope of every young wanderer whom the Summer leads, with parents and friends, away from the confinement of the city. The natural battlements of the Palisades once past, the travellers approach the Highlands, a cluster of bold and beautiful hills, through which the river winds, and certain points, as „Anthony's nose“ and „Cro'-Nest“ are familiar and classical to the reader of Knickerbocker's New-York and Drake's airy dream of Midsummer, the poem of the „Culprit Fay.“ In the heart of the Highlands is West Point, the military Academy of the United States. Nor is it ill-situated, if Liberty be indeed a „sweet, mountain Nymph“; for surely the Highlands are such mountains as Nymphs would love and every young military scion at West Point might well deem that in that neighborhood he should be a very Numa of liberty.

Ten miles above West Point and two or three miles beyond the northern limit of the Highlands, upon the westbank of the river, lies Newburgh, one of the more important Hudson-towns. As you perceive in the beautiful engraving, the land rises rapidly from the river, so that the view from the gardens, just under the ridge of the hill about 300 feet above the water, dominates the town entirely and stretches far up and down the river. Newburgh, distant 60 miles from New-York and 84 miles from Albany, is the capital of Orange County and is a flourishing place.— The Hudson at this point is a mile wide, and Newburgh, being built upon the steep hill-side, presents from afar a very pleasant and stately appearance to the traveller. Staying, he finds a characteristic American town. Newburgh has 10 churches, a courthouse, a jail, several seminaries and public institutions for various purposes. The population is 6000, and numerous sloops and steamers entertain a brisk trade and intercourse with New-York. The Albany Steamers stop at the place. The Hudson River-Railway has a station at Fishkill upon the opposite shore, with which a steam-ferry constantly communicates. A branch-railway connects the town directly with the Erie Railroad.

Just south of Newburgh stands a little, old-fashioned house in the centre of a large lot, commanding a broad and beautiful view of the river. This house, in March 1783, was the head-quarters of Gen. Washington at the time when the famous „Newburgh letters“ were addressed to the army for the purpose of inciting the soldiers to mutiny; — an attempt which was repressed by Washington with dignity and energy. The house and grounds were sold a few years since to the state of New-York for 20,000 Doll. The spot is now quiet and deserted. In spring the grass twines and tangles luxuriantly around the lofty flag-staff — the liberty-pole, where on every national anniversary floats the American banner. It is a shrine of patriotic pilgrimage, and apart from its personal associations, reveals to the spectator one of the finest prospects upon the Hudson.

The river at this point, as seen in the engraving, is about a mile broad. — To the south is the bold, dark mountaingate of the Highlands; upon the eastern bank the range of the Fishkill-hills is piled against the horizon, and northward gleams the glassy surface of the river, stretching in languid summer-calm between low and shrubby banks. The bay, a fine sheet of water, which Newburgh overlooks, is in winter frequently frozen over so that the inhabitants of the shores go to and fro upon the natural bridge thus formed. Nor are there the most graceful of winter-sports unknown. The youth of both sexes, as in the north of Europe, may be seen every sunny day in winter darting and gliding upon skates, and the matrons pushed upon sledges by the men. In other seasons the stillness, that inwraps this basin, is interrupted by the swift gay steamers, the heavy sloops which drag slowly along, and whose huge sails glisten in the sun, and the fishing-boats, appearing like whitewinged water-birds from the surounding heights.

No American can stand on the balcony of the humble-looking house of Newburgh, hollowed by History, without an exulting bound of the heart as his eyes sweep over the spacious landscape around. Was it not well, he asks himself, to strive at the risk of life for a region so stately, so fertile, and fair, — a region the natural features of which, its majestic rivers and the endless ranges of noble hills varying this boundless horizon, — suggest and inspire the freedom for which our fathers bled? Standing here, with the same summer-beauty around him that now touches you, Washington beheld for the last time his glorious army, which he had led to victories that gave hope to a world unborn. Could he then, amid the enobling feelings of the moment, have escaped that thrill of patriotic pride, that you now experience, as you gaze upon the scene he saw? That scene has for us a still deeper beauty by the charm of past events; for we cannot lean from the balcony of this house admiring the landscape, overlooking the river and the high banks upon which „Washington's head-quarters" stood, without renewing our thanksgivings to God, our homage and praise to liberty and national independence, and our reverence to that man, who, the pride of his own country, is the greatest, wisest and best committed by our millenium to immortality.

CALCUTTA

Published for HERRMANN J. MEYER, 8. North William-Street NEWYORK.

CALCUTTA.

Though the maintenance of peace be proclaimed by the powers of the old world, its society is living in perpetual warfare. Stability and progress, tyranny and selfgovernment are the watchwords of the contending parties, of princes and nations. If the auguries of my prophesying heart prove true, the hour will be soon born, that sets the old continents, trying to end their process of social transformations, in flames and blood. The impulse toward change penetrates all quarters. It has become as irresistible in Asia, as it has been in Europe since the commencement of this century, and all eyes are now directed toward India, where the past ten years have brought about great events, and prepared still greater ones. The two rival-powers, Russia and England, have overstepped their boundaries. The British trident is planted on the Persian borders, and for a long time, a Russian army, eager for conquest, keeps steadfastly fixed its eyes upon the Turcoman steppes. Russia and England, till lately separated by a space of five hundred geographical miles, and by independent states and nations, are now divided by the narrow interval of a hundred and twenty miles, and by a kingdom, where despotism, anarchy and weakness join in ruining the state and the people. Persia cannot inspire either respect or fear. Where will the antagonistic movement of the two giants end? A final collision between them is unavoidable. Upon the high table-land of Central-Asia, where the primeval tribes of the human race stand forth like the ruins of the older crusts of the earth, from the superincumbent strata of younger nations, will it be decided, whether the despotic Slavonian, or the free Saxon element is to complete its march of victory and conquest over the eastern Hemisphere. Under these circumstances, Calcutta, the Capital of the Indo-British empire, acquires an unusual interest.

Calcutta is situated in the Delta of the Ganges, upon the deep Hoogly, or western arm of that celebrated river. Its distance from the sea is about a hundred miles.

We will make our journey by the overland-route via Alexandria and Cairo and take the steamer at Suez. Babel-Mandeb is behind us; we pass cape Guardafui; we bid a last farewell to Africa, and, favored by the Monsoon, our boat glides like an arrow over the Arabian sea, towards the Bay of Bengal. After a short stay at Bombay, Ceylon, the isle of the traditions of Paradise, is the first land we again behold. At a distance almost of thirty leagues from the shore, we spy the mythic Adam's peak, gleaming like a bright cloud on the horizon. It is gradually stepping into the foreground like a giant, till, as the steamer leaves the coast, it takes the shape of a cloud once more, and at last disappears. We do not make land again before we reach the height of Orissa, off the coast of Bengal. The shore is desolate; it stretches out in flat monotony; but in bright weather we may clearly discry from the steamer's deck an immense building, imperishable as the monuments of Tentyra and Luxor, and striving with them for preeminence in vastness of proportions. It is the temple of Juggernaut, as famous as it is infamous, where avaricious priestcraft slaughtered thousands of human victims to the Idol every year.

The steamer carefully avoids the coast, for it abounds with shallows and sandbanks. The nearer we approach the end of our voyage, the greater are the dangers that attend it. A signal is hoisted to inform one of the pilot-boats, that cruise near the mouth of the Hoogly, that its assistance is needed, whereupon a small boat makes toward us, with a pilot on board, who undertakes to steer the vessel over the bar, a precaution, to the neglect of which a large number of vessels continually owe their destruction. Within the bar the river is a league in width, and its numerous smaller outlets enclose a flat, alluvial Delta, which, at high tide, scarcely lifts itself above the surface of the waters. Upon one of these islands, close to the bar, fortifications are thrown up, and batteries erected; a telegraphic line extends from here to Calcutta. Some hundred yards around the station of the telegraph, the thicket of tall cane has been cleared and a few houses are visible, dwellings of officers and clerks, with neat gardens, laid out upon the embankments thrown up in the form of terraces. They offer a lively contrast to the dreariness and wildness of the surrounding country. The whole establishment is fenced in with high palisades, not for protection against human enemies, but against the tigers, which haunt the jungles of the Sunderbund, — a name which applies to the entire Delta between the Hoogly, the Ganges proper, and the Burampooter. It is remarkable that in this now uninhabited district, undeniable traces are found of a high civilisation, and of a numerous population in ages long gone by. Occasional diggings along the shore bring to light coins, metal ornaments, and objects of glass and burnt clay in great number, mostly of an age prior to that of Alexander the Great, and according to a tradition, preserved among the Bramins, the capital of a great Indian empire once flourished here. It was probably an irruption of the sea which, in an instant, destroyed the city with the whole population, and swept them from the tablets of history. It happened only five and twenty years ago, that a similar occurrence engulfed all the villages to the very gates of Calcutta, and buried thousands of human beings in the flood.

Large, heavily-laden vessels, drawing a great depth of water, cannot reach Calcutta except at flood-tide, and they wait for this in Diamond Harbor, which is also the station of the steamers, employed as propellers. Vessels, of more than eight hundred tons burthen, are obliged to discharge part of their cargoes into barks, which then follow them up the stream: a great inconvenience to trade, latterly however, in part, remedied by a rail-road, which has been laid from Hoogly Point to Calcutta. It is no longer necessary for larger vessels to proceed to Calcutta; they can take in their cargoes at the mouth of the Hoogly.

Approaching Diamond Harbor, the scenery of the river-banks gradually changes its desolate character. Cultivated lots of land become more frequent, and from the velvet-verdure of luxuriant rice-plantations, the humble dwellings of the Hindoos are seen peeping forth. Farther on, the tropical cocoa-nut-tree spreads out its fanlike leaves, at first singly and sparingly, by and by more numerous and in groups; the palms are joined by the pisang and other trees with their splendid foliage and fantastic growth enlivening the bamboo-huts, now clustering together into villages. Thus onward, ascending the scale of culture step by step, the desert, occupied by wild beasts, is gradually transformed into the most enchanting landscape, where every thing breathes prosperity, peace, and cheerfulness; where village succeeds to village, park to park, where the proud summer-palaces and mansions of the sons of Albion, the masters of the East, rival each other in splendor and magnificence.

At last, at a distance of ten American miles, gilded spires overtop a gray cloud of smoke, and the dense throng of ships and boats on the river, and that characteristic hum which proceeds from a crowded and busy population proclaim the immediate proximity of Calcutta.

The first building of the city that strikes the eye of a stranger, is the colossal green-house of the botanical garden; a splendid establishment, worthy of British pride and sway, and unique in its kind. A double row of elegant dwellings, adorned with balconies and colonnades, connects this building with the city proper. The episcopal palace, in the gothic style, situated at some distance from the river, and shaded by palms and teak-trees, presents an admirable view, one that deeply moves the Christian spectator, when he remembers, that, on this spot, scarcely a hundred years ago, Bramin priests offered to their idols human victims.

Farther onward, the river bends almost at a right angle, and upon the tongue of land which it skirts, appear the extensive buildings of the dock yards of Kydpora. Here ships of a thousand tons burthen are built of the costly and almost indestructible teak-wood, and the yards will bear a comparison with the largest establishments of this kind in New York and Liverpool. — Now, that the steamer has rounded the neck of land, the traveller gets a glimpse of the city of Calcutta itself, which extends for three miles along the left bank of the Hoogly.

Calcutta offers from this point a vast and, grand aspect, though the general view is defective in beauty and elegance. It has something unwieldy, something oppressive to the spectator, as indeed is the case with every large city that is built in a plain. The towers, whose glittering spires, when seen at a distance, shone through the cloud of smoke, and so highly exalted the expectation, seem, when approached, to disappear; they have withdrawn into the depths of the chaotic mass, and would leave the prospect very naked, were not their place supplied, in some measure, by a forest of lofty masts with their fluttering streamers, rising from a thousand vessels moored in the river, which, with their unceasing stir and bustle, proclaim, that in the capital of the Indo-British empire no monarch but trade sits upon the throne. A strong citadel, Fort William, stands to the east of the city; yet to judge from the appearance of its environs, which are desolate and devoid of trees, the God of war plays here quite a subordinate part. The works of the fortress are considered impregnable.

The interior of Calcutta displays in some quarters of a late date the splendor of European architecture, in the old ones however, all the filth, and all the poverty of a closely crowded Indian population. The European portion extends from the fort a quarter of a league to the west. The centre is formed by the palace upon the esplanade, where the governor general of British-India keeps his court with all the pomp of an oriental prince. With the royal colors waving on the top, it towers with an air of majesty above a row of palaces which adjoin it. All these noble buildings are erected in the Grecian style, and surrounded by shady groups of trees, giving to this part of the city a picturesque and imposing aspect. The quarter is inhabited by the Croesuses of the European population, and those high civil functionaries, that are entitled to appear at the levées of the viceroy. Their life combines European refinement with the luxury of the East. The streets and squares next to this aristocratic quarter are inhabited by Indians of rank, and by those Europeans, whose station and wealth are inadequate to entitle them to the honor of an invitation to the governor's soirées. The remaining portion of the city, and by far the largest, compose the Black city, as it is called, an ugly, narrow labyrinth of small houses of dried bricks painted red, of filthy pagodas, and wretched bamboo-huts, the primitive dwellings of the common Paria. In this part of Calcutta where the streets, seldom paved, are covered with a layer of thick mud, half a million of men are crowded together, while the more elegant quarters contain scarcely the tenth part of this number.

In 1752, the population of the city, including the nearest villages, amounted to 409,056 souls, inhabiting 51,133 houses. In a pamphlet issued by the Calcutta school-union, I find for 1819, the number of inhabitants set down as being 750,000; later authorities vary in their estimates from 600,000 to a million. The truth, probably, lies between both ends. The movement of the population is exceedingly variable, and in times of great epidemies, which are very frequent and destructive in Calcutta, the Hindoos leave the city by thousands and disperse into the surrounding country.

Society in Calcutta divides, with the pedantry of oriental etiquette, into a long scale of classes, which have no social intercourse with each other, and of which each bears a peculiar stamp. The English society of rank occupies the first line. To this belong the civil functionaries and lawyers (whose profession has a golden soil in Calcutta), the military officers, and merchants of note. Disposing freely of the treasures of European civilisation, and in the possession of large fortunes or incomes, either as salaries or as the product of their speculations, these circles miss none of the forms or pleasures of the refined society in European capitals. But a peculiar feature stamped upon the intercourse of these exclusives, is the endeavor of the functionaries as well as of the merchants to amass fortunes as quickly as possible, and large enough to enable them to spend the evening of their days in luxury and repose in Europe. No European settles here to spend his money, and if, at times, a merchant, seduced by an immoderate desire of gain, passes his whole life here, this is a rare exception, not the rule. The governor-general takes the lead of society. With royal air he keeps afar the less aristocratic and less wealthy Britons, by not inviting them to his soirées. These, thus neglected, unite in small coteries, or live by themselves, too proud to mingle with the Portuguese population (grocers innkeepers &c.,) who stand a degree lower in rank, and form a third class. The numerous Mahometans, the former masters of the land, keep retired and isolated; Hindoo society however divides into an endless scale of rank from the pensioned ex-king and Rajah, down to the despised Paria, the lowest of all. — Occasional European residents of note — Americans, Frenchmen and Germans, — attracted by the interests of commerce or navigation, and staying for a longer or shorter period of time, associate with one of the two first-named classes, to which by their recommendations or introductions they can lay claim. As a general rule, foreigners do not meet with a very liberal reception. Another important part of the population deserves the more attention, as it is rapidly increasing in number and making decided progress in influence and civilization. It is the so called half-caste, a mingling of British and Indian blood, mostly of illegitimate origin. They are in general a handsome race, many of them possessing large fortunes, which, aided by the charms of the females, often lead to alliances with the highest classes. Intelligence, good breeding and refinement are frequent acquisitions among these mulattoes, who monopolise many a profitable branch of the trade of Calcutta. That with the interior of the country and the coasts, is, almost exclusively, in their hands. — As a peculiar appendix of the population the European Miss claims some notice; the member of the chivalric order of Love. A cargo or two of these young ladies of good families and small fortunens are shipped annually from England to India to be married and after some years to return as rich Nabobesses, who may glitter and shine in the routs and assemblies of the English metropolis; a prospect which is frequently realized.

The influence, which the British sway exerts upon the higher circles of Hindoo society, and the gradual transformations which it is producing, is remarkable. It is true, Braminism contests obstinately every inch of its former territory against the intruding flood of western life; but it is daily losing ground in the unequal strife, and retreats more and more into a narrower and lower sphere. All the weapons of European culture are here continually active against Braminism, and are laboring restlessly for its final remove. In more than a hundred free schools, on the Lancastrian plan, are the sluices of instruction opened to the Hindoo down to the lowest Paria; twelve Bengalese newspapers and journals, two of which are distributed gratis, are strewing the seeds of European knowledge and thought in the guise of attractive entertainment, and the many institutions for the higher intellectual improvement of the natives, are zealously attended, now that the doors to office and dignity, both in the civil and military departments, are thrown open to the Hindoo of talent and capacity. In the interior of the land, however, we scarce behold a sign of British influence. There the Indian bears the stamp of his primitive originality, as decidedly as he did three or four thousand years ago. His theocratic constitution is still an unconquered bulwark there; it protects him against every change, a strict and unalterable system of castes puts every man into his proper place, which he cannot overstep; his European masters stand opposite to him, as strangers and conquerors, and if he should pass beyond the limits prescribed to him by custom, he would effect his own ruin. — It is otherwise in Calcutta. There the Native is daily exposed to the assaults of European civilisation. He is laying aside his prejudices; not at once, but by imperceptible degrees, and private interest is doing the rest. Already the father sees no longer in his son a genuine Hindoo, and his grandson will appear still less so. The arm of the Bramin, to the present day so powerful in the interior, is broken in the capital. Many Hindoos of rank have already publicly adopted the garb and manners of Europeans, and even their philosophers, laughing at the excommunications of their priests, explain in public schools the absurdity of the Bramin faith. One of the wealthiest men in Calcutta, Tagore, of the Bramin caste, gives balls, soirées, and dinners in his palace, which in splendor and taste rival those of the governor; and the European, invited on such occasions, beholds, with surprise, an assembly of Hindoos conversing upon politics, science, and philosophy with a freedom, adroitness, and soundness of judgment, that would do honor to the best society in Europe. Those Hindoos of distinction, however, who, by strict seclusion, endeavor to keep themselves free from European influence, are an indolent, degraded, effeminate race, who seek to hide their want of power and esteem under silly splendor and pompous show. — In such a manner is England working, unhindered, toward her object; this is avowedly, to form out of the better class of the Hindoo population in Calcutta a ripe and sound kernel of improvement, which, when grown to a tree, may at some future day, spread its branches over all India, and, to the benefit of civilization, take the place of rude Moslem ignorance, and of Braminism, which fetters the human mind in senseless stupidity.

As a commercial market, Calcutta holds the first rank in all Asia. It is the great emporium not only of the traffic of the mother-country with her Indian empire, but also of the trade of both with other parts of the continent. It is also a ware-house for the importations and exportations of the Australian and African colonies. Its inland-trade is immense, chiefly by the Ganges and its branches, which are navigable for a distance of 1500 miles. The introduction of steam-boat-navigation has greatly increased the means of communication with the provinces and during the last year forty one steamers plied upon the Ganges alone. The discovery of coal-beds on the banks of this river opens new prospects to industry and speculation, and the rail-roads now constructing to Bombay and Madras promise to unlock the southern and western provinces to the grand centre of business. The commerce of Calcutta gives employment, at present, to more than 800 vessels, and upwards of 20,000 river-boats keep up the trade with the interior. The commercial capital is estimated at 400,000,000 Doll. All the products of India and Asia figure in the list of exports from Calcutta and the European imports comprise, beside vast amounts of specie, most of the products of British manufactures.

Institutions, tending to promote the commercial interests and to advance science, as banks, insurance-companies, docks and bazars; universities, colleges, observatory, botanical garden, and innumerable societies for artistical, scientific and charitable purposes are crowded in the metropolis of the British-Indian empire and Calcutta may have indeed some claims to the proud denomination of a Capital of Asia, bestowed or her by the last governor-general.

The ROMAN AQUAEDUCT in SEGOVIA

(SPAIN)

Published for HERRMANN J. MEYER 164. William-Street. NEW YORK.

THE ROMAN AQUEDUCT AT SEGOVIA IN SPAIN.

The people of the Gracchi has disappeared, the dust of the Cesars is blown away; another Rome stands now on the seven hills, another race has taken possession of the classic ground: but in spite of all changes, on whatever side the nations that composed her vast empire turn their regards, whether to their courts of justice, or to their codes of law; to their political institutions, to their schools, or to their languages; everywhere they see and feel the hand of ancient Rome, the once irresistible mistress of the universe. —

Rome's dominion connected civilisation with splendor and terror. It was the period of great virtues and great vices; a period, when the spirits of many nations vanished before the genius of a single city. The idea of a universal monarchy was carried out by Rome alone. During ten centuries did the Giant of the Capitol continue to grow, until he stretched his unwieldy limbs over three quarters of the then known globe. Nations formed his flock, and his crook was his will at the point of the sword. He inexorably destroyed, with a hand of iron, every vestige of nationality in the vanquished; customs, religion, language, and form of government were crushed by his ponderous foot, and Roman life and civilisation filled up their place. Thirty generations lived in war and victory in order to fix the yoke on the neck of a subject world. Thirty successive races celebrated triumphs on the Capitol, saw their fellow-citizens wear laurel-crowns, and laden with the earth's spoils, march over the Forum with kings conducted in fetters, and captive-generals chained to the victor's car, saw the treasures of the globe flow towards their city in a continuous stream:— but bearing on their bosom the load of blood and guilt that accompanies the subjugation and pillage of the weak by the stronger. The day of retribution arrived. While the eagle of the Capitolinian Jupiter looked on the known world as his dominion, at a moment when it was least expected, the temple of the Thunderer himself became desolate, and the fate of the deposed Deities, whom he had assembled in the pillared hall of the Pantheon, proved to be the lot reserved by Destiny for himself, the majestic ruler of the Gods. Just when his power seemed at its zenith, faith deserted his altars, and „like the baseless fabric of a vision“ he vanished from the eyes of the deluded multitude. These were stirring times. The empire was torn with internal dissensions, towns and cities were laid waste by incendiaries; political factions convulsed the State, proscription and plunder were the order of the day, Rome's streets swam in the blood shed by the executioner or the assassin. Terrible days had dawned over the City of the World; and, in spite of her outward splendor, happiness and joy had no abode within her walls. Gone was all trust in the power of the gods, and the temples were pointed at in scorn; contempt smote their priests and deserted were the altars. In this long starless night suddenly a new light broke in: Jesus Christ. The mild and elevating doctrine of an eternal God, who loves mankind and judges them with love, the doctrine of immortality and everlasting peace as the price of virtue, flowed into the wounded souls of the nations like streams of healing balm; the Cross brought from the Golgatha on the Jordan was erected on the Golgatha on the Tiber. It became a token of reconciliation between Man and Heaven; it was the harbinger of a new Era.

Long before the Emperors of Rome themselves professed the Christian faith, had the benign influence of Christ's doctrine made progress throughout the empire. The vast majority of the better society were, in secret, Christians. The word of the Messiah was the bond that linked together the noblest hearts from the Pontus to the pillars of Hercules, and under its influence the spirit on which the Roman policy was conducted, underwent a total reform. For Humanity this change was a blessing. —

Rome was at this juncture at the height of territorial power. Her thirst for conquest was satisfied. Christianity condemned the rapacity of a conqueror. The maxim was no longer to enlarge the state, but to preserve it. The solicitude of the imperial rulers was now chiefly directed to the greater security of the frontiers. Hence arose those gigantic long-extended fortifications in Scotland, Thrace, the Asiatic provinces, and Germany, the authorship of which, on account of their stupendous magnitude, popular tratition often asscribed to the Devil. The Roman empire having bulwarked itself against external ennemies, the activity of the government was enabled to display itself in internal improvement. Nations overcome with the sword, and now considered as members and constituent parts of the Roman state, were to be made sharers in all the advantages which universal dominion by its unity in legislation, executive power and administration is enabled to bestow; they were to be attached to the stability of the empire by the strong tie of their own Interest; and this design was carried out with that energy of execution exhibited in everything undertaken by Rome. Those legions which were not required for the protection of the frontiers, were employed in the execution of works of public utility; they constructed roads, excavated canals, deepened rivers to make them navigable, and laid out harbors for the convenience of commerce: the labors of peace steeled their sinews for those of war. All that could contribute to the material welfare and to the intellectual development of the provinces, was encouraged and promoted by the State in the most liberal manner. Trade and industry enjoyed unrestricted freedom; agriculture was ligthened of its burdens, and animated by commerce throve rapidly; throughout the vast conglomerate of countries, wealth and prosperity were diffused to an extraordinary degree, and the Arts and Sciences in their different branches were fostered and furthered by enlightened patronage. The provincial cities, notwithstanding the rapidity of their growth, contained edifices that might vie in splendor with those of Rome herself: theatres, baths, halls for public assemblies, tribunals, temples, churches and triumphal arches: works, whose remains after almost two milleniums still astonish the world, and bear irrefragable testimony as to what Rome once was. —

Amongst these works we must not forget to mention the aqueducts. In truth, they belong to the most colossal and, at the same time, most praiseworthy undertakings by which the Roman spirit was characterised, or that the human mind ever conceived and executed. Almost every city of consideration in the Roman empire was furnished with an aqueduct. Whilst in our own times, in spite of our boasted improvement in civilisation, the capitals of powerful and extensive kingdoms suffer from the want of clear, clean, healthy spring-water, the Romans acknowledged it a duty of the State to procure the very best, and it discharged this duty with a magnificence, nay, even a majesty, which surpasses our boldest projects. If here and there a modern architect has endeavored to soar to the height of the Ancients, these feeble imitations were scarcely ever dictated by a regard for the public welfare; they have been erected to gratify the caprice of the mistress of a prince, or the ostentation of a monarch; they are monuments of dynastic arrogance, of boundless extravagance, and a mockery of the national distress. The feelings excited by their view are those of indignation or regret; they give neither pleasure nor respect. Louis XIV. would throw aqueducts over valley and stream and bring the pure element from a considerable distance, in order to feed the fountains and puerile water-works of his palaces and gardens, or to supply some artificial lake, destined to bear the decked-out gondolas of a fawning court, while the principal cities of his realm received bad water through rotten pipes of wood. In such royal works the people were never thought of. — And these gaped-at wonders, the issue of a frantic extravagance, what are they, in spite of the millions they cost, when placed beside those majestic constructions of the Romans? Child's play compared to the work of man! While the ancient aqueducts, after 20 centuries, still call forth our admiration and seem to defy the hand of Time, those modern buildings sink in ruins. —

The structure of the Roman aqueducts has, at all times, been an inexhaustible source of study to the Architect. On them the latter may learn how to combine, without prodigality, the highest degree of grandeur and fitness of design with elegance and extreme durability. Vitruvius and Frontinus have described the method of proceeding observed by the Roman architects previous to laying out one of these immense constructions. After having ascertained what quantity of water would be requisite for the city in question, all the springs, within a distance of 50 miles, and situated above the level of the place to be supplied, were carefully tested not only in regard to quantity but also to quality. The main object, namely, to procure the wholesomest water that was to be had, was never sacrificed to considerations of expense. As soon as the capital-question, what springs were to be chosen, was settled, canals of solid masonry were built, through which the water was conducted either in metal tubes or in stone channels. If mountains traversed the line, the canal was carried through them; if valleys were met with, it passed them on arches, like a bridge; if the depth to be overarched was considerable, several rows or tiers were constructed one above the other, attaining occasionally the height of 200 feet. At certain intervals the water was collected in large reservoirs (*Piscinae*), both for the purpose of clarification as of increasing the hydraulic pressure. At the place of its destination it was received in large vaulted cisterns (*Castella*), whence metal pipes conveyed it to the different quarters of the city, and distributed it among the baths, private houses, gardens, etc. The expenses of maintaining the aqueduct in repair, were covered by a small tax levied by the state. — The most gigantic and imposing constructions of this kind were to be seen in the immediate neighborhood of the city, where the pomp and splendor of the empire were concentrated within a comparatively limited compass. The architecture of these conduits was carried in the greatest perfection. In the time of the emperors, more particularly, a magnificence was displayed in their erection, which borders on the incredible. Several of them brought the water a distance of 60—80 miles, over valleys and through mountains. „When we consider“, says Pliny, „the immense quantity of water conveyed by the collective aqueducts for the use of the many baths, fish-ponds, fountains, artificial lakes and cascades, for the numberless private dwellings, for the gardens and villas of the environs; when we view the works themselves by which this service is effected, these mighty canals, whose towering tiers of arches level the loftiest mountains, and bridge over the most spacious valleys, or sometimes pierce the rocks and traverse large forests, and bear the weight of towns and castles on their backs, we must confess, even in Rome itself, which has so much that is grand and glorious, that in the world there is nothing more worthy of our admiration. The city of Rome possessed 14 large Aqueducts. The first of these was the Aqua Appia; it was built 305 years before the birth of Christ. Forty years later, the celebrated structure raised by M. Curius Dentatus conveyed to Rome the excellent springs with which Tibur (Tivoli) was environed. This aqueduct is 20 miles long and almost entirely subterranean. Of the whole number there are, at the present day, but three remaining. These, however, suffice to afford a copious supply of water to all the houses and public fountains of modern Rome, as well as to most of the gardens and villas of the environs. The rest are ruins and constitute a prominent and imposing feature in the Roman landscape. Nothing can surpass the aspect presented by these venerable remains, which, draped with pendant ivy and crowned with rampant shrubs, on all sides approach the Eternal City, traversing hill and dale, in long, and often unbroken, array. —

During the period of a line of good Emperors, when, with few exceptions, the State, free from inward dissensions, enjoyed the blessings of peace and order, the benefit of aqueducts was extended to nearly all the larger towns of the provinces. The ruins of hundreds of these structures still exist, and often constitute the sole memento of a departed greatness that has left not even a name behind. Others, however, still fulfil the purpose for which they were originally designed, and may perhaps be destined to supply nations as yet unborn. —

One of these is the celebrated Aqueduct of Segovia. It conducts the exellent springs near Ildefonso in one collected mass to the most elevated point of the city, the lowest parts of which it traverses on a double tier of bold and lofty arches. The supply of water is sufficient for a population of 100,000, and this was the census of the Roman city in the reign of Trajan. The modern Segovia, however, is but the shadow of what it formerly was. Crazy, mean-looking dwelling-houses, and often mere huts lean for support on the solid masonry of the Conquerors, and an idle heedless multitude is rambling about, too indolent even to cast a look at the great works above them, though their hats are off in an instant when an Alcalde crosses the street. The contrast is revolting and the question involuntarily suggests itself: where is our boasted progress during 2000 years? The question cuts to the quick; but luckily the Spaniards, now stupified by despots and priests, are not mankind. Progress is to be sought for in other quarters. Nevertheless a mournful feeling occupies the mind on seeing this Roman monument, which Nature, as were it her minion, has gorgeously decked up to the topmost ridge with ivy, grass, and creeping plants dangling their vary-colored flowers. — The most glorious cities of old bear all the same fate. The ruins of Palmyra decorate a desert, and the wandering Arab pastures his steed in the sanctuary of the Theban temples. Culture is migratory, and in the great drama of Humanity judgment should not be formed on isolated scenes. Look up! Worlds in ruins revolve round every sun, and in vain do the fragments follow each other. They never meet again. Their longing for re-union remains ungratified. And shall we blame the Author on that account? Dare we ask Him why these atoms chase each other? Let us rather consider and comprehend the Universe as a whole, and trustfully believe that the Creator's worlds manifest his wisdom and love, and proclaim,

For ever singing as they shine:
„The hand that made us is Divine."

THE VALLEY OF CHAMOUNI IN SWITZERLAND.

Deep in the bosom of the Alpine world, and far from railways and post-roads, lies the valley of Chamouni, from whose bottom rises the monarch of European mountains, Mont-Blanc. The vale of Chamouny, winding between the walls of snow-topped mountains for five leagues, is narrow and seldom widens to above an American mile. It is watered by the Arve, a gushing glacier-stream often forming cascades. Several hundred shepherds with their families inhabit the romantic spot and a small, ancient chapel, the Prieuré, is their common place of worship. The dale is rich in meadow-land and forms, with the lofty glaciers and ice-fields, the waterfalls, torrents and rocks towering up on its sides, or covering the green sward in colossal and vary-shaped blocks, a scenery of most charming contrast. In the winter and spring, the landscape is a picture of seclusion and repose; in summer, however, it is constantly frequented by strangers and tourists of all nations, for whose reception four large hotels often prove insufficient. The young girls of Chamouny then hire themselves out as waiting-maids to the hotel-keepers, the young men as guides, and both reap a rich harvest. They have the good and wise custom, to save their gains and when they have set up for their own to expend it on the improvement of their property or on the purchase of live-stock. Nowhere are there to be seen finer herds of cattle and the trim attire of the mountaineers, their dwellings, and the neatness of their furniture, present a pleasant picture of cheerfulness and comfort. The most skilful and boldest chamois-hunters are inhabitants of this valley.

A century ago, this interesting portion of the Alps was entirely unknown to the travelling world. In the year 1741, two Englishmen, Pocock and Windham, in endeavoring to ascend Mont-Blanc, strayed thither, and as they described their discovery in the most attractive colors to their rambling fellow-countrymen, the swarm of tourists soon found their way into the quiet mountain-nook. Since then its population has increased tenfold; splendid hotels have been built, paths and roads have been made, and the natural beauties in the neighborhood of the valley rendered accessible by the industrious shepherds. The memory of the discoverers is still preserved in the name given to an enormous block of granite upon the Montanvert. It is called the Rock of the two Englishmen.

One of the existing three mule-paths is by preference used for reaching the valley of Chamouni. The first winds from Evian, on the lake of Geneva, across Samoens; the second runs from Martigny over the Col de Balme; the third, the most convenient, leads from Evian, through Sallenches and Servoz. The latter is preferred by the tourists in general and we have chosen it for our own excursion. —

On a bright morning in July, with the rise of the sun we set out from Evian. Rose-colored clouds gleam in the sky; the lake is bathed in a purple glow; the sun clothes the great Saleve in glittering gold, and the invigorating mountain-air blows cool upon our cheeks. Our mules trot briskly through Chesne, the last cheerful village in the canton; upon the height we bid adieu to free Switzerland, and find ourselves in the dominions of a monarch; we are in Savoy. Even without the royal escutcheon set up by the way-side, even without barriers and custom-house, we should have at once remarked it. Upon the Geneva-side, intelligence, cheerfulness, moral dignity shone in every face; industry, and her daughter, comfort, looked forth from every peasant's cottage, over every garden-fence; here, stupidity stares us in the face, poverty and wretchedness, with scrofula and cretinism, grin at us from every hovel. Decay and degradation are every where visible, and of the fruits, which the soil of priestly and monarchical sway bear in every clime, there is no want.

But Nature, how wonderfully beautiful, how grand, how sublime, how glorious, art Thou here! We see the Savoy Alps in their white gleaming garments, and beneath them, as, at the gate of a magic world, lies the village of Faucigny, jammed-in between the perpendicular walls of a deep chasm. We make this romantic spot our first resting-place. The inn is large and commodious. At all hours of the day, it swarms with wandering bands of various nations.

From there we proceed toward Sallenches, through a land, adorned with the grandest, and, at the same time, the loveliest scenery. Calm and quietness are the fairies of these dales. What majesty in these heights! The wild, rushing Arve, hastening to the stately Rhone, is our constant companion upon this path, from which we behold alternately glaciers, frozen seas, and the velvet Alpine meadows with their herdsmen's huts, and our ear listens to the noise of waterfalls and to the distant thunder of the dreaded avalanche. The clouds are already tipped with evening-gold, when we reach Sallenches. From the windows of the inn, where we have taken up our quarters for the night, we see Mont-Blanc directly before us. His head still beams in purple light, while the mist is already covering the valley with its dusky veil.

In Sallenches we hire fresh animals. We can trust ourselves to them with perfect security; for they know each step and stone upon the way. We ascend the steep pass. On the right hand we have the Arve, which leaps from valley to valley; on the left precipices; before us, mountains tower toward heaven. At one spot in the path, the eye, glancing through a ravine,

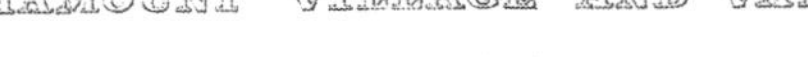

C. Reiss del.

CHAMOUNI VILLAGE AND VALLEY

(SWITZERLAND)

Published for HERRMANN J. MEYER 164 William-Street NEW YORK.

falls upon the Lac-de-Chede, by whose emerald waters chamois are grazing. Near Pont-de-Chevres, a wild cataract leaps into the abyss below; farther on rise the ruins of the castle of St. Michel, in times of yore the magnificent residence of a dynasty, now the retreat of the eagle and the vulture, who build their eyries there. Then we cross the Pont-de-Pelissier, beneath which the foaming Arve rolls onward throug a dark fearful chasm; at last, we enter the valley of Servoz, with its cottages and soft meadows. It is a mountain-basin, which, some hundred years ago was a lake. In Servoz we stop to dine, and enter the hotel St. Louis, well known to all travellers in Switzerland. It is admirably conducted, affording every convenience provided the crowd of strangers be not too great. Here, for the first time, we drink genuine glacier-water mingled with Burgundy. It is the best refreshment in hot weather.

After having dined we direct our course to Chamouni. The mountains rise higher and higher in front of us, and Mont-Blanc, the giant, steps forth, in outlines full of majesty. Dazzling glaciers hang over the green valley-sides, and, here and there, are piled up ice-clad masses of rock, which gleam in the sun-beams, like vary-colored jewels. Between this landscape and the path, the Arve dashes onward in the ravine, while from its banks, the grazing-ground of herds, resounds melodiously the tinkling of cow-bells, and Echo repeats the love-song of the shepherd. We enjoy a picture of rural loveliness in the midst of Alpine grandeur.

Evening comes on, and mean-while we reach La Prieuré, the head-village of the valley, and the goal of our journey. Clean, well furnished hotels, and agreable, obliging hosts receive us; the attendance surpasses our expectation. All the inns of this place face Mont-Blanc, and in the presence of its glory, at sunset, the guests of each *auberge* assemble upon the balcony around the tea table. It is a happy, transient hour. The rosy summits of the mountain, glow and fade away each evening; but for him who has once seen them, the remembrance holds fast through life.

CIVITA CASTELLANA IN ITALY.

The Power of description is limited to the narrow sphere of words and becomes tiresome, if not enlivened by the power of thought. Mere sense of beauty is insufficient to fix constantly the attention of the reader. The traveller, who is making his notes of impressions, is naturally ever recurring to the same exclamations of his pleasure. I saw a thousand beautiful sceneries during my travels; and whenever I was tempted to describe them, I could not forbear the thought that it would be better to keep silence on a past world of exultation.

Our engraving represents Civita Castellana, the famous citadel in the Abruzzi, the living tomb of the Italian patriots. I take out my note-book. What shall I quote? „Civita Castellana is the diamond lock of a string of pearls, the chief ornament of a very romantic landscape. Situated on the road from Fuligno to Rome, built upon a lofty rock, surrounded by deep gorges and bathed by the waters of the Preja on their way to the Tiber, it commands a grand prospect. The surrounding country is now but slightly cultivated and thinly peopled; but in the classic days of Rome it was a garden, and Falerii, — on the site of which Civita Castellana is erected, once the capital-city of the Falerii, — was already a flourishing place before the foundations of Rome were laid. Its subjugation cost the Romans a long war, and when it was finally taken by them, they razed it to the ground, and compelled the inhabitants to build the new town in the plain. Of this latter the ruins of an aqueduct, of a theatre, some towers and walls remain.“

CIVITA CASTELLANA
(ITALY)

The CASTLE and MONASTERY of ILLOCK

(HUNGARY)

So much the note-book. Nothing distinguishes it from a dry quotation of a tourists-guide. It is „a text without a sermon."

The reader turns away disappointed. Patience! The clergyman is coming.

ILLOCK IN HUNGARY.

Far in the interior of Hungary, where the Drave unites with the Danube and separates countries and races, near the confines of Sclavonia, a little fortress looks down from its mountain-top upon the rivers and and plains below. This is Illock, the castle; and the neck of the height bears a cloister. All the country around is classic. Here eighteen centuries ago, Rome, with the help of German warriors, conquered the land and yoked the free people of Thrace; from hence her consuls and emperors brought the captured kings and generals of the vanquished for the decoration of their triumphal processions, to dazzle the eyes of the idle, staring, ambitious multitude of the seven-hilled city; — and here, where several military roads crossed, sprung up numerous Roman cities and colonies, and were erected by the emperors those extraordinary works of fortification, on the possession of which has ever depended the occupation of the most important strategic points of the country. As far as the eye can reach from the towers of Illock, the landscape is a battle-field, where, from times of tradition to the present day, hired warriors and independent peoples were wrestling, robbers with the robbed, oppressors with the oppressed, freemen with the slaves, who had come, at the command of their masters, to deprive nations of liberty. Near Illock had Rome obtained a central position for her power, by which she held the countries of the Lower Danube under her iron yoke. Those extensive and impregnable fortifications, which she constructed in the marshes between the Drave and the Danube, served as the stationary-quarters for the veterans, who had exhausted themselves in the battles of the Republic and the Empire, and for the formidable German legions, whose strength and valor converted all battles into victories. It was there that the Romans attempted to establish a lasting and firm support of their power by military colonies of German warriors, of the existence of which numerous traditions and the names of many places still give testimony. The populous Teutoburgum (Citadel of Teut) was situated in this region.

By a singular freak of fate, a new Roman power has sprung up on the same spot, where so many ruins of buildings and monuments are witnesses of the supremacy of ancient Rome; for Illock, with the surrounding country to a great distance is the property of a race of Roman princes, the Odescalchi. The coincidence looks somewhat like the irony of fate. While the ruins of Roman temples strew the ground and her gigantic works, the mile-stones of her power, are fallen; while thorns grow on the graves of Rome's cities and aqueducts; while her roads and her amphitheaters are demolished; while her obelisks and columns are overthrown, and the tombs no longer protect the dust of her heroes: — we see on the rock, from which the emperors, surrounded by their proconsuls and generals, looked down on a world that was subject to their power as far as thought could reach, a prince of modern Rome sipping his Tokay, and with servants in brocade-coats and silk stockings to carry the commands of his Serene Highness to the overseers of his serfs. Happy Odescalchi! It was a strange dream which summoned thee to reestablish on the Danube the empire of Rome and build the hut of thy frail existence over the graves of the conquerors of the world. Yet thou hast performed thy task, it must be allowed, with sense. Illock is one of the finest principalities of Hungary, and the interior arrangements of the castle are worthy of its refined master.

In the late war, which has ended with a result so tragical for the fate of Hungary, the name of Illock has often been mentioned. On the breaking out of the Revolution, the Odescalchi left the country. The first bloody scenes of that drama — the frightful struggle of the Magyars with the Servian race — were played in the vicinity. Afterwards Illock changed masters several times between the contending parties, as the god of battles gave now this, and now that side, the advantage. The most bloody conflicts took place in its neighborhood during the spring and summer of 1849, when Jellachich and his generals, with their Croats and Servians, encamped in the old Roman fortifications, and for months stood on the defensive against the daily attacks of the Hungarians. The Magyar-courage of that time did not shrink back before impossibilities; for the position of the Servians in the Roman entrenchments, which are protected in front by wide marshes, and in the rear by the rivers Drave and Danube, could scarcely be assaulted, not to speak of being carried. Incredible valor, and a profusion of blood were sacrificed in vain before these works. The bravest generals fought in succession on the Hungarian side — the old Damjanich, the bold Leiningen, Perczel, and the high-minded Kiss, — all of them heroes, who have recieved the order of immortality from the hands of the Austrian executioner.

The ghosts of the thirteen generals, who perished at Arad, the spirits of others who were cut off in the dungeons of Munkatch, the inumerable victims, whose fate is still shrouded in mystery, they haunt not the bed of old Haynau, who got his due by the whipping of the London rabble; no! their curses rest on the Judas who betrayed them, and with them his country, — on the wretch who treacherously plunged into the abyss the noble people that idolized him and looked up to him for salvation. Him, the traitor, may the Furies pursue through Eternity! To every Judas-deed clings a Judas-curse: and if Görgey did not to himself the same that Judas did after he had betrayed the Lord, — if Görgey has not yet hanged himself over his threshhold, we can only perceive in this circumstance the awful justice of God which took from him the last redeeming trait able to awake sympathy: — his *courage*. Who but a Görgey could endure, or would be willing to endure, the *existence* of a Görgey?

Only *one* mental quality was developed on a large scale in Görgey — *that* quality which is apt to turn man into villain — *selfishness*. Görgey was the slave of egoism, so long as we can follow his career. Selfishness perverted and corrupted his very nature. It made him false from head to foot; it filled him with hypocrisy and deceit; it made him incapable of a moral judgment ŏn his own conduct. All the brilliant qualities with which he so long deceived the world, were destitute of the moral basis.

We wonder not that there are persons, who still attempt to defend Görgey. It was an easy matter for the princes, who profited by the treachery, to find venal pens to play the advocate of the traitor. Yet their efforts will ever be in vain. It may be said of the bloody hand of Görgey, as of the little hand of *Lady Macbeth*, „All the waters in the ocean can not wash it clean“. In vain have his pleaders exhausted all the treasures of their sophistry. Not a single conviction damning Görgey has been shaken; not a grain's weight of the load of public contempt has been taken from him. Where undeniable facts speak, as in the case of Görgey, no pettifogging lawyer can alter the public judgment.

The deed of Görgey was neither the suggestion of a moment, nor of a noble thought, as some have tried to represent it. He had long before conspired against Hungary and against her Government. The catastrophe of Villagos was only the *closing scene* of his false game. Görgey never conducted himself like an honorable character. While he flattered Kossuth to his face, he craftily did every thing to undermine his influence; and while in the company of his intimates he ridiculed the measures of the executive government, he never ventured, on a public occasion, to express an opinion in opposition to Kossuth. Görgey's *duty* was clearly determined by his position. He was a general, and as a general he was bound to *obey*; he was a Hungarian, and as a Hungarian he was bound to defend his country to the last breath. When by his intrigues he had displaced Kossuth; when all the power and all the authority of his country were lodged in his hands; when Hungary, not discouraged by two lost battles after so many victories, resolute on self-sacrifice, and ready to go into death for freedom and independence, received him as dictator: even then ultimate success could not fail to freedom's cause, if Görgey's soul had been animated with a spark of the true hero. Görgey, we allow, was not destitute of the qualities which constitute the great commander in the field. His calm and sang-froid in battle gave him a decided superiority; he gained the army by his courage, the generals by his intellectual power, the lower officers by his commanding look, the people by his exploits; and he possessed an advantage which is rarely given to men in high positions: he never lost his temper. His iron heart yielded to no affection of the soul except to one: — self-love. The taciturnity and the reserve of his manners and of his character, moreover, drew a halo round his head. This was so effective, that it even forced his enemies to indecision. Görgey wanted only one thing to change the role of the great villain for that of the great man: morality. All his dazzling qualities could not disguise this want and hence he never inspired trust even to his most intimate acquaintances. General Görgey could not give that which a man of honor can give. This explains why he was suspected a traitor by all who knew him best long before his treachery was accomplished. Perczel openly charged it upon him; Nagy Sandor broke with him; Klapka, his old friend, used to say, „I cannot comprehend him"; Guyon declared his conviction, that Görgey would labor for the triumph of Russia, as soon as the Czar would pay his price, and the noble-hearted Kiss said: „he will sell us all, and with us all Hungary"; but in spite of these convictions none of these men were so mean to accuse Görgey publicly on mere suspicion. Kossuth alone had a duty and a right to do it; it was, indeed suggested to him by his officers; but his pure and elevated soul was unable to regard Görgey as a Judas. „Görgey" said he, „is an egotist; but he is a Hungarian and no Hungarian is

20

a traitor.“ He knew indeed that he was capable of aspiring to the supreme power; but he was far from believing him to to be a villain. Kossuth was a virtuous and great man: he could not descend to the baseness of Görgey even in thought. When the terrible fact of the contrary broke in upon him, Kossuth had no longer the acknowledged power to make good the error. He had surrendered the dictatorship to the traitor. To raise his arm against him afterward could only be done by an act of illegality. Such a proçeeding Kossuth's elevated mind scorned. He is not to be blamed for it; but the fact is ever to be lamented. A good cause needs not the sanction of written laws, and a bad one often seeks it, though it cannot justly claim it. — If Kossuth had shot the traitor Görgey at Villagos before the front of his army, such a punishment by re-inflaming the heroic spirit of the army, might have saved Hungary, and with Hungary the freedom of the west of Europe, — now a prey to Russia and her crownbearing vassals.

Kossuth, always ready to sacrifice every thing else for Hungary, refused to sacrifice his respect for the law. Yet it will never be denied, that he suffered more than death for his fatherland. When he left Hungary, he left all dear to him behind; he took nothing with him, but a broken heart and his poverty. Not even the pillow, on which he reposed his head, could he call his own; so poor was he even at that time, when he had the treasures of an Empire at his uncontrolled disposal. The purity of his character was never behind the elevation of his mind. This fact has been decided with unexampled-unanimity by general judgment. This judgment is his best reward. When driven into exile, the world hung listening on every breath of his lips; England and America watched over his safety; when the hour fixed for his liberation struck, he was conducted from the prison-house like a conqueror in triumph and the proudest nations of the earth rivalled each other in receiving the pennyless fugitive gloriously, like a sendling of God. They saw not merely the man in the virtuous Hungarian, they welcomed him as the representative of the principles to which they own their happiness, their independence, their wealth, their renown: — the principles of popular freedom and self-government.

On the opposite side, General Görgey, the lost man, has nowhere a moral support. He might think it an easy matter, to sport with the happiness and freedom of a people, and to reward popular confidence with treachery. The tragic end of his friends and comrades, the terrible fate of those who, lying in chains, now are daily appealing to death for deliverance and invoking the vengeance of God on the author of their sufferings; the unparalleled misery of his fatherland: all this is accumulated in a mountain of guilt, which will for ever torture the immortal soul of the wretch, who is reduced to live on Russian ducats, the price of his infamous acts. In vain does the traitor attempts to hide himself in obscurity and to weaken his own guilt by slandering those, he sacrificed. The sentence is irrevocably pronounced, and the most tolerant and human disposition can never remove the least particle from it without wronging justice. —

Every traitor ripe for the gallows has an official advocate, and Görgey had no lack of them. They have spoken of his error and his intention to appease his country. What mortal may truly imagine, a Görgey, that crafty, sharp, intricate man, could have believed in the magnanimity of Austria and Russia? — Not to you, who have the face to make such an assertion does the sober judgment appeal; for the tools of tyranny are of course destitute of moral feeling; but to you, in whose soul the laws of morality and honor are respected, I call: look at the immortal patriots, the victors on so many battle-fields, the old Aulich, the valiant Damjanich bending under his wounds, the undaunted Perczel, the noble, youthful Leiningen, Kiss, who laid his immense fortune, together with his life on the altar of his country, and all the others, who stood under the gallows on that fearful August-morning; imagine the scenes of terror, when the rest of the Hungarian generals and high officers were dragged forth and condemned to dreary dungeons for twenty years or for lifetime, and when their limbs were put in irons; imagine the condition of those, who, belonging to the noblest families in the land, were enrolled as privates in the oppressor's army, of those young enthusiastic souls, who must now bow to the will of an Austrian corporal, and sleep on the straw of the Austrian barracks; and if this is yet unsufficient to arm your judgment, — than cast your eye on Hungary herself, that magnificent country, which the hand of God has so richly endowed with all the boons which can delight and bless mankind, — and then ask: who dares say, that the treachery of Görgey has given peace to Hungary? Peace? No, not even the peace of a churchyard! Devotion, faith, love and resignation shed their blossoms on the tombs; on the battle-fields however, where hundreds of thousands of Hungarians sleep, who have paid the price for the freedom and independence of their fatherland with their lives; on the ruins of the countless towns and villages, which have been devastated by fire and sword; on the mounds, beneath which the happiness of innumerable families is buried: — there wander other spirits than those of reconciliation and forgiveness.

No, no! As long as Austria's intolerable yoke galls the neck of the nation, there will be found in Hungary no other peace, than the peace preluding a war of extermination, the stillness before the storm, the calm before the earthquake. A nation as quick and vigorous in thought, as free and bold in speech, as prompt and resolute in action, as ready for sacrificing life and property for the One and All: such a nation will only wait the first tidings and trumpet of political reformation for the rise of fettered nations, to sally forth and re-assemble under the standard of honor, liberty and national independence. And than the name of Kossuth will be a watchword to the generous people, as was once that of Washington to the people of New-England, and the prayers of the modern Peter of Amiens, which now fall on so many deaf ears and on so many hearts unmoved in the blessed land of freedom, — will be fulfilled.

BREMEN

BREMEN.

I had taken my passage on board a small craft at Nienburg. An accident had occasioned delay, and shortly after midnight on a Sunday morning — it was in July — I heard the old master rousing up his men, in order to reach Bremen before the first ringing of the church-bells. He was evidently ill at ease. „On the Lord's day I never let an oar be touched," said he, „but my cargo ought to have been in Bremen yesterday and necessity has no law!"

The trampling of the men on deck, the splashing of the heavy oars, the creaking of the rudder, soon put an end to my sleep. I crawled out of my berth and out of the small, low closet, black with smoke, and dimly lighted by a bit of window a single foot square, which in those days was called a cabin, and came upon deck. The full moon lingered still above the horizon in the West; the stars twinkled; the Milky Way spanned the heavens with its arch of worlds; in the farthest East, hardly visible, the heralds of approaching day, a few stripes of rose-tinted clouds, appeared. The moon cast across the waters the long shadows of some slender alders and poplars, which here and there were grouped upon the shore, and their shapes seemed to dance fantastically upon the glittering waves. It was one of the most pleasant scenes which I ever saw. The vessel glided gently down the widening river. The twilight gradually encreased, the moon went down, the sky grew paler and paler, the stars one after another disappeared, and the morning mists played on the path of our boat. The stillness of night gave way to awaking life. The water-fowl, startled by the splashing of the oars, flew whirring and screaming from us; now and then we passed a raft floating lazily down, or were overtaken by some swifter vessel than our own. Church-towers and chimneys peeped inquisitively down upon us from over the grass-clad dykes, and a light cloud of blue smoke above every roof appeared like a morning-offering to God and a sign of calm and peace. Fishing boats lay here and there in green coves, or some larger vessel with furled sails, solitary and melancholy, like a man without friendship and without love.

Purple and gold now „*Laced the severing clouds in yonder East.*“ — The mists fled the waves. Brighter and brighter grew the morning. Larks soaring in the air warbled their hymns, the little singers of the bushes performed their concerts, and our master whistled joyfully, when above the tree-tops, in the distance of a mile, we saw pennant-bearing masts and lofty towers. „Morning hours have gold in their mouths,“ said the old man, „we shall come to anchor in Bremen right early.“

The sun now rose in all his splendor. The whole landscape glittered and sparkled, bathed in the morning-dew. How beautiful, thought I, is this flat river-landscape so often decried for its monotony and want of beauty. The gilt clouds illumined trees and shrubs with their borrowed brilliancy; the branches waving in the morning breeze melodiously rustled their choral song; screaming waterfowl skimmed the surface; the bells for morning-prayer were audible from the villages right and left, mingling their tones in sweet harmony, and inviting the soul to devotion. Here and there we saw parties of church-goers passing along the top of the dykes, and gleeful, playing groups of children; all around us was Sabbath, holiday and contentment. When, by and by, both right and left, windmills, villas and countryseats crowded nearer together, and the houses formed continual rows, looking upon the river and showing their shining fronts; — when the masts of ships and various craft thickened to a forest, covered with sails as foliage, and their streamers waving in honor of the sabbath; — when the stately towers, rising from the depth of the city looked directly down upon our vessel: then we could no longer doubt that we had reached our journey's end. And so we had. The men towed the boat to an open place at the quay, drew in their oars, pushed a plank from the deck on the stone pier — we were in the port of Bremen.

Nearly forty years have since passed away. Those days were not the days of steamboats and railroads. A passage by the river from Minden to Bremen occupied not less then seven days. Nor was the journey much quicker by the mail-coach; it was a half-week's ride over the heath between Hannover and Bremen. At present the steam-horse traverses the same distance in six hours. When at that time a voyage to America was undertaken, prudent folks made their last wills and testaments; now it is a mere pleasure-trip. The earth has become smaller — man has not become happier.

Bremen as a city can hardly be called handsome. The splendid and imposing outside-show of many continental capitals is not to be looked for. Bremen is distinguished for something better; the first glance gives you the pleasing impression that it possesses a vigorous, industrious, comfortable and happy population. It does not summon the stranger to „behold and admire!“ but it makes him feel comfortable. He will not miss enjoyment in a city, where integrity, modesty, industry and morality are combined with good-breeding, cultivation of mind and knowledge of the world, without pretension or ridiculous haughtiness.

The broad channel of the Weser, which 54 miles farther down empties into the German Ocean divides Bremen into two portions of unequal size: the Old and the New town. A stone-bridge crosses the river from the Old Town, which is the most populous, to the left shore. Beyond the limits of the ancient ramparts, the suburbs stretch off into the open country. The circumference of the city including the suburbs, is reckoned about six miles. The space once occupied by strong fortifications, razed to the ground in the beginning of the present century, is laid out into public walks, forming a park, which surrounds the city in a semicircle and elongates on the river-banks at each extremity. It challenges comparison with the finest grounds of the kind in Germany. Calm sheets of water alternate with running streams, open spaces with shaded nooks, clumps of shrubbery with thickly-planted woodland, lawns with flower-gardens, cultivated with a care, which would do honor to a Dutch gardener. The proudest streets open upon this park, the noblest houses overlook it, and many points command extensive views over city and river, fields, meadow and forest.

The architectural physiognomy of the ancient parts of the town is of the old German stamp, such as we admire in Nuremberg, Augsburg, and Lübeck: — small-fronted houses of solid masonry, the lofty gables turned toward the streets, with balconies in the front or turrets at the corners. They breathe an air of cleanliness and comfort. The ancient wealthy Hanseatic City looks well in her stately garments. — In the new town the architecture is of course modern and elegant, seldom splendid or pretending. The houses are built with a view to neatness and comfort, and with few exceptions, they do honor to the taste of the architects. Shining palaces, such as were recently erected by so many rich merchants at Hamburgh, loaded with magnificent decorations to hide the poverty of ideas and the want of good taste, are seldom or never to be met mith in Bremen. The total number of houses reaches 7000 and the last census showed a population of nearly 60,000.

The city is fast increasing. A fresh and active spirit is visible in her life and in spite of the thousand honorable years, which Bremen counts, there is no sign of weakness or decay. Everywhere growth, improvement and development are to be met with; and in this, respect Bremen is not behind the thriving cities of North-America. That the constant and most intimate intercourse with the glorious Republics of the United States reacts favorably upon Bremen, invigorating life and urging onward, is a fact, and this intercourse is generally acknowledged to be the main-spring of her prosperity.

Bremen has few places or squares and none of peculiar beauty. The Market and Münster-place are worthy of notice, the one or account of the Town-Hall, the other for the celebrated Cathedral, their chief ornaments. The Cathedral, one of the most ancient places of christian worship in Germany, is neither very large nor beautiful. Its celebrity is mainly owing to its crypt, — (vulgarly called the „Bleikammer“ or Leadchamber) — a vast subterranean vault for the dead supported by pillars and walls of huge thickness. The peculiarity of this crypt — a circumstance which has never been satisfactorily explained — is, that corpses placed in it do not decay. They are preserved entire, and gradually dry up to complete mummies. When I visited the place forty years ago some fifty open coffins were placed in rows; the dead were children, boys, men in all stages of life, girls, women and ancient dames. All seemed but to sleep. Faces and hands had remained perfect; they appeared to the touch as smooth as parchment. Some might have been there for centuries, for they were clothed in the fashions of the middle ages.

Among the rest of the churches Angari Church with its tower of 324 feet, the highest in Bremen, is most worthy of note and the days of the Hanseatic league have their noblest representative monument in the ancient town-house. A colossal statue of Roland, the hero of Teutonic yore, stands in front of this building, a work of early art, uncouth and rude both in form and workmanship. Yet the principal attraction at the town-house is, as is the case with the Cathedral, subterranean. It is the celebrated wine-cellar, filled with the richest and costliest growths of the Rhine. Each drop of it may be valued by pistoles. The „Hochheimer“ of 1624, stored here, originally purchased for 37500 Doll., as the saying goes, if calculated by compound interest, would now represent a capital of 16,000,000 pistoles, or 61,000,000 Doll.

Is this not an enviable property for the magistrate of a Republic? Truly no emperor can boast of such a one, and a more original idea for the investment of the public funds could never have entered the brain of even a Law or a Biddle. The most celebrated apartment in this financial establishment is the „vault of the Apostles;“ so named, because on the heads of the twelve giant-casks, which contain the twelve best growths of the past century, the figure of an Apostle, as patron saint, is carved. The place is still pointed out as a matter of curiosity where a secret staircase conducted from the council chamber, affording to the fathers of the city easy access to their beloved saints. Those jolly days are gone by, and the passage has long since been walled up. Yet wine and pleasure have not migrated, and though they have grown somewhat more democratic, it is no injury to either. Whoever will pay the price has now liberty to sip the true Rhenish care-destroyer at its purest fountain; and no person of note visits Bremen who does not partake of civic hospitality in these halls. Music and Song then resound through the vaulted Temple of Bacchus until the crowing cock scatters the carousers.

Besides the structures enumerated there are worthy of being mentioned; — the Exchange, the Schutting (place of assembly of the city-militia), the ancient Palace of the Archbishop (now the senate-house), the Seefahrt (hospital for Seamen), the Post-office, and the extensive Waterworks upon an island in the river which supply the public fountains and dwelling houses. The buildings of the various charitable institutions for the old and sick, for insane persons, for the deaf and dumb, for widows and orphans, and the workhouses, are less remarkable for their architectural beauty than for their excellent regulations and management. The Duty of kindness and sympathy towards our poor and suffering brethren, has been ever extensively performed in Bremen.

Taste for science and art is generally cultivated; more so than is commonly supposed. Numerous institutions are in its service. The new Hall of Art is a fine edifice, the Theatre commands good talents, and in the beautiful building of the Union, with its large concert-room, Music finds cultivation. The Museum, an institution of long standing, furnishes, as well as the Library of the Union, a solid foundation for general instruction, and places the means of reading and study within the reach of every body. The Museum-Library numbers more than 70,000 volumes. No important work in modern literature will there he sought for in vain. The City-Library is very valuable for its collection of works of a more ancient date. Private-cabinets and collections of Art and Natural History are numerous and easy of access. The Observatory of the celebrated Olbers, whom the city of Bremen has honored with a marble statue from the chisel of Steinhauser in Rome (a native of Bremen), is shut up since the death of its founder. — Much has, in late years, been done for schools and in this respect Bremen has gone, a head in Germany. The good influence of these exertions upon the rising generation is apparent. A spirit for scientific research and learning is active among all classes and it is honored and respected. The preparatory and high-college, the scientific, mercantile, technical, and naval schools, and the Seminary are models in their arrangements and management. The city prides herself justly upon some immortal names in the realm of Genius: Adam von Bremen, Treviranus, Heeren, Olbers.

Commerce and Navigation are the pivots on which the affairs chiefly turn. The advantageous situation upon a navigable river, by which the town is connected with the very heart of Germany, the spirit of enterprize and the well-founded credit of her merchants, who unite large fortunes with the experience and the practical knowledge of generations, and that high commercial character, which is the growth of centuries, have, in spite of the „evil times and evil spirits that press and haunt poor Germany“, built up a mercantile greatness, which is only surpassed by that of Hamburgh and Trieste. The maintainance of such a position is no easy task for Bremen. Hamburgh, with a back-country three times as extensive, is a powerful rival and Trieste, the special favorite of the absolute rulers of a great empire, has but to open her lap to catch the rich gifts, which pour from the cornucopia of exclusive privileges. The merchant of Bremen however is indebted to his own labor and enterprize for every success. He prudently embraces every spot of the Earth's surface in his plans, and his flag is met with on all seas. While the trade of Trieste is satisfied with the low and lucrative position of brokers and commission-merchants, in whose magazines and warehouses the foreign merchants, seeking a market, bring their wares, and while the business of Hamburgh is to a great extent of the same kind, the Bremen adventurer is accustomed to speculate entirely at his own acount and peril. In consequence he is ever busy to examine all corners of the world, in hopes of spying out some opportunity for a profitable operation. When the monopoly vanished with the overthrow of the Spanish and Portuguese rule in South-America, the merchants of Bremen were the first who explored these new channels of trade; when the ports of Australia were thrown open, they appeared in her ports before all others; Hamburgh had not even thought of its first expedition to California when Bremen-vessels were anchoring in the harbors of San Francisco, Monterey and Mazatlan. Her ships visit the arctic seas of Greenland and Davis's straits, they sail regularly to Archangel, Odessa and the ports of the Mediterranean, they transport the pilgrims for Mecca or Medina to the Arabian ports, they cross the waves of the Persian Golf, and upon the whole extent of both the Eastern and Western coasts of America there is no port which they do not visit, and where the interests of Bremen are not represented and protected by a mercantile house or a consul of the little republic. In the United States the Bremen flag, next to the English, is the most frequent and stands in high reputation and credit. The merchant-marine of Bremen is nearly as extensive as that of all Austria; it equals that of Hamburgh. These facts are never spoken of with ostentation, and the Bremen people, like the Dutch, are best pleased, when the envy of their neighbors and rivals thinks it fit to ignore them.

The Bremen citizen is the man of prompt action; and in his character as a patriot he has at all times proved himself the same. When Germany collected for the support of the national cause in Schleswig-Holstein, Bremen contributed 100,000 Doll., while Hamburgh, though far more opulent, gave the tenth part of that sum, and the proud capital of Prussia, Berlin, but a trifle.

At a later period, when, in Hesse-Cassel, those brave men, who held fast to their right and to their constitution, to which they had sworn fidelity, were receiving the princely wages for doing right, persecution and ruin; — it was again the people of Bremen, who afforded prompt and generous assistance, and furnished the largest sums for the support of the sufferers; and her hands were not slow in giving assistance to the many thousand victims of tyranny and despotism, who were thrust pennyless into foreign countries, while the very towns, whose voices had been the loudest in boasting their zeal for the greatness and freedom of Germany, could find no cent for the maintenance of our Exiles! Even in this present time of barefaced oppression, Bremen stands up firmly for her rights and honor, nor will she be frightened by threats, which but need to be firmly repelled to shew their weakness together with their injustice. A true and noble spirit of independance, which more or less penetrates the population, finds its strongest development in the mercantile classes. The merchant has seen the world, has travelled in distant lands, knows the habits and customs of nations under their various aspects, and his practical, experienced eye easily detects both the good and the evil, and finds out their hidden causes. Most of the Bremen merchants have spent some years in the United States. They consequently are entirly free from the prejudices of our scholars of the closet, of the wise men of our colleges, who never stir from home, and seek the experience of life in their books. The Bremen merchant adopts the Yankee-word „Go a head!“ though he practises it in his own way; not by dangerous and sudden leaps, but in a firm and measured pace: for he is of opinion that no fortune can be secured, but what is honorably and gradually acquired by constant labor.

The Bremen merchant is also a man of foresight and caution, and in public life, as citizen of the republic, he follows the principle „Trust but know well whom!“ This being his compass and fundamental maxim as well in trade, as in politics, he abhorrs swindlers and visionaries, who would tear the old society to pieces, only that they might try to make a new one. As a man of order and method, he is not willing to change liberty for license. Demagogues and heedless adventurers, whose element is disorder and anarchy, find no favor with him.

It need hardly be mentioned that the building and outfitting of ships are flourishing branches of trade in Bremen. Both are carried on to a great extent and are tending to a much greater development. Many mercantile firms are proprietors of whole squadrons of merchant-vessels, ploughing the seas in all quarters and by the transport of goods and men doing service to all nations. The shipping-interest has of late years found its main support, and a germ of a rapid and extensive increase in the German Emigration. Nearly one half of those, who wander to the seaports of the Atlantic shore, to save themselves from tyranny and oppression, and their families from ruin, go to Bremen, and if there was a rail-road constructed from Eisenach to Lichtenfels, which is the only link wanting in a direct railroad-communication between North- and South-Germany, the trains of Emigrants from the Southern states would augment by tens of thousands.

The comfort and ease, with which the sea can be reached by descending the Maine and the Rhine, conduct some forty or fifty thousand Germans annually to the Dutch ports and to Havre, who otherwise would naturally prefer Bremen, where the laws, official arrangements, and various associations work hand in hand to ameliorate the lot of the Emigrant and to protect him from fraud and extortion.

By authority of the Republic an Intelligence-Office for Emigrants has been recently opened in Bremen, which under the guidance of men of high character gives counsel and assistance to applicants gratis. The Emigrant-House at Bremerhaven, whence the vessels actually start for America, is the most extensive Establishment of its kind and a cheap and comfortable shelter to the wanderers before sailing.

The agents for emigration and the ship-owners of Bremen possess a long-established reputation, and the government keeps a watchful eye upon their business. Laws regulate the number of persons to be taken by each vessel, and also the quantity and quality of the provisions and stores for each voyage. Complaints, which are so frequent respecting the transports from Havre, Liverpool and Antwerp, are very seldom heard of at Bremen.

For the Emigration to Brazil, Australia, California and Central America, regular lines of vessels are established or in preparation. Two large steamers, fitted up with elegance, start every four weeks from Bremen and New-York; several others ply weekly between Bremen and England, and some small boats on the Weser keep up the communication with the interior of Germany. This river-navigation extends now to Wanfried on the Werra. It could be easily extented to Meiningen, and it might be prolonged up the Fulda-River to Hersfeld by certain improvements on the banks and the remove of a few mills which obstruct it. Rafts of timber for ship-building float directly from Werningshausen near Meiningen down to Bremen. Farther up, the Werra and its branches, in autumn and spring, carry smaller rafts, the produce of the Thuringian Forest, destined to the Weser-towns. — Those branches of business which depend upon shipbuilding, as ropemaking etc., are extensive in Bremen. — A manufacture which twenty five years ago was of little note, has latterly attained an astonishing importance, employing at least ten thousand hands and a capital of 4 millions. It is the making of cigars. Bremen offers peculiar advantages for this business, of which, as cigar-smoking became more and more universal, speculation hastened to take advantage. Bremen is known as the principal tobacco-market in Europe, and consequently the manufacturers have at all times the best choice of the raw material. The cigars are shipped in vast quantities even to North-America. The flourishing of this new branch has caused the decay of an old one: — the establishments for the manufacture of snuff and cut tobacco are rapidly declining. Another once very lucrative branch of the Bremen trade, sugar-refining, is equally in decay, since beet-sugar has taken the place of the colonial product. Brewing is a valuable item in the Bremen industry, and the export of porter is large. There are some extensive establishments for the manufacture of vinegar, whitelead, leather, whalebone, and for the refining of oils.

The commercial greatness of Bremen rests upon the most solid foundation — the international trade. While Hamburgh is the principal seat of the German inland-trade, having a back-country extending to Austria, Bremen has brought most of the traffic with the North American States to her own port. The attempts of Prussia to draw a portion of this great business to Stettin have miscarried, and Hannover has never renewed her former attempt to make Emden the rival of Bremen.

Bremen's main article of export was formely German Linen; but after England, by the introduction of flaxspinning by machinery, obtained the lead in this manufacture, the Bremen linen-trade has been reduced to one fifth of its former amount. — The aggregate total-value of Bremen's exports byond sea may he estimated at about 11,000,000 Doll. annually. The imports are considerably greater. Bremen is a market of note for the coffee and sugar of the West Indies and Brazil, for the tobacco and rice of the United states, for colonial produce in general; for blubber and oil; for grain, rapeseed and flour; for bones, salt, pork, butter, rags, etc. etc.; for rum, spirits and French wines; for Russian hemp and flaxseed; for the lead of the Hartz, and the wood of the Thuringian Forest. — The marine insurance-companies of the place enjoy a good reputation; the insured capital amounts annually to from twenty to twenty five millions, and is constantly on the increase. Their terms are favorable and in accordance with the spirit of the age. They give the insured full security. Since 1815 Bremen has a privileged Bank; and an office of Discount, founded on liberal principles, is a benefit to business at large. From the demoralizing effects of stockjobbing, and from the swindling in public funds and shares, the Bremen Exchange has, to its honor be it noticed, kept untainted.

A heavy prejudice to the shipping interest of Bremen, — one which was formerly a great drawback to its development — was the want of a good port at the mouth of the river, as the city is unapproachable to vessels drawing more then seven feet of water. However in the year 1829 Bremen purchased of Hannover for 100,000 Doll. a lot of land large enough for a haven near the mouth of the Weser and excavated there a basin 2600 feet long, 300 feet wide and 18 feet deep, sufficient to receive her whole merchant-fleet; and a second basin, quite as extensive, was nearly completed at the close of the year 1851. Magazines and docks have been built on the quays and a flourishing town is rising upon the spot. Such is the origin of Bremerhaven, a noble and useful monument of the energy and public spirit of the little Republic.

There is no room in this work for the history and the life of the State of Bremen from her first origin. It has ever been a history of struggle, clashing interests, open collisions; and there has been no end of patching and mending the robe of the State, according as the aristocratic or democratic element gained the upper hand. A long period of absolute patrician rule fixed the authority of the state as an heir-loom in the hands of a few families, and the membership of the supreme council was handed down in a longcontinued and regular course, and confined to a certain number of influential family-names. That was the golden age of Oligarchy. The Patriciate divided the sweets of office among its members and left other things to take care of themselves. Napoleon, the conqueror, put an end to this state of things. The restoration in 1816 attempted to bring back a part of the former patrician privileges; but still the power of the senate was limited; and its attempts to attain a greater independence of the democratic influence of the citizens failed in the commotions of 1830, and led exactly to the contrary result in 1848. Since then Bremen has adopted a reformed constitution, which leans decidedly to the democratic side. To demolish this constitution the reaction is at present trying all its might. In consequence, a contest is taking place between the political parties of the city, more bitterly than any where else in Germany.

The courage and firmness exhibited in this contest between the aristocratic and democratic elements in Bremen are to be considered as no bad indications of the character of the population, for such a battle presupposes the existence of strength and vigor in the public mind. A right and good issue of the unbloody war will in time be found and the public will be in the end a gainer. That the aristocracy try to maintain their influential position; that the more they lost, the more firmly they hold on to what remains; that they will not voluntarily retreat farther, but, after having lost their exclusive position they are now determined to defend themselves to the last: — all this we find honorable and right. As Christianity maintains the doctrine of perfect equality before God, so Democray teaches precisely the same regarding parties and opinions. All political sects have claim to fair play. The Democracy, standing on the opposite side, use also their right by the demand, that the supreme authority in the state should never again become the exclusive possession of a privileged, patrician class, and that all the citizens should share in the legislation either directly or indirectly. They affirm the folly of attempting to maintain any longer those artificial restrictions, which have already been broken through on all sides; they consider privileges null and void, because they invade the rights of others; they scorn the laws, made to restrict the free exercise of trades to certain persons, and the claim of the priesthood to regulate the Freedom of Conscience, on the ground that by priestly intervention the very substance of Freedom of Conscience is destroyed.

C. Reiss del.

THE OBELISK OF LUXOR

IN PARIS.

The bitterness of the contest is now at its height. It is supported and nourished by the universal sway of despotism in Germany. The Bremen aristocracy has for the present a very advantageous position. It will last and vanish with the foreign support; for it has none in the hearts of the people of the republic.

THE OBELISK OF LUXOR, IN PARIS.

What dost thou *here*, in the presence of the day, thou dumb witness of the ages of darkness? What is thy business *here*, thou messenger from the realm of shadows, among the living? What brought thee from thy quiet grove of palms into the midst of the stirring city? I see carved upon thy sides mysterious symbols, the Caduceus and the key of Hermes: — comest thou perhaps as a priest of fate, or wouldst thou, as soothsayer and magician, prophesy to the nations of Europe their destinies?

Ah, if thou couldst! If thou couldst interpret the marks and lines which are written on their hands; if thou couldst read their fate in the stars; if thou hadst power to rehearse to us the tablets of futurity; if thou couldst tell us by name the fruits which will come forth from this germinating and growth, this sprouting and shooting, budding and blossoming in the realms of Europe; if thou couldst, wiser than Champollion, decipher the hieroglyphics, which cover the gates of ages unborn and couldst give clear outlines to the misty shapes which cover the horizon, and fill our hearts now with terror, now with hope!

But thou canst do nothing of all this. Thou art come hither by command as the wretched slave of that tyranny and that craft, which cheat nations and falsify history; thou art but a despicable instrument of the vanity of kings, like all monuments of thy kind. That monarch who ages ago erected thee in the far land of the Nile, with the special mission to proclaim to distant times the falsehood of his renown, was perhaps no better a man than the heartless satrap, who cast thee down, or the foreign king, who erected thee again in his capital, to flatter the vain thirst for glory of the very people, whom to cheat and to corrupt was the aim and object of his government. In thy appearance upon the Place de la Concorde in Paris, Obelisk of Luxor! thou hast nothing to rejoice mankind, nothing to elevate the patriot, nothing to awake esteem for the motive, nothing to reconcile us with its intent. Thou art but an altar for the idol „Gloire“ to which the French nation has so often brought, as a sacrifice, the best of her treasures — the blood of her sons, her freedom, her rights, her true honor.

Mehemed Ali, viceroy of Egypt, presented to Charles X the two obelisks, which adorned the entrance of the great temple of Luxor, upon the site of ancient Thebes. King Charles despatched a vessel to bring over one of these monoliths, each of which was seventy two feet in height. It reached Havre in safety, where it was transferred to a flat boat, which was destined to transport it to Paris. Here, as it was about to be raised upon the quay, in the presence of a crowd that stood gazing in wonder at the stranger, the machine broke, and the enormous stone fell into the stream.

There lay the child of the sun, buried in the mud of the deep during the winter, and not until the following year was it raised from its bed, and conveyed to the spot, where it now stands. — Will this obelisk, which has stood for four thousand years upon its old pedestal in Thebes, remain as long upon its new one? Or will there not come a day, when Egypt will reclaim it, as the Prussians once reclaimed their Victoria, and Venice her Lions of St. Mark? Who will foretel the issue of the strife with the African Atlantide, in which France has involved herself? Who will foretel the development of that eventful, stirring, and mighty drama, the first act of which is now performing in Algeria? We have to remember, that the two grand elements, which inspire nations, Religion and Patriotism, are at stake in this contest. The Arabians are contending for the Penates upon their domestic altars, and for their national existence. In my opinion no one can foresee what will be the issue of such a strife in which the religion, liberty and independence of a brave people are at stake, and how far it will lead; for it has made its way into the unfathomable depths of the human heart, it has fastened with a strong, deep grasp upon the burning souls of the sons of the desert. Peace between France and Africa is but a truce. France has hazarded a contest with a savage people of primitive character. The Arabs are fanatics for their faith, their nationality, their country; they do not want self-sacrificing courage, and such a people, suddenly thrust, as it has been, from its solitude upon the stage of history, cannot but gain strength with the continuance of the struggle. The truth of this argument is proved by history, and what happens on Mount Caucasus is its newest illustration. It needs but a slight gift of prophecy to foretel that France's conquest in Africa will sooner or later change into a contest *à outrance*, like Odin's contest with the Capitolinian Jupiter, and notwithstanding all the triumphs, trophies, and crowns of victory hitherto gained, it is possible that, in this war, France may yet end like ancient Rome.

SARATOGA LAKE.

(BY GEORGE WILLIAM CURTIS.)

Saratoga Springs are the Baden-Baden of America. The fashionable summer season assembles here the gay travellers from every part of the country, and from the first of July until the middle of August the throng of brilliant society is greater at Saratoga than at any other spot. With the decline of summer the fashionable hosts move eastward to New York, where the season is closed with not less festivity than it commenced.

The legend at Saratoga is that the springs were discovered by chance in the rambles of a stray hunter some seventy years ago, who resting in the ardor of the chase among the pine trees upon the plain, drank of a spring whose waters were mineral. At that time and for many years later Ballston Spa, not many miles removed, was the favorite summer resort for health and fashion. About a quarter of a century since Saratoga began to rise in importance, was visited more and more every year, until poor little Ballston dwindled from its distinction, became melancholy, like an old mistress, and is now known to the eager traveller hurrying thro

SARATOGA LAKE

it in the cars to Saratoga, only as an uninteresting village with a very white church. — Old Mistresses, too, have been known in their decline, to present the same glaring front of piety.

This gay resort lies only two railroad hours away from the great route to Niagara, and perhaps most of the pilgrims to the cataract turn aside at Schenectady, where the railroads join, to run up and look at Saratoga. Every summer assembles there a multitude of old habitués whose holiday is their Saratoga visit, and to whom Saratoga and the summer are synonymous. They have a theory that their health requires the water. They go as surely to the purlieus of the congress spring, as the swallows fly northward. And they sit upon the piazzas and stroll about the walks playing the young man, and remembering with a fond melancholy the days when youth was not a play, but a happy reality.

In the first days of the brilliant career of Saratoga, Congress Hall was the most popular hotel, and most of the stories of that period, relating to Saratoga life, lay their love scenes upon the lofty-columned and long piazza, and their serenades under the garden windows, of this hotel. The glory of Congress Hall has now passed across the street to the United States, which is one of the most spacious and striking buildings of the kind in the world. It is built around a large court which is laid out in grass-plots kept always fresh and green, and overshadowed by handsome trees, which impart a pleasing and harmonious dimness to the silence of the enclosure. It is surrounded by piazzas, and at its farther end there are a half-dozen cottages containing two or three rooms which are let for the season, at a high rent. In the court after dinner, the band plays while the guests promenade upon the piazzas or sit in the parlors which overlook it; and the universal air of leisure enjoyment — the palatial spaciousness of the hotel, — the throng of gaily-dressed promenaders, — the murmur of the music, and the soft Summer languor of the air, combine to make the aspect of Saratoga poetic, and to recall to the musing observer, some faint image of Bocaccio's garden.

The resources of amusement are very few, and they are found, almost entirely, within doors. In the early morning the few conscientious visitors who have really come for health, repair to the various springs, chiefly to the famous Congress spring whose waters are bottled and sent all over the country, and drink the waters. The morning after breakfast is devoted to bowling, billiards, dancing in the parlor and flirtation by the young men and women who are seeking to brim every moment with pleasure, and to lounging, smoking, chatting and reading the papers by the elders — the habitués and the parents. After dinner all Saratoga drives to the Lake. The road is not interesting, except from its loneliness, and the long pine-reaches are strangely thronged with the light carriages whirling out of sight, for the moment they vanish the scene is as solitary as if only Indians inhabited Saratoga. To the equestrian loitering along the road, the faintly waving outline of the distant Green mountains, and the broad, friendly stretch of sky, — are sadly critical of the bustle and glare; they reprove the unheeding hurry of the life that dashes by him. And sometimes, returning, when the crowd have gone before, he sees the splendor of a glorious sunset dying over the woods and fields, and, impatient of the hotel-life, takes the train for the north and the quiet shores of Lake George. —

The lake is a sheet of islanded water, and of most glossy calm in Summer. Its banks are low and varied. The lake is ear-shaped. The solemnity of the old pines that surround it is relieved along its edges by the fringe of water-lilies. Boats are here for the romantic or the adventurous, and moonlight parties, with music, sometimes enchant it upon lovely evenings. It lies in strict seclusion, and the old settler, — Barhydt by name, — who once held it as his undisputed fishery, lived upon its shores for some time after Saratoga was the fashion, but quite unmindful, and somewhat disdainful of its gay society. In his day he entertained visitors in the homely Dutch way — would cook a trout for the hungry and romantic citizen, or give him a glass, leaving the compensation quite at the citizen's discretion, and a little grieved that the world would not let him dream his dreams alone, as he smoked his Dutch pipe by the lake-shore. Old Barhydt and his pipe have both gone from the memory of the time. A spruce, little cottage-like inn, now stands upon the bank over the lake, devoted to the entertainment of men, and famous for delicate fish-dinners and fried potatoes. It is de rigeur at Saratoga to dine at the Lake — and to pay likewise. Every afternoon scores of carriages and saddle horses are tied in regular lines to the adjacent fences. Nimble hostlers and waiters in white jackets run busily about, while parties from the United States are rowing upon the lake, or sipping sherry-Cobblers on the piazza. They are from every part of the country and of the world. But the weary votary of pleasure from the old continent galled with Baden-Baden, sated with the Rhine baths, and incurious of Heligoland, is pleasantly thrilled by a shock of surprise as he glances among the groups who may not entirely please his fastidious taste, but who a few years since were poor with no hope but their hearts and their arms, who now, thro the benign operation of institutions, whose great and peculiar praise it is to give every man an opportunity, are enjoying those fruits of leisure which under other institutions are only assured to a few favorites of Fortune.

ROUSSEAU'S HERMITAGE IN MONTMORENCY.

The small watering place of Montmorency is distant about three leagues from Paris. The romantic traditions of the middle ages hover around the name, and we think involuntarily of tournaments and royal courts, of knights in gleaming steel, upon richly caparisoned steeds, and of fair dames, in gold, and velvet, and silk; of the pomp and pride, of the vices and the craft, the wealth and rapacity of the nobility — and of the rudeness, the ignorance, the poverty, and the helplessness of the people in those times of old. All this has changed. The castle and race of Montmorency have disappeared from the spot of earth, to which they gave name and fame, and in these grounds, where a man of humble birth never dared to appear except as a servant or petitioner — the cheerful artisan and laborer with some francs in their pockets, spared from a week's wages, now roam and look proudly and scornifully at the old ducal escutcheons, thinking: we are better than you. — The gloomy spirits of the the steelcoats have fled, the genii of sport have entered, and song and dance, amusement and pleasure flutter about the charming Montmorency, with its delightful grounds, its hotels and restaurants, since it has become the Sunday-resort of the gay Parisian. The visitors seek pleasure here, and no where is it offered them in greater variety. On a bright Sunday in

THE COTTAGE of J. J. ROUSSEAU

in Montmorency.

Published at [illegible] North William Street NEW YORK

summer, the grounds are decorated, as if for a festival of Saturn; everywhere are resplendent joy and abundance: music in hundred places, dancing beneath pavilions, or on the green swards shaded by oaks a thousand years old, carousing in every saloon, clinking glasses and loud merriment on all sides. Neither rank, nor wealth, nor office, nor refinement, divide the joyous crowd. Equality is the law for all, and all serve one ruler: Pleasure. Who will blame them for it? The care-pinched life of the greater portion of the people has scarcely any other joy than this Sunday-dream, which for a few hours transforms an earth full of toil into an Eden! Remembrance of the happy moments dispensed on such a Sunday, must often feed a life of want, and the few honey-drops must sweeten an existence of bitterness. — —

Yet it is not the knightly forms of the past, nor the sylphs of pleasure alone that render Montmorency attractive and fashionable — it is clothed with a deeper interest by a name, that stands a grand ornament of mankind. What is the faded splendor of a ducal race, when compared with the starry crown which, in the night of Eternity, beams round the name of „Rousseau"? What is the influence of the whole line of the Montmorencys, compared with the influence of that single writer? The earth is full of his renown. The storms of time have wafted the seeds which he scattered over oceans, mountains, and dales, and they have grown up in distant zones and climes. Rousseau was a poor man in worldly goods, but a Croesus in imperishable treasures. No splendid monument presses his ashes like the dust of yonder dukes; but his Ideas are monuments of everlasting durability. Rousseau is dead; but every day celebrates his resurrection. How many writers, lawgivers and statesmen have been born in this single man, and how many more will kindle the immortal spark at the flame of his Genius!

Three quarters of a century ago, the valley of Montmorency was an unknown spot to the Parisian world. The roebuck bounded amid the foliage of the forest, and the extensive grounds were occupied but by a few dwellings of gamekeepers and laborers. Upon his lonely wanderings,

Rousseau once chanced to stray hither, and was so pleased with the peaceful spot, that he hired a small cot where he lived for many years like a hermit. — The little house has since been known as Rousseau's Hermitage, and has been preserved with care.

I quote the graphic description from the pen of my high minded friend, the late Dr. Börne. — „Wanderer —“ he exclaims, „look at those chestnut trees! they have known Rousseau, and their shadows have soothed his glowing soul. In yonder cot he dwelt. Look in at the window! It is Rousseau's; but he is not at home. There stands the little table at which he wrote the Heloise; there is the bed, in which he rested after his labors. — Sacred valley of Montmorency! There is no path in the woods, in which he has not strayed; no hill that he has not walked in meditation! The clear lake, the dark forest, the blue mountains, the fields, the villages, the mills — they have all seen him, and he has greeted all, and loved all! —“

Love is the right word. Rousseau's power flowed from this highest of all sources. When the strong man rules, he has to fear the stronger; what the prudent mind resolves is crossed by malicious fate; yet Love-deeds are everlasting, for there is nothing stronger than Love. „Even the Gods are Love's subjects“ — says the old proverb. How many tyrants have lived, since Rousseau wrote his „Contrat Social?“ How many nations have trembled at their lifted arms, and bowed to their swords? for how much crime, shame, wretchedness and slavery have they to answer? And where are they, these men, who forced their subjects to revere them as earthly Gods? They have passed away, and nothing of them remains but a name loaded with curses, and a handful of dust, while Rousseau sits in the teacher's chair from century to century, and the influence of his Genius on mankind embraces eternity.

WASHINGTON'S HOUSE

MOUNT VERNON

Published for Herrmann J. Meyer, 164 William-Street, New York

WASHINGTON'S HOUSE AT MOUNT VERNON.

(BY HORACE GREELEY.)

At Mount Vernon on the right bank of the noble Potomac, some fifteen miles below the city of Washington, (which lies on the other bank, at the head of ship-navigation on that river) rest the mortal remains of George Washington. There is no mountain in the neighborhood, though the name borne by the Washington Estate might lead to a contrary impression; but the placid river is here broad and beautiful, and its wooded shore rises steeply to an elevation of some fifty feet, where it breaks into an irregular or undulating table-land, partly covered with brush and under-wood, and partly devoted to those branches of cultivation common in that part of the Union. The mansion in which the illustrious man lived and died is of modest dimensions; it is in part built of wood and already showing symtoms of decay. The adjacent buildings, inhabited by negroes or designed for herding cattle, or the various requirements of rural economy are insignificant, and give still more unequivocal signs of delapidation. The garden contains some rare and valuable exotics — probably presents to its former master, or collected by his care — but they, too, are wasting and decaying. The whole aspect of the place is sombre and dreary; unless you look away from it through a fringe of trees upon and across the river; and if my recollection is accurate, no other house is in sight — nothing but a few fields bespeaking niggard soil or heedless tillage, belted by woods which fill up the outline presented to the vision. America has hardly a scene less animated or inviting.

And yet to this lonely and ungenial spot, unwelcomed by the residents, who could hardly fail to be annoyed by the visits of so many strangers, the steps of many pilgrims are daily directed — all anxious to gaze at least once in their lives on the stone which covers the ashes of WASHINGTON. So the rude and boisterous squatter from the far West, the swarthy, sanguine planter from the South, the keen but cold New-Englander, the immigrant or traveller from the Old World, though diverse in every thing else, and mingling in careless hilarity or eyeing each other in stern distrust as the steamboat bears them along the Potomac to or from the national Metropolis, instinctively remove their hats and gaze in earnest reverence as they pass the hallowed spot, where all that was mortal of the Patriot, the Hero, the Statesman sleeps the sleep that knows no waking.

And this reverence is a tribute well deserved, as the briefest glance at the leading incidents of his life will serve to establish.

GEORGE WASHINGTON was born in Westmoreland County, Virginia, on the banks of that same Potomac, but nearer its mouth, — on the 22. of February 1732. His great-grandfather, belonging to a family which held a good position in the middle walks of life, had emigrated from England to Virginia seventy-five years before. George enjoyed but moderate educational advantages. He fitted himself for the vocation of a surveyor, and was, while a stripling, employed in that capacity by Lord Fairfax, an extensive proprietor of Virginia lands. When twenty-one years of age, Gen. Dinwiddie employed him as a messenger to the French commander on the waters of the Ohio to remonstrate against the erection of a line of forts down the Alleghany and Ohio, whereby the limits of Virginia were invaded and the security of her people threatened. He wandered in November and December through the dense wilderness then existing from tide-water in Virginia, across the snowy Alleghanies to the forks of the Ohio, thence passed up the Alleghany to Franklin and the French creek to a point near its source (now Waterford, Pa.) where he found the French commander, delivered his letter, and received one in reply. Setting out on his return on the 15. of December, he reached the banks of the Ohio on the 28. and narrowly escaped drowning in an attempt to cross the Alleghany on a raft while that river was open in the channel but frozen some fifty feet from each shore. Thrown into the water by the violence of the current filled with running ice, he recovered his position on the raft, but could not reach either shore with it, and was obliged to spend the night on an island where a companion had his fingers and toes frozen. Thence he repassed the Alleghanies in mid-winter and returned to Virginia.

The next year saw him (at 22 years of age) Lieut. Col. of a regiment of colonists raised to resist French aggression, and the Colonel soon dying, the command devolved on Washington. In July he was besieged in Fort Necessity, in the Alleghanies by a very superior French force, and ultimately forced to capitulate, after the loss of fifty-eight men. Though unfortunate, he and his comrades were publicly thanked by the Virginia Legislature for their gallantry. He retired from the colonial service, disgusted at the order by which the British regular officers were authorized to out-rank their colonial brethren; but the next spring Gen. Braddock, on setting out with a strong British force from Alexandria, near Washingtons new home, Mount Vernon, on an expedition against the French forts on the Ohio and Great Lakes, invited Washington to act as his aid, and his offer was accepted.

This expedition had a most disastrous result. Leaving Fort Cumberland, Md. on the 12. of June, it reached the neighborhood of Fort Du Quesne (now Pittsburgh) on the 8. of July, and on the 9. after crossing the Monongahela, fell into a French and Indian ambush of inferior numbers, by which it was nearly destroyed. The General was headstrong, rash and ignorant; the soldiers, fired at with deadly aim by an inivisible foe, fell into the wildest panic, and, after discharging a few rounds irregularly and fruitlessly, fled in utter dismay and disorder, while the officers bravely courted death and were shot down by dozens as they vainly attempted to rally them.

Gen. Braddock fell mortally wounded; most of his staff were cut down; while Washington had two horses shot under him and his clothes riddled with balls. The British loss amounted to six hundred killed and wounded, with all the artillery, ammunition and stores. But for the conduct of Washington and the colonists in covering the retreat, it would have been much greater. The wreck of the army retreated across the Alleghanies completely demoralized.

Col. Washington was now entrusted by the Legislature with the chief command of the Virginia forces, employed in repelling Indian and French hostilities along the frontier, until 1758, when he resigned, and was soon united in marriage to Miss Martha Custis, a lady of fortune and great personal worth. For sixteen years he pursued at MOUNT VERNON the quiet life of a planter until 1774, when he was chosen by the Virginia convention one of the seven Delegates from that state to the Continental Congress then assembled at Philadelphia to devise and adopt measures of resistance to British aggression and tyranny. Though fresh from his quiet fireside and the plow and never an orator, he at once took rank among the members of that body most eminent for good sense, patriotic firmness, and sound judgment, with ready and abundant information. He was re-elected to the next Congress; and, after the conflicts at Lexington and Concord had rendered a bloody issue inevitable, he was unanimously chosen by that body Commander-in-chief of the American forces, which position he next day accepted with unaffected modesty declining any compensation for his services. This appointment was made on the 15. of June (two days before the battle at Bunker's Hill); his commission was made out on the 19.; on the 21. he set out for the army, consisting of a hasty assemblage of volunteers, then beleaguering Gen. Gage in Boston; the royal forces in that city numbering about eleven thousand, while their besiegers were nominally seventeen thousand, of whom two or three thousand were sick or otherwise ineffective. Discipline was hardly known, even by name, in the American camp, and every thing but valor required for the conduct of the campaign, especially in a siege, was wanting. A month after taking command, he discovered that all the powder in the camp was but half a pound a man — the amount having been grossly overrated (through a blunder) in previous returns. Had Gage but suspected this deficiency, he must have chased and routed, if not utterly destroyed, the force which held him in siege.

Having partially supplied his pressing wants, Gen. Washington twice proposed an assault on Boston, but was overruled in counsel by his officers. On the 1. of October, Gen. Gage was recalled; being succeeded by Gen. Howe. Washington, whose army was reduced by the expiration of enlistments at one time to 9,600 men, being hardly equal in numbers to the well-trained regulars in the strong town, was never in a condition to risk an assault; or, at least, such was the judgment of his officers. Finally, on the 17. March, 1776, after the Americans had stormed and fortified a position on Dorchester heights which commanded the town, so that the British were reduced to the alternative of assailing it or abandoning Boston, Gen. Howe evacuated the city, sailing for Halifax with eleven thousand men and a fleet of seventy eight vessels. The Americans took possession that same day.

Washington had no doubt that the British would next attack New-York. Accordingly he concentrated his army there in April. Gen. Howe arrived off that city on the 28. of June, and by the middle of August, had an army of twenty-five thousand men, encamped on Staten Island; Washington had sixteen thousand on his rolls, of whom but half were regulars fit for duty. In order to hold New-York, it was necessary to defend also the high grounds of Brooklyn on Long Island opposite that city, from which it is only separated by a narrow strait, known as the East River. The attempt to do this was unfortunate and resulted in disaster. The American force on Long-Island, numbering five thousand, was outflanked and surprised on the morning of August 27. by fifteen thousand British troops, with a loss of twelve hundred, mainly prisoners, including the Generals Sullivan and Sterling. The British loss was trifling. Gen. Howe declined an assault on the American entrenched camp, but prepared to besiege it with the aid of heavy artillery and the cooperation of a powerful fleet. Washington saw that his evacuation of long Island was inevitable, and accordingly drew off his troops, under cover of a dense fog, on the night of the 9. without molestation or loss, save that a heavy cannon was abandoned.

The British now commanded the navigation of both rivers and compelled Washington to withdraw from New-York. Indecisive actions or skirmishes followed at Kip's Bay, Harlem and White-plains, between Washington's dispirited, diminishing and retreating army and detachments of British troops, the advantage being generally on the side of the latter. On the sixteenth of November, Fort Washington, the American's stronghold on New-York Island, seven or eight miles above the city, was assaulted and carried; the American loss being two thousand men made prisoners and a great amount of military stores. Washington crossed the Hudson, retreating with from four or five thousand men, through New-Jersey, pursued by Lord Cornwallis with ten thousand. Finally, on the eigth of December, the American army now reduced by disasters, sickness and the expiration of enlistments to three thousand, was driven across the Delaware into Pennsylvania.

The spirit of the country was nearly broken; that of Washington was undaunted. On the 20. he addressed a letter to Congress demanding one hundred and ten new battalions and urging the folly of the short enlistments and other hand-to-mouth measures hitherto relied on in the vain expectation of a speedy termination of the war, Congress, on the one hand, having declared the Colonies independent, while the British cabinet manifested no disposition to redress even one of the grievances which had driven them into rebellion. Congress responded heartily to his appeal by investing him with almost dictatorial powers. He was joined about this time by some battalions, raising his force to five thousand men; and with this little army, on the night of the 25. he re-crossed the Delaware nine miles above Brenton, attacked in two columns the

British-Hessian force which held that town, partially surprising and completely defeating it with a loss of more than a thousand prisoners and dead including Col. Rahl the Hessian commander. Washington recrossed the Delaware before night, in order to secure his prisoners; but returned to Brenton on the 30. He was assailed there on the sixth of January by Cornwallis with a superior force, but night closed the conflict without serious advantage to either party. During the night, Washington decamped and silently marched with the greater part of his army toward Princeton, in the rear of Cornwallis, intercepting at Stony Brook a British brigade marching to re-enforce his adversary, of which one regiment was cut to pieces and the remainder thrown back on New Brunswick. The British loss in this action was severe; three hundred were taken prisoners. The Americans lost few men, but among them were General Mercer and several other officers of great merit. Washington pursued the flying regiments as far as Kingston, and then moved to Morristown, some thirty miles from New-York, where his winter quarters were established. With a beaten, discouraged and undisciplined army, ill supplied with provisions and munitions, the great general had baffled and cut up an enemy flushed with victory and of thrice his numbers, recoveriug almost the whole State of New-Jersey and thoroughly reviving the spirit of the people.

The next summer, after some manœuvering in New-Jersey without decisive results, sir William Howe abandoned that state, crossed to Staten Island and encamped his army, leaving New-York strongly garisoned. Washington knew that Philadelphia was his object. He marched to meet him. On the 25. of August, Howe debarked at the head of Ely on Chesapeake bay. On the 10. of September, the battle was fought on Brandywine creek, some thirty miles South-West of Philadelphia, in which Washington, misled through false information, was finally defeated by the superior force of the enemy. Though this defeat necessarely drew after it the loss of Philadelphia, neither Washington nor his army lost courage. They took a strong position in front of the ennemy. — General Washington's foe was weakened by the occupation of Philadelphia where he left a strong garrisson. His chief force encamped at Germantown, some ten miles inland. This place Washington determined to take by surprise. Accordingly he assailed it on the early morning of the 4. of October, attacking the British in four columns. The attack was at first successful, but, in the obscurity caused by a dense fog, Washington's columns was mistaken for the enemy, and after some severe fighting, during which one of the American battalions most advanced nearly exhausted their ammunition, a parley was mistaken for a signal to retreat and the Americans retired in disorder, though pursued but a short distance. The British kept the field; yet the fruits of victory were earned by their intrepid assailants. Sir William Howe was shut up in Philadelphia; and this result of the Campaign following close after the defeat and surrender of Burgoyne at Saratoga, doubtless aided in determining the French Court to take the side of America in the contest.

Washington wintered in log huts at Valley Jorge, twenty miles from Philadelphia. The winter was most severe and his army suffered dreadfully from lack of food and clothing. The only important event in this dreary period was the exposure of the „Conway Cabal“, which had for its object the transfer of the chief command from Washington. It served only to center in him more firmly the confidence of Congress, the Army and the Country.

On the 2. of May, 1778, tidings was received of the Alliance between France and the United States. Sir Henry Clinton, on the 18. of June, evacuated Philadelphia retreating on New-York across New-Jersey, closely pursued by Washington. On the 28. the British were attacked by the latter in a strong position near Monmouth Courthouse, and nothing but a gross disobedience of orders on the part of Gen. Lee, who headed the attacking division prevented a signal victory. As it was, night closed the combat. Washington, sleeping on the field among his soldiers, expected to renew the battle at dawn and confident of his power to annihilate the enemy; but Clinton stole away during the night, leaving his wounded and his baggage behind. Washington's plan and dispositions were admirable; his bearing throughout the battle was truly heroic and inspiring;

and the opinion was universal among his officers that only Lee's treachery or madness deprived him of a victory which might have terminated the war.

The British were now out of reach, and, embarking at Sandy Hook, took shelter in New-York. Washington moved by Brunswick to Stony Point, where he crossed the Hudson under very different auspices from those which marked his abandonment of that river two years before. An attack on New-York, in conjunction with the French fleet under D'Estaing, was projected, but found impracticable, and, after two or three fights, that decided nothing, the army went into winter-quarters some forty miles north of New-York. Washington visited the Congress at Philadelphia during the winter, mainly to discountenance an invasion of Canada, which was a favorite project in many quarters.

On the 1. of June, 1779, the British fleet sailed up the Hudson and captured Stony Point, which they garrisoned; on the 13. of July it was surprised and stormed by Gen. Wayne, who made 600 prisoners. There were several desultory conflicts between detachments this season, mainly in New-Jersey, in which the advantage was generally with the Americans. The same state of things continued through the next year, 1780; the conflagration of the war chiefly raging in the Southern States, which were in good part overrun with the British. Sir Henry Clinton continued to hold New-York as his head-quarters, sending out predatory detachments, by means of his fleet, to ravage the coasts of Connecticut and even of Virginia. Washington held his head-quarters in or about the Highlands, defending the passage of the Hudson, covering New-Jersey so far as possible, and protecting New-England. Meanwhile the treason of Arnold at West Point and a revolt in the Pensylvania and New-Jersey troops during the winter of 1781, attested the still doubtful fortunes of the contest. The British were gradually transferring their troops to the South. Gen. Gates had been badly beaten at Camden, and the Carolinas completely overrun. Gen. Greene, who succeded Gates in command, had fought several battles with various results, but on the whole had gained ground and revived the spirit of the people. The traitor Arnold, with a fleet and heavy force had burned Richmond, the capital of Virginia, and laid waste a large portion of that State. Cornwallis advanced from the Carolinas into Virginia at the head of a large army, watched and harassed by Lafayette with a far inferior force. Gen. Philips with 2000 men sailed from New-York to join Cornwallis. At this critical moment Washington concerted with Rochambeau, the French commander, an attack on the British stronghold, New-York, which they had threatened during the Summer, but never actually assailed. On the 14. of August Washington received a letter from Count de Grasse, the French admiral, then at Hayti, informing him that he should soon sail for the Chesapeake with his whole fleet and three thousand men. This intelligence caused an immediate change in Washington's plans. He resolved to the deliver the South from the enemy. He left the North with Rochambeau and took his head-quarters at Williamsburg, Virginia. The demonstrations against New-York were made as imposing as possible, while the allied troops under General Lincoln were silently drawn off to the greater part and put in motion toward the South, marching through Trenton and Philadelphia to Ely head, whence they were conveyed down the Chesapeake in transports and landed in lower Virginia. De Grasse arrived as he had promised, landed his troops, and Washington concerted with him and Rochambeau farther operations. Barras arrived about the same time from Newport with another French squadron. The fate of Cornwallis was now sealed. That General perceived the storm gathering around him, but, supposing that the British fleet would command the Chesapeake, had fortified himself at Yorktown, at the junction of the York and James Rivers. The period of apprehension and preparation allowed him was but short. On the 28. the allied forces moved down from Williamsburg; on the 30. the investment of the place was completed; on the 6. of October parallels were opened within 600 yards of the British lines, and several batteries erected to destroy the fortifications. On the 14. two redoubts, 300 yards in advance of the British works, were carried by storm and the guns turned against the besieged town. On the 16. a sortie was made and repulsed. The British, disconcerted, attempted in vain that night to escape in boats. On the 17. several fresh batteries were opened and so deadly a fire poured into the town that its farther defence became manifestly impossible. At 10 in the morning Cornwallis beat a parley, asking a suspension of hostilities for 24 hours in order to give time for adjusting the terms of surrender. On the 18. Commissioners met to settle the affair; but, delay occurring, Gen. Washington early on the 19. despatched articles of capitulation to Cornwallis stating his expectation that they would be signed by eleven o'Clock and arms delivered three hours later. The British General, having no alternative, acceded. He had lost his best troops by the bombardment and the daily contests, which reduced his army to 7,000. These laid down their arms and became prisoners of war. The British ships in the harbor were surrendered to Count de Grasse. The allied army, amounting to 16,000 men, had lost during the siege only about 300. This great triumph decided the war; and all credit of this great achievement is due to Washington. The conception was his, the rapidity of movement and the mystification of Clinton were as essential as the masterly combinations and the vigorous execution which perfected it. On the very day that Cornwallis surrendered, Sir Henry Clinton despatched 25 ships-of-the-line to the Chesapeake, with a *Corps d' Armée* 7,000 men strong. They arrived off the capes of Virginia on the 24., only to hear that they came too late. General Washington left Yorktown on the fifth of November, and spent the winter in Philadelphia.

In May, 1782, Sir Grey Carleton landed in New-York as British commander-in-chief in America. Expectations of a general peace were prevalent, and the British, desisting from invasions or predatory excursions, remained quiet in New-York. No serious hostilities were attempted on either side. The French army moved slowly from Yorktown to Boston, and in December embarked for home. Washington's winter-quarters were at Newburgh, where new and serious difficulties broke out in the army, which all his magnanimity and unequalled influence barely sufficed to overcome. In the spring, definite tidings of peace were received, and a solemn proclamation of the close of the war was made to the American army on the 19. of April, 1783, just eight years from the day on which the first blood was shed at Lexington. On the 18. of October, Washington disbanded his victorious troops and on the 25. of November the British evacuated New-York, and the few American soldiers remaining in service entered the city in triumph, headed by Gen. Washington and Gov. Clinton. On the 4. of December the former issued his affecting and celebrated farewell to his army, and on the 23. resigned his commission to Congress, then in session at Annapolis, and retired the same day to his humble farm at Mt. Vernon. In thus bidding adieu to the camp and to power the great man hoped that his public life was at an end, and that the evening of his days would be spent in the unbroken enjoyment of quiet by his own fireside, and in the prosecution of those rural studies and labors most congenial to his tastes and desires. But the designs of Providence and the pressing needs of his country were not thus to be satisfied. Within three years the absolute necessity which existed for a more intimate Union between the several States of the Confederation and for a stronger Federal Government had been thoroughly demonstrated. In the absence of a Tariff, the whole land was drained of its specie by excessive importations of foreign fabrics, leaving its Currency worthless, its Industry prostrate and its Commerce bankrupt. No progress was or could be made toward paying the State Debts, which had been contracted in the course of the revolutionary struggle. A convention of delegates from the several States, to revise and remodel the Federal pact, became indispensable. Such a Convention was therefore summoned to assemble in Philadelphia on the 2. Monday in May, 1787; and Washington being one of the delegates from Virginia, was unanimously chosen President. That Convention labored arduously, deliberating in secret for more than four months, and the result was the Federal Constitution whereby the previously allied States became a powerful Nation. Washington was from first to last among the warmest and firmest advocates of a more perfect Union, which this Constitution established. His name stands first on the roll of its signers; and his great personal influence, exerted to the utmost in its favor, was barely adequate to overcome the violent and desperate resistance which that constitution encountered when submitted to the people for ratification, especially in the leading states, Massachusetts, New-York and Virginia. The party spirit and partisan divisions which this controversy excited did not cease with the adoption of the constitution, whose friends were then known by the name of Federalists while its enemies, soon discarding the name Anti-Federal for the more popular designation Republican, and ultimately Democratic, were enabled to take control of the government so soon as the chief impediment to their triumph had been removed by the death of Washington. Luckely this event did not occur till 1799, when the constitution had commended itself by its practical workings to the judgment and affection of the people so much that any direct proposition for its overthrow would have been received with derision.

In April, 1789, Washington was chosen first president of the United States. Be accepted the office and discharged its grand duties with wisdom. He was re-elected at the close of his first term of four years, and served gloriously through his second. A third election he peremptorily declined. On the 15. of March, 1796, he issued his Farewell Address to his countrymen — a document still regarded by the nation with profound interest and reverence. On the 3. of March, 1797, he bade a final adieu to political life.

His eight years of civil administration were stormy, eventful and full of embarrassments. The revolution then raging in France excited the warmest sympathies of a majority of the American People. The coalition of despots for the overthrow of French liberty was regarded by that majority with intense hostility and indignation; and the great influence of Washington was barely adequate to withhold his countrymen from plunging into a general European war. He saved them from that calamity even at the risk of his personal popularity. The assumption of the State Debts contracted for the prosecution of the Revolutionary struggle was another measure of public justice and wise policy which was carried under his auspices, against the vehement opposition of the Democratic party. So with the establishment of a National Bank, the creation of a Navy, and most of the leading measures of his administration. Though his election as President was not directly opposed, yet party spirit did not spare him in its denunciations; the measures which he sanctioned were often carried through Congress by slender majorities; nay — a vote of thanks tendered to the great magistrate by that body at the close of his public life was stoutly resisted; and the leading Democratic organ did not blush to thank God „that the only man whose name had power to uphold corruption and misrule was about to take leave of public life!“ When, two years later, he once more was called by congress from his farm to the command of the army raised in view of a collision with the French Directory, which then seemed imminent, these attacks were renewed; but his death, which occurred very suddenly and unexpectedly in the 14. of December, 1799, hushed for ever the voice of calumny and detraction. Friends and foes united in deeply deploring the irretrivable loss, and the nation went into mourning. Even now party-spirit is silenced, party-feeling is forgotten by the Americans as they recount the services of Washington or gather around the tomb at Mount Vernon.

To a just estimate of the character and deeds of WASHINGTON a knowledge of the circumstances under which those deeds were performed, and that character perfected, is essential. It must be borne in mind that he was but a militia colonel and an obscure farmer, when first chosen to the Congress by whose unanimous voice he was soon appointed leader of the Revolutionary armies. Neither eminent as an orator nor as a writer he had commended himself to implicit confidence only by the excellence of his character, the clearness of his understanding and the wisdom and soundness of his judgment. As a military man, he had been prominent but in the defence of a backwood-fort which he was obliged to surrender, and in a defence which was famed over the whole continent as one of signal and almost incomprehensible disaster. His first campaign as commander-in-chief was marked by a series of unlooked-for and dispiriting discomfitures, whereby the American army was reduced from 25,000 to little more than 3000 men. His whole course, during a seven year's contest of fluctuating but oftener adverse fortunes, was watched by rivals, ambitious, confident of their own superior abilities and covetous of his office, who habitually spoke of his want of daring intrepidity as the chief obstacle to the success of the Revolutionary arms. Especially after the brilliant achievement of Gates at Saratoga, resulting in the capture of Burgoyne and his army, the contrast between the services of Washington and those of his subordinate gave his enemies an opportunity of detracting from the merits of the former. Yet it is recorded, to the honor both of Congress and the Country, that the confidence of neither in their chosen chief was for a moment withdrawn. Others might be trusted to lead a detachment or head a charge, but for the conduct of a campaign or the general direction of the war no other was thought of but Washington. And though, during his military career, he encountered reverses oftener than he achieved triumphs, yet no one has since disputed his right to rank among the most eminent commanders of his time. The surprise of the British at Brenton, followed by the success at Princeton; the able dispositions whereby he covered states from invasion with an inferior force, and always avoided a surprise where he personally commanded, fighting only when and where he chose to risk a battle; and finally the masterly combinations and rapid movements which resulted in the capture of Cornwallis and his army, fairly justify his claim to a place among the great Captains of all time.

It must never be forgotten that the armies he commanded he was required also to *create* — that the government he served had for the most part neither means, credit nor inherent power — that Congress was but a collection of delegates from thirteen independent States, invested with little authority and flying from place to place before an advancing enemy — that the soldiers he led were not merely undisciplined levies, fresh from the plough and the shop, but that they were called forth on short enlistments, so that their turns of service often expired just when they could least be spared, and before they had struck a blow for their country, or even been trained to steadiness under fire — that their cannons, munitions, horses and forage were almost always deficient — that his troops were paid, when paid at all, in a depreciated paper currency, of which a month's pay would hardly buy a breakfast — that operations in winter were necessarily suspended or greatly restricted on his side because his soldiers were unclad and often unshod: — while on the other hand the British armies were composed of war-inured regulars, abundantly provided and regularly paid in coin, commanded by experienced officers, and serving steadily from first to last, having the sea and powerful fleets for their base of operations, which enabled them to change the theatre of war at pleasure, transporting all necessary munitions with one-tenth the cost and labor involved in similar movements on the American side. When these circumstances are duly considered, it must be felt that no struggle was ever commenced against forces more disproportionate than those encountered by Washington, and no contest ever maintained with more spirit and skill, worthy of a great general.

There have been greater men, intellectually, than Washington — men of profounder mind, broader grasp, more dazzling capacities, more brilliant achievements, more signal genius: but in the combination of greatness with goodness, — of character with action — of love of Liberty with love of Order — of eminent Military with admirable Civil qualities — of patriotic devotion with the absence of personal aspiration — the world has decidedly not known his equal. Other men, even in the Revolutionary army, may have been superior to him, in some one quality; but his was the calm judgment and masterly appreciation, which combined their various abilities into one harmonious and effective whole. So in civil life — Hamilton possessed a larger and loftier command of the science of practical Statesmanship, while Jefferson had a keener foresight, a deeper appreciation of popular tendencies and sympathies — a truer philosophy of the nature and scope of purely popular institutions: — but the consolidation of the National

ERLANGEN

(BAVARIA)

Published for HERRMANN J. MEYER. 6 North William-Street, NEWYORK

Liberties, the foundation of the National Greatness and Security were due to neither of these, save in subordination to the controlling influence of the Father of his Country. And still, when Faction rages and Discord rears her snaky crest — when the violence of party threatens to shake the grand and glorious work of the Union — the solemn voice heard above the roar of the tempest, calming, soothing and reconciling, is that of WASHINGTON: the altar on which discord is hushed and antipathies are buried is the grave at MOUNT VERNON.

ERLANGEN.

Equality is one of the Three Words symbolically inscribed upon the banners of humanity. Nature is at constant war with all inequality; her laws are perpetually active and her strength is unceasingly exerted to restore the equilibrium, whenever and wherever it is disturbed. Hence the ebb and flow of air and ocean, hence thunder and lightning, hence storm and inundation, earthquake, pestilence and seasons of sterility. The battle is also waged in the awful depths of space; shattered planets fly around the sun, and the irregular courses of the stars prove the disturbance in the equilibrium of the universe.

To the nations of Western Europe, the inequality of civilization and culture has ever been the most fruitful mother of their woes. It is the stumbling-block which prevents the regular progress towards a happier futurity; it is the rampart which protects despotism; it is a wall stronger, higher, more insurmountable than that of the Chinese; it is the nursing mother of all despotical, Dionysian powers — the magic ring, which enables the defeated tyrant to rise again with increased strength; it is the rock on which peoples in their struggles for freedom split; and it is the consciousness of this inequality, before which turns pale the expectation of the philanthropist that good fruits may be brought forth by that great catastrophe, which is now impending. In the immeasurable distance, which divides those enlightened men, who serve as interpreters and intellectual champions of freedom and human rights, from the stupid, indolent masses of the people, yawns the grave of hope. Show me but one nation in continental Europe battling against monarchy and absolutism, among whose masses prevails a rational idea of Liberty, Equality, Fraternity — an idea firmly rooted and active in thought and deed! There is none! Absolutism knew well, what it did, when it everywhere so regulated all the institutions of the state, that intellectual cultivation should for ever remain open to, and be the necessity of but the few, and the masses be consigned to ignorance and the condition of Helots. Frederick II. wrote upon the margin of a plan for school-reform which was laid before him: „Stick to the Catechism and the four rules of Arithmetic. When a potentate teaches his peasants any thing more, he does like that fool, who sawed off the branch on which he was himself sitting.“ — This doctrine of royalty is as old as monarchy itself. Whatever kings may have appeared to try in a contrary direction, they have never done in real earnest. Their intentions reduced themselves in most cases to mere phrases spoken to deceive the credulous.

Wherever the Liberty and Selfgovernment of the people have gained sway, it is generally the first object of those at the helm, to reform the system of public instruction and to break the fetters and fences of mental development. Yet intellectual culture is not an advantage which may be gained in a day; it is not a property which may be divided among men like fields or meadows, goods or money, through the application of some communistical law. What the erudite scholar or gentleman has acquired from teachers, books, reflection, and by the intercourse and exchange of ideas with other men of cultivated mind through a long series of years — these his mental treasures, his various scientific knowledge, his experience and his ability to judge of events and things, can never be attained by the multitude, purposely reared in ignorance, by reading newspapers and books for a year or two, or by listening to the discussions of ale-house politicians. After such a course of instruction the ignorant may think himself wise, because some indistinct ideas of his abject condition and the rights of man are dawning in his soul; but he is just as incapable then, as he was before, of rising to a full consciousness and appreciation of those rights and to that courage, necessary to a manly and persevering defence of them at the peril af his life and all his earthly goods. The ignorant, uncultivated man who in his simplicity is so easily excited in the days of revolutions, and but too often made the tool of any one who will flatter him and clothe his silly notions of liberty in words, will easely forsake the true patriot, who courageously, firmly, faithfully defends step by step the sanctuaries of his rights in the days of oppression, and how seldom will he show sympathy to strengthen his champion in adversity! Generally he has for him not even a mark of good will or affection. How many of those, who have sacrified themselves for the maintenance of popular rights, have been trampled on, by command of the tyrants, by the people themselves, and have been forgotten! The sting, which pierces the deepest in the patriot's heart is the want of hope on considering the moral and intellectual condition of the masses. The Catastrophe will come; it is unavoidable; but who can say that it will lead to the peaceful rule of Liberty?

When Attila „the Scourge of God“ had entered Rome, with the intent to blot it from the face of Earth, the Roman Bishop went to meet him holding before him the Christian Cross, and before the power of that symbol of love the sword of destruction fell from the hand of the barbarian. When humanity, chained to the corpse of polytheism, seemed destined to perish in its corruption, then by Christ's word of love a new life was awakened, and his death on the cross paid the penalty laid on a guilty world. Shall in the old seats of civilisation the words of warning now spoken to implore justice and humanity have no effect? Alas! they will have none, for the waves of enraged despotism dash mountain-high, and its maniac laws make every word of warning a deadly crime. Nevertheless the attempt must be constantly made by those who, faithful to their calling, judge of their duty by the monitor within and not by the consequences. And they may be sure that the day will come, when the nations of Europe will trust none but them, who in the days of the rule of terror valiantly raised their voice for liberty, equality and fraternity, in spite of all personal dangers.

What was I about when taking up the pen for this article? I would describe my railroad-excursion from Plauen to Erlangen, and I have completely forgotten it. — Hark! The locomotive comes wheezing and coughing along; another half hour and the train is crossing the boundary between Saxony and Bavaria, and speeding to the station of Hof.

„This frontier“ remarked a fellow-traveller as we were passing it, „divides the North from the South Germany.“ „„There is no fear of a separation, for all that““, say I. „„But it is a melancholy fact, that in these days of dull despotism, no argument can be found for the unity of North and South save that basest and meanest one — the personal rivality of the rulers. The German railroads are a constant protest against German disunion, though they of course, can effect hardly anything against the combined pride, ambition, covetousness, hate and envy of the different states and princes. Fiscal interest, fear and suspicion are the iron clamps of their Union. Do away with these, and they would tear one another to pieces.““

Let us look out upon the landscape. The blue tinted rows of the Erz- and Fichtel-Mountains throw their arms out far and wide and furrow the country with delicious little vales, in which, man has fixed his abode. Now and then a manorial seat appears in sight; but most of the houses are mere cots, which often bear the face of poverty. The railroad does not descend into the deep grounds. It keeps along the mountain-side, and the locomotive flies on above the green dales with its long train, and across the gorges in the forest on lofty bridges or on the edges of dizzy abysses. The roads in this irregular, broken country are continually ascending and descending; we see them running along by the brookside, or winding again upward to the top of the heights. For the railway, however, a level was to be constructed in this hilly country and for a part of the tract it has succeeded well. But beyond Hof, on the ridge where the waters that belong to the Rhine and Elbe divide, the mountains plunge so steeply down into the valley of the Maine, that the laying out of a line practical for railroad-construction was hardly possible. The difficulties at this point were in fact of such a nature that the skill of the mason and architect could be of little avail, and the road was of necessity brought down by a succession of curves. Here is the celebrated „Inclined Plane“ down which the locomotives with their trains roll 400 feet to the station of Schorgast, to the fright of the passengers. Further on the tract pursues its course into the valley of the Maine, along the declivities of the Fichtel-Mountains. Prospects of great beauty are presented here and there on this part of the way, till the hoary castle of Culmbach, a town renowned for its beer, draws near and Franconia opens its shrine of rich and beautiful scenery. Franconia is a delightful portion of the German soil, full of beauty and fertility, and romance lurks upon its mountains and heights. The ruins of cloisters, and chapels, the resorts of pilgrims, are scattered about, and old feudal castles peep out of the green forests and recall the days, when the proud knights held their congress at Ratisbon, and their confederation was strong enough to carry on long wars with the neighbouring powerful princes.

Nearly all the towns have citadels and are protected by fortifications and walls. Trade and business flourish in most of them and their energetic populations are the descendents of those citizens, who in times of peace cherished the arts of peace, but when the defence of

26

their rights rendered it necessary, fought with lance and sword, like the boldest of knights, and were ready to suffer every calamity, before they would part with an inch of their liberties. The Emperors had the good sense to honor this spirit with grants, donations, endowments and privileges, and it was the custom in those days, when the emperor rode his way to Nuremberg to administer justice, or to hold the imperial diets, that the citizens of such towns, completely armed, accompanied the ruler of the empire on horseback and formed his guard of honor. — As far as Bamberg the majority of the population are Catholics. Protestantism has the upper hand in Nuremberg, and reminiscences of those days when the Zollern sat there in the old castle as counts and officers of the Empire, kept alive strong feelings of sympathy for that dynasty, until recent and sad experience did away with it for ever.

At Bamberg the railroad has passed from the valley of the Maine into that of the Regnitz, which it keeps as far as Nuremberg. Before reaching Erlangen, the river, the canal and the hill of the Altstadt are so crowded together, that the railroad had to be pierced through the hill, whence in a long curve it approaches the city. From this point (that from which the accompanying view is taken) Erlangen, in the midst of a broad, well cultivated valley, and surrounded by a wreath of villages, presents a pleasing and friendly prospect. Nor does the interior of the city shorten the good impression. The broad, clean, regular streets aud squares and the stately dwelling-houses, perfectly justify the reputation of Erlangen, as one of the handsome cities in Germany. It is a very quiet place too, almost too quiet. The population (about 10,000) seems lost in the vestment of a large city.

The celebrated University is the axis, round which the intellectual and material life of Erlangen turns. It was founded by the dukes of Franconia and was, soon after its opening in 1732, removed from Baireuth to Erlangen. Parsimoniously endowed and rather repressed than aided by the government, a development on a grand scale was impossible, though the University kept up the reputation of cherishing a spirit of true and severe scholarship and of sending forth men of great learning. The relations beetween teacher and pupil contrast advantageously with those, which prevail in many larger universities. The social circles of the professors are opened to the students, and they find easy access to respectable families. In consequence the student's manners and morals are improving and he is saved from many dangers, which exhibit themselves in their worst form, where the young men are cut off from polite intercourse.

The University of Erlangen is proud of many men of celebrity, whose names shine in the Republic of Letters; Martius, Steinheil, Liebig, Goldfuss, Bischoff, have opened new paths in the domains of Natural History and Physics, and their fame is spread throughout the world. Schelling in Berlin, Osann in Würzburg and the poet Rückert were Alumni of the University.

Erlangen — the town — is very ancient. Her foundation carries us back to the times of Charlemagne, who removed the conquered Sclavonians to this region. The place received new and strong elements of prosperity, when after the revocation of the edict of Nantes, the Margrave Christian offered the town as an asylum to the banished French protestants. They built the „new city," and established various branches of industry, which still flourish here; the manufactures of looking-glasses, stockings and gloves employed, in the days of their prosperity, thousands of hands. Changes in commercial relations and the closing of many of the outlets to their products, have of late much reduced the manufacturing activity, and inflicted a deep wound on the former prosperity of Erlangen.

CAPE HORN.

A thought of the Almighty God created the world; and the creating thought rules and preserves it. God's breath is working in men and he makes them the executors of his decrees. Thus he has acted through the Prophets and Apostles, through the great inventors and explorers of science, and his inspiration works in men like Marco Polo, Humboldt and La Perouse, who remove the veil from unknown lands, and whose discoveries have an enduring and beneficial influence upon the progress of civilization.

Half a century had hardly elapsed after the discovery of a the western hemisphere by Columbus, when the form of the American Continent was already well known. Its coasts had been carefully examined and conceptions had been formed of the mountain-ranges and the hydrographic net in the interior, which, as the maps of those days prove, were by no means far from the truth. There was however one capital point, on which error prevailed. The new world was supposed to extend itself southwards indefinitely into the polar regions, and the strait through which Magellhan first sailed was thought to be the only channel by which the Pacific could be reached

CAPE HORN

Published for HERRMANN J. MEYER, 164. William-Street. NEW YORK.

from the Atlantic. Tierra del Fuego was held to be not a cluster of islands, but part of the continent, stretching away to an unknown extent towards the south pole. Drake was the first to shake this belief. He had passed through Magellhan's Strait, when he was met by a storm, which drove him upon the southern extremity of Tierra del Fuego, where he found a place of refuge in a rocky cove near Cape Horn. His opinion, that Tierra del Fuego was an island, was not able to combat successfully with the universal prejudice and was by degrees forgotten.

Forty years later a rich Dutch merchant, Isaac le Maire, a jew, equipped two vessels for the express purpose of attempting a voyage round the southern point of America. His object was to open a new route for the commerce with the Pacific, and free it from the dominion of Spain, which not satisfied with the dangers and delays — two to three months being often required — of the passage through the straits of Magellhan, had erected fortifications on its shores with the intention of closing it entirely against other nations. The expedition of the patriotic merchant proved succesful, and the southern cape of America washed by the waves of the Pacific — a mere island of rock separated from Tierra del Fuego by a narrow channel — received its name Horn from the village on the Zuydersee in which stood the summer-residence of the rich Isaac.

The nature of the country corresponds in part only to the opinions, which had their origin in the relations of the early voyagers, and which have been transmitted down to the most recent period. Cape Horn lies in nearly the same degree of latitude as Edinburgh. Tierra del Fuego extends from the 52. to the 56. degree, and its climate where the coasts are low, is not colder than that of the Baltic shore of Prussia. But it is an alpine region, traversed by a continuation of the Cordilleras, which at the southern extremity of the island, plunge abruptly into the ocean in steep promontories several thousand feet in height. On the southwestern side sea and land wage eternal war. The arms of the ocean have swept away the land, as they did upon the western coasts of Scotland and Norway, and won their way in deep channels through the gorges of the cloudpiercing mountains, dividing this part of Tierra del Fuego into an assemblage of smaller islands. The eastern coast on the other hand, spreads out flat and level, and has precisely that naked, desolate, sterile aspect, which the older adventurers depicted; while in the alpine region of the West, romantic vallies like those of Switzerland produce a luxuriant vegetation, and the most beautiful forests crown the heights. The main ridge of the Cordilleras rises from two to three thousand feet above the line of perpetual snow (6000 to 8000 feet above the sea-level) and all the splendor of the glacier-world exhibits itself in this region not less than among the frozen mountains of Savoy.

The most imposing scenery is that of the westerly part of Magellhan's Strait. With inconceivable violence the mighty flood has there wrought out for itself a passage through the mountain ridge 6000 feet in elevation, where the granite masses rise up from the depths in perpendicular or overhanging walls, enlivened only by the cries and motions of millions of sea-fowl, that build their nests in the crevices of the rocks. Darkness and gloom rest upon the cliffbound floods and render the passage so hazardous to the voyager already encompassed by dangers and horrors, that it would certainly be nevermore attempted were not the doubling of Cape Horn equally hazardous. For there the storm never ceases to rage, and demands its annual sacrifices of human lives and property. A shipwreck on Cape Horn is almost always certain death; for the shores, lined with a wall of rock rising as it were to the heavens, overhung by glaciers and veiled by falling torrents, present few accessible spots, and those who trust to boats for deliverance are generally swallowed up by the surges. The demand of humanity for the erection of a lighthouse, with a station for life-boats and an asylum or place of shelter for the shipwrecked mariner, is still, to the disgrace of the great naval powers, unheeded. And yet the passage around Cape Horn is one of the most important on the globe, and the number of those, who attempt it, is now prodigiously multiplied on account of the brisk trade from Europe to California.

Ere we leave Tierra del Fuego let us glance at its master, Man! — Does this dwarfish, shapeless creature, from whose quadrangular skull, beneath the low forehead, stare those small lifeless eyes, indicative of the stupidity of the mind within, really belong to the human race? Well may we doubt it. The heart which fain would embrace all humanity with its sympathy, the soul, which would gladly behold in all men on earth an undoubted, though unequal, relationship by common origin, find themselves restless and disturbed. What, you ask, is this creature with the thick bone thrust through the underlip, the being that, with beastly appetite, gorges himself upon the fat of penguins, and poisons the air with his noisome effluvia — is *this* creature my brother? Where is that breath of God, which separates man from the brute, and what ground is there to claim that sympathy which is deeply rooted in a common origin? In the presence of the natives of Tierra del Fuego, those rude beings of deformity, in whom no spark of the soul has ever kindled into a flame, the doctrine that a *single* family born of *one* mother has peopled this globe falls to the ground.

The greatest enigma on earth is man. A veil which no science has yet uplifted conceals the history of his creation. He fills the whole earth. No race of animals bears the slightest comparison with him in this important point. Dearly has he purchased this pre-eminence. In the polar regions, his noble form shrinks to a distorted and dwarfish figure and his spirit is frozen into insensibility. Under the equator he is parched and withered and in the regions of the tropics he wears himself out by the indulgence of brutish lust and raging passions alternating with periods of languor and exhaustion. We see whole races of men, where the clime has been unpropitious, whose activity is consumed in the narrow circle, which the mere supply of their physical wants draws around them, and even in the bosom of civilization, how many millions of men are to be found, in whom every thought of the feeble understanding revolves exclusively round their immediate necessities in how many does the fettered soul sink under the anxiety and distress, which are renewed with every morning's dawn? We see races of men, whose intellects remain dull and unawakened during life, wandering at random over the wastes like migrating beasts. They win no smile from the desert, no property but the booty gained by the watchful eye and the rapacious arm — by theft and murder. We see others who know no joys save those with which the greedy hand supplies the palate. We boast of the progress and treasures of civilization, and yet gloomy night still broods over the masses of mankind! Beside the few hundreds of thousands in whom the culture of the mind is active, stand hundreds of millions, into whose souls no gleam of light ever penetrates, and who in misery and mental darkness make the long journey from the cradle to the grave. Thoughtless of the past, with no idea of, or faith in a better futurity, they are neither conscious of their brutish condition, nor have they a conception of any thing lying beyond the circle of their absolute wants. They die and pass away with the feeling that, when they die, they will become dust from which they have sprung. Those to whom religion points out a state of eternal bliss, have at least one consolation; but even this easy charity is extended to the minority only; for most religions place the kingdom of eternal punishment and woe on the borders of the grave, and in the hour of death they fill a cup of anguish and fear. Wretchedness follows the majority of mankind through life — terror is their outfit for eternity.

Man divides, like branches from a parent stem, into numerous races, sharply distinguished from one another in character and form. There is one race highly gifted by preference. The Caucasian race has for thousands of years been constantly at the head of the higher development of humanity. The Caucasian is the guardian of the sacred fire; to him belongs the apostleship of civilization. Therefore power was given him above the rest, and by this power he scatters the sparks of light over the earth, and erects in all zones the altars of human improvement. In antiquity its sphere was narrow — now, how wide it extends! 2000 years ago civilization had not yet made its way beyond the countries bordering upon the Mediteranean. It has since traversed the oceans, and as the sway of the Caucasian race has gradually extended to all continents, its civilization has been grafted on other races, and those who would not receive it, are vanishing from the earth. Still, while the chosen stem of the East has pushed forth its shoots in all directions, overshadowing even the new world with its branches, it has lost vigor and activity in the old; its roots dry up and wither; civilisation fled from its offspring once powerful and cultivated, and the degenerate, demoralized nations, perish or sink into barbarism. Turn your eye to Armenia, to the coasts of the Euxine, to the curse-smitten countries of Persia, to modern Greece. What do you behold? In one quarter barbarized tribes, in another nations worn out and feeble, vegetating in a dreamy, impotent existence, hardly recollecting the mighty past, and incapable of vigorous resistence, unworthy of Freedom, bearing patiently the yoke of Slavery.

Even the German people, the standard-bearer and treasurer of civilisation, in its ancient seats struggles in vain for a renovation of its ancient power and liberty, and has not solved the great question presented to it. There is much that calls for earnest reflection. So great a nation, which within the space of one generation has thrice suffered herself to be betrayed by her princes, and to be yoked again without a firm resistance — a nation, which now for the third time, submits to be deprived by craft and perfidy of dearly purchased freedom — such a nation has certainly entered the period of decline, unless she rises unanimously and shakes off her treacherous oppressors. The decay must soon be manifest. But though the ancient stem will rotten — in the far West will its transplanted shoots grow up to unrivalled greatness, and while the fathers are bearing the chains of slavery in the old world, the star-sprinckled banner of her hardy sons will wave victoriously in the new, and with pride and glory, enjoying the full happiness of Freedom, they will, ere the century closes, deliver the rest of the world and at the same time rule it.

Alas for the poor Indians on Tierra del Fuego! There is no hope even of saving their bare existence. The bearers of Civilization bring them certain death. Their chilled soul will perish in the flame of the distilled liquors, the use of the gun accelerates their selfdestruction and the Missionary renders them not happier and more contented by taking from them their ancient gods and planting the cross upon the mountain tops. Since an intercourse arose between the natives and the American and British whalers, intemperance, disease, and intestine feud have decimated that unhappy race. These causes are hurrying them on to utter extermination, and the time is not far distant, when in the list of the Indian tribes the name of the aborigines of Tierra del Fuego will be struck out for ever.

The OPERA HOUSE

A MASKED BALL AT THE OPERA HOUSE IN PARIS.

It is *Lundi gras.* The night is intensely cold, the vault of the heavens is painted in the deepest blue, the stars sparkle, the milky way — each speck therein a sun — girdles the firmament, and spans its bright arch in quiet majesty above the huge metropolis. Paris seems wrapt in slumber. On a sudden a thousand spires raise their voices, all the clocks strike twelve, the witching hour, and the scene is changed as by magic. Tumult succeeds to stillness, carriages rattle, doors are thrown open, the windows grow brighter, the streets noisy and amid echoing laughter, strange, unsightly forms, — not men, not women, — beings without names in the garb and attire of all times, of all nations, ranks and conditions, — trip masked through the crowd. Whither do they go these heroes and kings, hand in hand with the gipsy-girl and the beggar-woman? Whither hastens yonder Cassandra on the arm of Tartuffe, those Roman matrons led by a courteous Abbé of the Regency and the *Cavaliere Servante* of modern Venice? All take the direction to the Opera House. Half Paris seems engaged in the masquerade there and all who can spare five Francs, will this night wear the cap, or at least enjoy the spectacle of folly. Let us follow the stream! — We enter the saloon. Down pours the dazzling light of sixty girandoles, each with a hundred gas-flames in vari-colored glasses. The boxes and benches are gradually filling. Thousands and thousands of peeping, prying glances cross each other in the chaos of fantastic masks. All is expectation; all hearts beat. Suddenly the walls tremble; a crash of trumpets, loud as the summons to the dead at the day of judgment, gives the signal; the storm of tones looses the storm of pleasure. As if smitten with St. Vitus dance, the masses circle in a whirlpool, delirium has grasped them, the fanaticism of pleasure has seized every soul; the frantic masks, men and women, shout and leap, and one entwining the other, they cast themselves into the mazes of the shapeless dance. Pleasure becomes intoxication, intoxication madness; in quicker, quicker time the music urges the couples onward in the giddy round, until utter exhaustion compels to pause. But scarcely has the breathless crowd had time to pant, the orchestra begins anew; the floor again trembles beneath the feet of the thousands, and these scenes, ever broken off and ever repeating, continue until bright day. The Opera-House, on this night, may truly be termed a mad-house The philosopher, who is accustomed to consider Paris in the grave attire of the open book in which Clio is writing her most pregnant pages, would certainly be at a loss to recognize her in this hurly-burly of vanity and nothingness. How can he find in this picture a likeness of the giant, who, when he moves his limbs and turns himself about, causes the earth to tremble, and makes thrones totter? who will find out the trait of the hero that need but lift an arm to liberate a continent from its chains? Who would think these masses hunting with madness after enjoyment, belonging to the same people that were fearlessly storming the Tuileries? Who would, on seeing these men in brocade-coats filling the boxes of the madhouse as spectators, think of the men in blouses at their hard death-work? Who can find in these scenes of the fanaticism of pleasure on the one hand and life-contempting enthusiasm for freedom on the other, the connecting link? In fact there seem to be two people in Paris who have nothing in common with each other but the name. —

C. Reiss del.

THE BOSPORUS FROM THE EUXINUS

THE BOSPHORUS.

On the shores of the Bosphorus stands the Genius of the Old World and holds up the balance in which its destinies are weighed. At this grand portal, where the highways of nations are crossing, those commotions and events frequently took place, by which crowns were broken and empires crushed. There, where the boundaries and dividing lines of East, West, and North end in a single point, and where so many nations slumber, and the graves of the civilization of three thousand years have a common burialplace: — at such a place it may not be unfit to pause and cast a contemplative glance upon the present condition of Society in the old World. —

Turning firstly toward the Orient we see three faiths, which divide the East: the Mohammedan, the Hindoo and the Chinese. All these religions are now reduced to mere forms; life has fled from them, and time augurs their decay and annihilation. The Mohammedan States are tottering, the Sublime Porte mocks her very name, and the intruding flood of European customs and manners accelerates the impending ruin. — Further eastward Christianity and British Rule are breaking into fragments the ancient empire of Brama's faith; and since the trident of England has forced the gates of China, the spirit of destruction is irresistibly developing his power against the grand work of Confucius. The ancient civilisations are fast passing away in the East, and with the strength and vigor of social organization wealth is vanishing. The skill and machinery of the West are drawing the gold from the mines of Asia, the pearls from her seas; and as the prosperity of the Asiatic nations declines, their science and learning sink into ignorance. It is an established fact, that Oriental Scholarship is at present more at home in Europe than even in the Orient itself.

What fate is impending over the nations of the East? This question has been decided long ago. A new life and its forms will fill the places of the old. Christianity and European Civilization will, in the course of time absorb the ancient faiths and cultures. Corroded in her very vitals, penetrated by the solvent power of the spirit of Europe, all Asia is now in a state of fermentation. The „day of promise“ has passed for ever from her nations and faith is fast forsaking their temples. The star of Christianity is the only light in the Eastern darkness. No longer shall the revelation of God be kept back from those populations or be veiled in symbols, which have lost their significance; and the germinating seeds of true knowledge shall fall anew on a soil, now overgrown by the weeds of idolatry and priestly deception. Christ's Doctrine, by spreading among the nations of the far East, will complete the grand work of salvation.

From the ruins of Asia we turn our eyes to the West. What a spectacle! How the billows roll on the Ocean of Humanity, how the surges beat its shores! A sharp ferment is working in Society, and though the banners of peace for the moment flutter in the breeze, we see everywhere the contest and shock of hostile opinions, of principles and men. New forces are hastening continually into the battle, and even the most despotic rule is not so strong to quiet the disturbed elements and to divert the dreaded catastrophe.

Europe is evidently on the eve of a change in her social relations. The East is passive and the influences which work upon her come from without; in Europe, however, the reform of Society rests on an independent development of her genius and on the intellectual strength and vigor of her own. There are now three grand principles which, in this great tournament, represent the banners of the contending parties. Love, reverence, and interest for the past unite in the principle of Restoration; Conservatism will maintain the *status quo* in property and authority; and the spirits of Reform and Revolution represent the principle of Progress. Each of these opposing powers acts affirmatively or negatively upon the great questions which shake Society, and this opposition preserves European life vigorous, active and creative. Formerly a fourth and most powerful agent held those three in fetters: — Religion. So long as blind religious creed predominated in Europe little space was given for opposition from other social principles. But the rise of critical philosophy has removed those bands, and the present exertions of the Church-Hierarchy to regain a lost position will finally result in the acceleration of their decay.

The sharply defined nationalities and their pretentions, and their rise in the shape of opposite parties in the various states of Europe is a phenomenon, which is intimately connected with the contest of the principles aforesaid. These feuds contribute to guard the fire in the ashes from which the phoenix will arise.

Every where in Europe the feudal nobility, the great proprietors of the soil, are the chief representatives of the principle of restoration. Under their banners are united all those, who think it possible to save more or less of that patriarchal system of old in which an immigrant or victorious chief sized upon a territory and divided it among his followers, who again as Manor-Lords could assemble their retainers about them for service, or for mutual protection and aid. This feudal nobility, enjoying great privileges in many countries, and taking rank and station next to sovereignty, regards with scorn all new forms of society and considers the relations of the state mainly from that point of view in which its own interests predominate. — Opposite this party stand Democracy and Socialism, representing the principles of Reform and Revolution. Democracy finds it absurd to view man as a mere appendage to the soil, and repudiates the aristocratic doctrine of servant and master, — a doctrine inconsistent with the principle of Humanity and the rights of man. Socialism spreading its banner before the innumerable array of the masses asserts, that man's claims stand higher than even the laws of property. After the doctrine of the socialist, the earth like the air is the property of all; and consequently the present possession of the soil by the old deeds of arbitrary power or government can convey no right of perpetual occupation. Every member of the state — the socialist argues in the same course of reasoning, — may take to himself so much of arable land to his private use, as suffices the necessities of life, and he is able to cultivate. The physical powers for that purpose being originally nearly the same, each man has to claim nearly the same portion of the soil. Null and void are consequently those seizures of large territories in ancient times; null and void the laws which still uphold those seizures for the benefit of the present possessors; and null and opposed to all human rights are those differences of rank and condition which have their origin in these usurpations and arbitrary laws. Hence Social Democracy demands the overthrow of all those institutions, founded, as in its opinion they are, on the wrong of the past, and it imperiously claims a new and equal division of the property of the soil as the groundwork of the reconstruction of human society. It recognises the earnings of labor as the most legitimate and just means of increasing individual fortune, and it holds the labor and skill, which handle the plough and turn up the sod, the industry which creates capital, and the trade that unites and connects the nations, to be worthy of respect and consideration above every thing else. This party, to which the majority of the masses belongs, is ready for mortal fight against all the interests and claims, that oppose them, and as a true consequence of their principles, they assert to have a perfect right to tear down, by main-force if necessary, every impediment to the restoration of the pretended original equality regarding the property of the soil, and the construction of a new political edifice upon the basis of such equality.

A third party, in downright opposition to social Democracy, bears the banner of Absolutism. The Absolutist would fain stand upon historical ground. All individual right in the state, he asserts, emanates from the right of the absolute monarch. As subversive in his tendency as the social democrat he denies to all governments, save the despot, the right of existence. He openly demands the restoration of absolute monarchical power by counter-revolution and tries to lead back the races of of princes to the high place, which they occupied in antiquity, when rulers, radiant with the halo of a direct divine mission, sat upon thrones and not only ordained obedience to the people as kings, but also enjoyed religious reverence as high-priests. Such a condition of things appears to them the true fountain of human happiness. They are fanatics of their faith and will with fanaticism pursue their object.

Men who deduce the original compact of Society from the perfect equality of individuals, bear on their escutcheons the motto „Free and equal as our fathers were!“ The Republican wishes to reconstruct the state on the original principle of society in a true democratic sense. He acknowledges no other power in the state, than that conferred by legal delegation of the majority of the people, and no other right of ruling than that of selfgovernment; no other majesty than that of selfgiven law, no other sovereign than the nation.

A fifth party is exerting its influence at present in the West of the old world less by its numbers, than by its quality. The most richly endowed spirits are attached to it, and they are ready for self-sacrifice, when the hour of trial strikes. This party of enthusiasts sees in the social edifice of Europe but the misshapen birth of imposture and treachery, in the codes of law nothing but counterfeit imposed upon credulous nations, as a means of cheating them out of their inalienable rights. The successful cheat, they assert, has turned all things topsy turvy, confused all ideas, and degenerated states into madhouses, where the unfortunate inmates are every moment exposed to be maltreated by the rods of the guardians. Monarchy and all that appertains to it they hold to be the product of demoniacal craft with which no compromise is to be made. Many have gone forth at all times to battle against this state of things as against a dragon, and many have offered up their lives in the contest. A holy enthusiasm enflames them to free their brethren from the fetters imposed by tyrants, and when they fall, apparently useless and vain offerings, their example ever draws new champions into the field.

A sixth and a seventh party rise prominent from the crowd, and are conspicuous in all states from the pillars of Hercules to the Theiss, from the Niemen to the Adour. They both scorn to support themselves upon the *status quo*, though in their ends they are complete antagonists. The one, consisting of the large majority of public officers and all those who are dependent upon the princely power for the comforts and necessities of life, make their duty to the established regal authority the only principle of their conduct, and set up obedience as their idol in opposition to Freedom, which to overthrow and destroy is their open intent. The authority of the monarchical power in the state stands in their view as an unquestionable fact. Their orthodox political faith defies all investigation. The supreme will of the ruler forms the sum and substance of their symbols. While the aristocracy deduces the right of monarchical rule from feudalism, the party under consideration — the Serviles — trace it to the absolute personal will of the monarch and consider the sword as the instrument by which subordination can be made permanent. Obedient to every dictate proceeding from the mouth of authority, this party knows nothing of opposition aud every sound they utter is an echo to the commands from the throne. They nowhere recognize a right of independent thought in the individual, and liberty lies beyond their powers of conception. Recognizing but subjects they know nothing of citizens in a state, and according their doctrine, all individual acts, in order to be legal, must be authorized by the ruling power. The Monarch „by the grace of God“ is the original cause and legal end of all that takes place in the state; authority is derived from him alone; and consequently the power of legislation rests solely in him. His will is, after their creed, law in all respects, for it is not possible to be master and servant in the state at the same time. The doctrine of the Servile even goes beyond that of the Absolutist. Public opinion is condemned by him as a mere phantasm, and a spirit of progress as a the demon of criminal opposition to the Majesty „by the grace of God“, a demon which must be driven out by all possible means. Constitutions they abhor, if they be not mere toys, which are given to nations to pacify them, as mothers appease illtempered children, and may be taken away again at will, when the purpose of granting them has been accomplished. The man, who claims constitutional rights and legally struggles to sustain and defend them, is considered by the servile as a rebel, and he terms an act of justice every act of persecution with which such a man is punished. This party has everywhere the strength of public authority in their hands; for, from the minister down to the beadle, and from the field-marshal down to the drummer, the great majority of the public officers are the sworn followers of the banner of servility. They are everywhere drawn up in array fully armed, a compact phalanx ready for battle and as they unite civil and military power, they are able to despise public opinion and tread it down. Every act of the monarch receives their approbation beforehand, every command of despotism their cheerful, voluntary, reverential obedience: the strong bond of common interest unites them firmly, and makes them determined to protect and assist each other. They do towards Liberty the office of the Hangman and — they boast of such service.

As open declared ennemies of the servile party the Liberals have drawn up in arms and encamped before them. „Ye fools!“ they cry contemptuously „do you think to change the state into a prison? And if you were able to do so, that you could accomplish it in spite of our opposition? Your will is indeed bad enough but your wishes go beyond your power. The days are past in which superstition and ignorance rendered it possible to carry out your intentions, and make the people passively submit to beastly oppression. The sand in your hour-glass of prosperity has long since run out, your power has lost its halo and sits upon thorns instead of its ancient comfortable couch. The present is your dying hour, every victory of yours is but a step farther towards your destruction, and your rejoicing at every advantage gained is mingled with the pangs of coming ruin. Your sword is no terror to us, though victorious at this present instant. By instructing the people we bring all your plans to nought and make your exertions vain efforts; and as every stroke of your arm brings upon you final defeat, so every movement you make costs you the ground on which you stand. Your courage must fail entirely if you compare your former with your present condition. What is become of the sanctity of monarchs in Western Europe, during the last half century? Do you not feel the earth tremble beneath your feet? And know: this change has been our work! We have hurled despotism from its throne and by establishing the doctrine of constitutional law made every overstep of power a crime. With every constitution, which we have wrung from you and from monarchy, the great principle of the original social compact is indissolubly connected, and though you would hide it by heaping thousands upon thousands of clauses and provisos around it, though by your sophisms you would deprive it of all efficacy: yet its light pierces the clouds gathered round it and at moments it shines with splendor and new force. Moreover, every invasion of the rights guaranteed in our constitutions places you before the world as faithless, lying tyrants, prays for vengeance upon your accursed heads, and calls for the thunderbolts of an avenging, almighty God. „— Such are the solemn declarations with which the liberal party marches against the servile throng. The social compact, the Liberals declare, must be acknowledged and become a reality, and princes shall no longer be its interpreters. This party deduces the rights of the people from the theory of the original laws of nature, and by advocating the maxim, that sovereignty is inherent to the nation — considered as a union of many individuals for social purposes — which sovereignty is but another term for the popular will, they consequently allow to the people alone the highest function of sovereignty that of making laws. To selfgiven laws alone, they assert, the nation owes respect and obedience. The fountain of princely power is not God, but the People, and this latter is not a mere appendix to the prince, as the servile party will have it. Between the people in its quality as sovereign and the people in its quality as subject, Governement is, according to the doctrine of the liberals, the mediator, and the prince, as its head, should make it his duty to keep up the equilibrium between the opposing principles. At the same time it should ever be present to his mind that he has to execute the legal will of the majority of the citizens, and he should remember, that his authority rests on the sovereignty of such majority.

Among all the parties of Western Europe the liberal and republican parties are those who in spite of the victories of their opponents, are sure of ultimate success. They are the legitimate offspring of the age, and consequently its rightful heir. In the nations of the West there is an irrepressible tendency to Democracy, and after every downfall it rises the stronger. To the future sway of Democracy are tending, though unconsciously, the labors and exertions of even the monarchical parties. Christianity itself assists Democracy by its doctrines and the idea is now spreading rapidly, that true Christianity and Democracy go hand in hand. Many of the modern sects are based on this doctrine. The „German Catholicism“, the „Free Church“ etc., are open manifestations of it.

While thus in Western Europe the conflict of opposing principles is going on, and victory and defeat follow each other on the battle-field of opinion, the practical questions of the age advance more conspicuously into the foreground. The desires of the masses, material in their character, point to an entire change in the social relations. Since the richer and higher classes in most of the states of Western Europe have attained a better position by means of those constitutions, that weakened the power of Monarchy, we behold them engaged in an ominous conflict with the demands of the people. The humble and the poor are beginning to combine and organize themselves; the phalanxes of communism begin to make front against the ranks of wealth and birth, determined upon an ultimate contest for victory or death. Questions, which concern the weal and woe of the lower classes, can no longer be put to rest by futile concessions in a semi-liberal sense, by sophisms and highsounding phrases. The amount of knowledge and instruction which has been dealt out to the masses, is just sufficient to bring them to some consciousness of their abject condition, and some reflection upon its causes and the means of relief. Sighing under the pressure of an unjust system of taxation, which everywhere presses heaviest upon the lower ranks, — (just those countries of Europe, which boast of the highest civilization and wealth, make by taxation any attempt of the poor to elevate themselves from utter misery hopeless and vain), — they demand urgently and unceasingly some fundamental relief from their burdens and their woes. The changes in the system of labor, which separate the manufacturer from the personal fate of the individual laborer, and place the latter in the slave-service of capital and machinery, combined with the general increase of population, augment the distress of the poor, nourish discontent, and urge forward with ever increasing force to a catastrophe and social revolution.

While the fear of it keeps Western Society in constant agitation, other dangers of no less import threaten it from the North. Yonder is Russia, an unwieldy dragon, stretching its vast carcass over three quarters of the globe, hiding a nation under each scale. Like the monster of ancient tradition, which, the offspring of the Nile, was at one extremity still in process of birth while the other raised its hundred heads mountain high — the Russian Empire, still laboring to assume a definite form, is the terror of the old world. Its growth is uninterrupted; it is continually drawing new tribes of barbarians within the circle of its sway. The permanent seat of a tyranny, at which humanity shudders, staining the pages of history with blood and crime, Russia's degraded populations have been taught to regard despotism as a paternal and beneficent rule, and to their understanding the idea of a better government than a despotic one is a stranger. In Russia none of those elements are to be found, which form the main-springs in the history of the nations of the West. Her Nobility possesses nothing of that chivalric spirit which combines pride and independence with loyalty; nothing of that romantic, adventurous feeling which urges on to heroic deeds; nothing of that noble impulse which adorns, refines and dignifies life. The Russian Church is withered to a dead form. The principle of active life is missing, philanthropy and humanity are unknown to her. To prolong her existence by sticking fast to dark, mysterious symbols, is the unique intent of the Russian Church and if she should absorb Catholicism and Protestantism, Christianity would be the winterfrost for the soul of mankind. To the people the Russian Church denies instruction. The Russian autocrat, combining the supreme ecclesiastical and temporal authority in his own person, has made the Church his serf, just as the Russian peasant is the serf of the proprietor of the soil by law, by custom and education. Denied the right of acquiring property, being themselves owned by their absolute masters, the Russian slaves, wanting pride, self-esteem and public spirit, will ever be the servile instrument of tyranny in the hands of their Czar. On this foundation Russian despotism has with iron consequence erected a throne, on which, for several generations past, men of talent have sat, ruling their gigantic empire with firm and skillful hands and leading it to universal sway. While on the one hand the Russian monarchs from time to time give themselves the air of preparing the emancipation of the serfs, and are willing to afford them protection against the proprietors of the land, they strike to the dust every longing of the nobility to rise from their own degraded position, — and unwearily, undeviatingly they follow up the one great purpose of assimilating the subjugated nations into one great Russian people, one in faith, one in language, one in obedience, — thus executing what Czar Peter, the organisator, planned out. Russia's giant-corpse presses with equal weight against both the East and West of the old World, and we see her with demoniacal craft everywhere busy in extending her sway, and arming herself, ready to enter into the councils of Europe as dictator, and at the same time, on the fall of the Oriental Empires, to become their universal heir. The monarchs of the West, agitated by the consciousness of their guilt, urged to cruelty by their fears, and driven by their terror to despair, are rushing headlong into the net of Russia. Many princes and sovereigns are merely the executors of the commands dictated on the banks of the Newa. On the sites of the prostrated altars of popular rights, the Caligula's of the age proclaim absolute monarchy as the symbol of divinity, and the Russian highpriest has sworn to maintain its worship, though all the civilized nations of the West should bleed beneath his sacerdotal knife.

Such is the sombre aspect which the Society of the Old World presents to the view. It would be utterly desolate and hopeless, if we did not look up to the one grand, grave, almighty and all-loving Spirit, sitting calmly in the midst of universal commotion, and giving law and rule to his boundless Universe. Our eye rests with confidence on that Spirit. It is He, that from the beginning has assigned to every error its limits; it is He, who has sent every criminal to trial; it is He, who has reduced every excess to its proper bound; it is He, who has at the proper time, broken or bowed every stubborn and malicious will. They who rejoice in cunning and deceit will vanish before Him, their pride will be plucked, their unrighteous power will melt away, the injustice they have committed will meet its due punishment. Nothing has ever stood before Him, save truth, honesty, equity and justice. Let Despotism veil her deeds in darkness, let her work be clad with deceit, knavery cruelty and brutal force; that Spirit who in our own days has uttered and executed his Verdict on the most powerful and crafty of all tyrants — that Spirit has undiminished strength to overthrow the demoniacal powers of the present ere their plans are fully ripe for execution. Their fall is sure; but the hour which will call all Europe to the battlefield, is known to God alone.

DESERT ROCK LIGHT-HOUSE

COAST OF MAINE

DESERT-ROCK LIGHT-HOUSE.

BY CHARLES L. BRACE.

The coast of Maine presents the most varied and picturesque outline of all our sea-board States. The traveller from Northern Europe will be reminded, in its innumerable bays and inlets, its succession of pretty islands, its quiet and sheltered harbors, its banks dark with the pine and the fir, of the shores of Norway and Sweden. — As in those countries, this peculiarity of its coast is destined especially to influence the future of this, as yet undeveloped State. — The bays and rivers, connecting with the farthest interior of the country, the stores of excellent timber, and the facilities for the produce and manufacture of hemp, promise to make Maine the great ship-building State on the Atlantic shore of the Western Continent. — At present, however, the most interesting feature of this coast, is its wild and picturesque beauty. The traveller, as he skirts the shores in the swift and commodious steam-boats, or more leisurely in the „coasting-schooners“, is continually surprised at the bold and changing scenery. At one time, the gray, rugged granite rocks, beaten for ever by the full sweep of the Atlantic tides face the sea; at another, undulating hills, frowning with the dark pine and spruce and hemlock, reach to the very shore; then come a group of peaceful little islands, sprinkled far out in the ocean, and each perhaps fringed to the water's edge with woods; then appears one of the broad quiet harbors, with a mighty river flowing into the sea — so wide, that the blue banks of the one side, are hardly visible from the other.

This coast, though well adapted for shelter from rough weather, is exposed to the most violent storms of the Northern Atlantic. The „Easterly blows" — so dreaded by the sailor on our sea-board — sweep in here with a force, which, at various times, has strown the whole shore from Cape Sable to Cape Ann with wrecks. — The danger is increased by the heavy fogs, which from June to September gather on this coast. One of the first cares of the Government, was to erect light-houses, at various points, where wrecks had occurred. It was not however till within about twenty years, that the Desert-Rock Light-House was built. The rock is a dangerous granite ledge, lying about twenty-eight miles from the nearest main-land, and about eighteen from the nearest cluster of islands, which form the East side of Penobscot Bay.

It contains some ten acres at low water, and not more than five or six at high tide. The waves never fairly sweep it, though the spray flies over it in all severe storms; but not so much as to destroy the growth of grass and a few vegetables on a half-acre at the top.

The writer of this remembers to have been informed that in a violent casterly gale, some six or eight years ago, the waves beat with such force on the rock, that almost every square of glass in the keeper's house was destroyed, and the outer door was broken in by a rock, weighing above sixty pounds, thrown up by the force of the breaking surf.

The Light itself is a fixed white-light, from common oil-lamps and reflectors.

It is not unfrequent, in the foggy season for vessels bound from Europe to St. Johns and other ports on the Bay of Fundy, to make this Light, as their first land-face, whence they can grope their misty way to port with more certainty, than if they try to find the dangerous shores of Cape Sable or Grand Menan.

B. Metzeroth sc.

The GIRALDA in SEVILLA

(SPAIN)

Published for HERRMANN J. MEYER. 164. William Street. NEW YORK.

The water around is deep and the landing on the leeward side is always easy, so that it has not been the scene of very great loss of lives and property. Still the lumbermen on the shores, or the fishermen among the islands tell of many a gallant ship, which has been dashed on these granite ledges, in the fearful autumn gales.

The Light-house and the Rock look, in the day, the very monument of desolation. The tall, solitary, white tower, with no signs of life about it, except a few screaming gulls; the gray old, silent rock, beaten and stained for ages by the Atlantic surf; the ceaseless, monotonous surge of the waves, leave an indescribable impression of loneliness and desolateness.

It is only in the night, when the sailor, long tossed on the Ocean, approaches carefully through the mist and the darkness that dangerous coast, that the bright twinkle of the Desert-Rock Light shows itself — what it really is — a beacon of Welcome and friendly warning.

THE GIRALDA, SEVILLE.

„Woe to the Land whose King is a Child!“ To this Biblical malediction: may be added. „Woe to the land that is governed by a weak and licentious Woman!“ — Poor Spaniards! The domestic laws of your kings have scorned these maxims, and for the royal gift you must do penance. Requital is the lot of the individual who remains deaf to the lessons of experience, and bitter is the fate of nations who will not hear the warnings of History, and indifferently or pusillanimously permit evil to be forced upon them by evil hands. The field which is sowed with tares, brings forth no wheat, and he who opens the door to injustice, lets misfortune into his house. Nine tenths of the sufferings of nations to be found on the face of the earth result from the circumstance, that the sufferers shrunk from direct opposition to the introduction of certain ruinous laws or institutions, which those in power forced upon them either by violence or fraud. They have swallowed the poison instead of hewing off the hand which treacherously tendered it. The atonement of the cowardice or indolence of nations is a miserable life of pain, repentance and sickness leading to untimely death.

Of such a fate Spain has been for centuries a fearful and warning example. If ever a land on the face of the earth bore upon its brow the stamp of divine favor, it is that of the Iberian peninsula. And what a revolting picture offends us, on casting our look on present Spain! As if Jehovah's curse of wickedness pressed upon it, her beautiful features are changed into ugliness. — God placed in the once so called garden of Europe a lordly race, well formed and richly endowed with the noblest attributes of the three races which then took the lead of the human family — the Roman, the Arab, and the German — and the land stretching forth like the clenched hand of Europe seemed destined to be the proud ornament of the freedom, happiness and honour of mankind. What is become of that hand which swayed the world? A crushed, wearied and bloody member, and what was once decked with gold and splendid gems, is now hung with iron chains.

A time was, when the Spaniards filled earth and sea with the dread of their arms and the glory of their deeds. In the sixteenth century there was no people greater or more powerful, none inspired with a stronger consciousness of its own might, or more deeply penetrated with glowing patriotism, none richer in all the blessings of civilization or more deserving of freedom, while religious faith and enthusiasm thrilled every fibre and inspired that feeling of invincibleness, which recoils at no hazard, and seeks for great dangers only for the sake of overcoming them. In those days half the world was beneath the feet of Spain, and the Spaniards lived and breathed in the proud consciousness that they were born to be the Earth's lords and masters. And their of Cortez and Pizarro well knew how to fulfil their mission. They plunged into the newly discovered lands of the West in search of gold and adventures, and to overthrow thrones and kingdoms. But from this very period, Spain, giddy of her fortune and glory abroad, neglected her prosperity at home, and the souls of her sons were bewildered in a universal pilgrimage to the shrines of conquest and robbery. The treasures which they brought back with them from America, excited the baser passions of covetousness and avarice at the cost of the nobler impulses of the mind. The strength of the nation was gradually exhausted by continual emigrations to the new world, and as it weakened and the public spirit degenerated, Royalty availed itself of the opportunity to increase its power and to extend its priveleges and prerogatives at the expense of popular freedom. While the Spaniards abroad subjected half of the American continent to their sway, chains were being forged for them at home, and while the colonies arose in splendour, the star of the mother-country waned and the blackest clouds obscured the Iberian sky. Night fell when at last the Bourbons — that race loaded with the curse and ruin of so many nations — succeeded in planting themselves on the Spanish throne. Then that shameless and arbitrary exercise of regal power stepped forth, which, emanating from the French court, spread itself little by little like a pest over Europe. What freedom yet remained in Spain, was either oppressed or degraded to empty forms, trade and industry were sacrificed to foreign interests, and the credit of the nation was ruined both at home and abroad by means of swindling financial operations, in order to provide the means for unbounded royal extravagance. What Kingcraft could not effect towards the destruction of the people, Priestcraft brought to pass. The Spanish clergy amassed incredilbe treasures. In her hands, which never ceased to feed the fires of the Inquisition, the fortunes of the citizens accumulated, and a third part of the entire surface of Spain became her property. The nobility were ruined at an extravagant court, and gradually the people became so brutalized, that they even lost the vivid recollection of their past greatness. Literature turned a beggar, science was no longer cultivated, art was dead. The state in all its relations was an image of weakness and decay when the storm of the French invasion blew across the Pyrenean mountains and awakened the nation to new life and action. Once more the spirit of old Spain appeared on the stage of History, when NAPOLEON with a bold grasp, shook from the throne the wretched and degenerate royal race, and declared the land to be his lawful booty. Then the Spanish people, to the astonishment of the world stood up in arms to regain liberty and maintain their independence. Spain became the grave of the invading armies, and for the first time the faith in the constant fortune and invincibility of the conqueror, gave way. The glory of Spain flared up during the five years of the peninsular war with a brilliant flame — but it was a transient fire – a Phœnix was wanting to the ashes, and a new Spain did not arise. Too long had the poison of despotism raged in the body of the people; no victories or warlike honours could effect an internal renovation, and as soon as all external opposition was withdrawn, and the Spanish soil was cleared of the presence of the enemy, the weary multitude relapsed into narcotic slumber. In vain did those fiery spirits who fain would raise the Spanish people to the blessings of freedom, try to excite them to the claim of a constitution and govermental reforms. The indolence of the masses and the craft of the Bourbon dynasty, who found no means too base, provided that they aided in restoring the golden age of unlimited royal power, were continually against them. The strife between these antagonistic forces kindled the civil war, and gave birth to the most brutal military despotism, that sacrificed the last patriots of the country.

In Spain we behold now a picture of national misery such as has never before been witnessed on earth. I do not mean to assert, that there are no countries quite as unhappy, for the sun shines on suffering nations all over the European continent; but the wretchedness of the people in Spain appears the more terrible, because the difference between the happy state of the land, as it might be, and that state in which it really is, is nowhere greater and more glaring. The philanthropist cares little for the boast that a Spanish monarch was once the lord of an empire on which the sun never ceased to shine. The lust of conquest belongs to the inexperienced youthful years of nations, and it never brings a blessing. But that so noble a race, that such a brave-hearted nation could sink so low, that it stupidly bows to the most despicable yoke, is grievous. Does it not appear as if the brave and strong man had become at once old and decrepid? Lazily and sadly the Spaniards trail after them their fetters, and scarcely a trace can now be seen of their former chivalric spirit, of their courage in battle, of their pride of freedom. And who is the cause? It must be repeated over and over again: Kings and Priests! Kings and Priests have murdered the country's pride and fettered its manliness. They have bound it in chains to quench every effort of its life, as they laid toll and tithe on every undertaking. They have oppressed the colonies until they rose and made themselves free. They have sacrificed fleets and armies to their thirst of absolute power and vanity. They have squandered millions after millions of the State's property upon the altars of folly and treachery. The kings and priests have for centuries done their utmost to destroy the nation and the empire. They have, with diabolical cunning, found out, and poisoned or ruined every source of prosperity. They have supported Inquisition and created Censorship, to fetter the liberty of thought and word. They have undermined and destroyed with the glittering vices of the court and by the unholy practices of the priesthood, the morality of the people, and have finally rewarded the noble strife of the nation for Independence with black ingratitude and sent her heroes and patriots to the dungeon or the gallows.

A civil war of twenty years has been ravaging the unhappy Peninsula. How often during this time have we heard the bells of Spain tolling not for prayer but for rebellion and fratricide; and how often will their melancholy peal ring a new over Spain before they summon to celebrate the liberation of the people from priestly darkness and princely chains! Will that day ever come? or will Spain breathe her last in fratricidal battles, or by the sentences of martial law? or will the nation linger on until some foreign conquering race mercifully plunges the steel into her heart, and shortens her agony?

We return from this digression to our engraving. — At the end of that bloody war of religions and races, — between the Christian Spaniard and the Moslim Arabian, between the Cross and the Crescent, — *Seville* the capital of a Caliphate, after a long and severe siege, was reduced to extremities. The outworks and suburbs were taken, and the besiegers summoned those within for the last time to surrender. But the Moors declared that they would not yield, unless their grand Mosque should be shielded from desecration, and unless this were granted they would fight until buried beneath the ruins of their city. In consequence a capitulation finally stipulated, that the temple which was honoured by the Arabians as the holiest in all Spain should immediately after surrender be levelled to the ground.

When King Ferdinand of Castile entered the city he was so much struck with the beauty of the edifice that he would not permit the execution of the order for its destruction, although this had already been commanded by his generals. To preserve the building, he broke his royal word. Be made of the Mosque a Cathedral, and from the lofty tower — *the Giralda* — Christian bells have been for well nigh four centuries tolling to mass and summoning the crowd to Christian worship.

TEHERAN

TEHERAN IN PERSIA.

The Name of Persia leads us back to the first beginning of chronology — to the threshold of History. Persia is the site of old Iran, the land hiding the mystery of our origin as tradition narrates it. There was the garden inhabited by the first parents of mankind, where blossomed and withered the forbidden tree, where language was stammered forth in the first tones of the human voice, where the necessities of life taught the first arts, and where the spirit of man developed the first shoots of that wondrous flower of human knowledge which now after a growth of many centuries, unfolds itself in thousand colours. In Iran it was, where the young race fought its Titan-battles with Heaven in the first of wars and in Iran it was when a revengeful God poured forth his floods over sinful Man and where the first bark rescued on the heights of Mount Ararat the last family of the perishing race. In Iran too, it was that man built the first hut, and in Iran we find the first beginnings and foundations of Society, the first laws, the first attempts to form a state. There the heroes and conquerors stepped forth, there the first minstrels sang who immortalized their names. And again in Iran it was that the right of the strong led to the rule of the one over the many — that Monarchy had its origin and from the same point the first propagators of monarchical doctrines went forth with the conquering. Thus originated the old kingdoms of India, Egypt, Palestine, Syria, Saba, Asia-Minor and Phrygia and from Iran those richly gifted children of God, the Greeks, begun their mission to vindicate and strengthen for ever the supremacy of the spirit over matter, and to bless the earth with the treasures of refinement and civilization. There too, in later times, Cyrus, that great hero, was born who resolved to subdue the world. With Cyrus, the founder of the Persian power, who conquered Babylon and subdued all Asia Minor, the history of Persia Proper begins, and never did it shine with more splendor than during the reign of this monarch and his successor Cambyses who united Egypt, Cyprus and Tyre to his empire. The later kings of Cyrus' race were fools or tyrants. They sat upon their thrones and wielded the sceptre like a sword, or, giddy of their power and absolute sway, played the part of gods. Execrable despots they slayed the nations with the iron rod. At last the storm with which Alexander the Great overthrew the kingdoms of the ancient world, also put an end to the dynasty of Cyrus. From this time reigned the Seleucides, a dynasty who were followed by the Alsacides, whose dominion over Persia lasted for nearly five hundred years (until 229). The constant wars with the Roman power began in these days and occupied the first century of the ensuing dynasty of the Sassanides. The period of their rule was a sad one until the conquest of the Arabs. Ancient Persia declined during the endless civil and foreign strife which raged during this period. Its cities, invaded, laid waste and neglected, disappeared, and the people gradually relapsed into a barbarous state. Several of the Sassanides were valiant and powerful kings, but their course was like that of meteors followed by flames of fire, and the lands over which they shot were reddened with blood. Kosru the Second subdued Central Asia, penetrated to the heart of Africa, laid Athiopia and Lybia in chains, and like another Timour, made Arabia feel his power. Such warfaring expeditions might result in brilliant conquests, but they were no blessing to the people. The strength and power of Persia withered in wars and strife, and the kings after the death of the second Kosru, were instances of weakness and dissention. The last of the royal race was a mere play-thing of parties and factions. Feud prevailed among the aristocratic families of the empire, and the kingdom was in a perpetual state of anarchy. To hasten her destruction, destiny sent against Persia the lion of the Saracen. Bearing in on hand the Koran, in the other the sword, Omar, the successor of the Great Prophet, stormed forth against the defenceless land, and exterminating its ancient government and religion, raised upon the tombs of the kingly race and amid the ruins of their cities, the Arabian throne, defended by the shield of the new faith and strengthened by the new ideas which now propagated all over the East. The Arabian domination lasted in Persia for well nigh six centuries (from 636 until 1220) until Chenghis Khan with his innumerable hordes of Mongols and Tartars broke forth from his steppes like a hurricane, destroying and laying waste half Asia. Before the ravaging hordes the Arab dominion in Central Asia gave way, and Persia remained for two hundred years subject to the Mongols, during which period every trace of its former civilization and refinement disappeared. Tamurlane was the last Mongolian ruler. Then the Turcomans entered on the stage of History and founded several dynasties. Persia was in those days waste and abandoned. It fell an easy prey to every daring chief who seized upon it. Utterly exhausted it was compelled to yield to the every invader. Not until the beginning of the sixteenth century was it that a firm hand grasped again the sceptre in the person of *Shah Abbas,* a great king (1587—1629). This man reorganised the kingdom, and by successful wars restored to it many provinces which had been conquered by neighbouring powers. His dynasty ended with Shah Nadir, who in vain once more elevated Persia to power. Nadir was murdered. At his death Persia fell asunder into four kingdoms, which made war on each other, and have never since been united. The Afghans ruled in Cabul and Afghanistan; Georgia, after a short independence, became gradually subject to of the Turks and Russians, and Persia Proper through a succession of unfortunate wars with the latter, has until the most recent times been continually losing its best provinces to Russia. Persia is at present a ruined state, externally weak and defenceless, and internally bleeding under the lash of the grossest despotism imaginable, subject to a system of government that consists in incessant plunder, oppression and torture. It will inevitably become the prey of Russia, as soon as England is obliged to retreat from Central Asia, no longer able to hold in check the ambitions projects of the Moscovite power.

Teheran, the present Capital of Persia, — (it was in the place of Ispahan elevated to the seat of government) — gives a true picture of the ruined state of the country. Although the youngest of the Persian cities, it is for the greater part a heap of rubbish. The Capital is a collection of ten thousand wretched mud huts, arranged as chance or accident would have it, into crooked, narrow, filthy lanes, from among or above which, the cupola of a mosque, the roof of a barrack, the walls of the palace of the Shah, a few poplars or some plane trees project. A dry ditch surrounded by a mud-wall encircles the city, which in every respect, presents a spectacle of misery, filth and and poverty. In no place is a vestige of order or governemental care to be found. The inhabitants pass on in indolence and melancholy with fear and reserve in their countenances, nor is a trace of intellect perspicuous in their doings and movements. On the face of every one we see it plainly written, that man is here only the slave of his ruler — that neither person nor property are in security, and consequently that no man keeps account with the future. Without thought or reflection they live on from day to day, uncertain, what the fate of the next hour may bring them.

Teheran contains about forty thousand inhabitants — little for the capital of a kingdom, which is as large as the original thirteen States of our Union and has a population of fourteen millions! The royal dwelling, the barracks, and the citadel occupy the third part of the city. The sabre is the sceptre. The Shah maintains an army, the strength of which is a guard of eight thousand men, a part of which is continually occupied in the collection of taxes, which is exclusively a military operation, a system of brutal extortion and plunder, that exhausts the last sources of national prosperity and public welfare.

For the Proprietor HERRMANN J. MEYER.

THE TOMB OF WASHINGTON

WASHINGTON'S TOMB.

BY CHARLES A. DANA.

The tomb where rest the ashes of WASHINGTON was constructed some fifteen years ago on a spot which he himself had long before chosen for the purpose. It stands on a hill-side overlooking a woody dell not far from the mansion of Mount Vernon, and is built of brick covered in front with a simple rough-cast coating that is much damaged by the influence of the weather. The pillars on each side the doorway are of freestone; on a pannel fixed over the iron door the visitor may read these words:

„*I am the Resurrection and the Life; He that believeth in me though he were dead, yet shall he live.*"

Our engraving presents a view of the walls enclosing the tomb. These walls are of brick twelve feet high; upon a slab above the iron gate is the simple inscription:

„WITHIN THIS ENCLOSURE REST THE REMAINS OF GENERAL GEORGE WASHINGTON."

The body of Washington was deposited here in 1837 in a marble sarcophagus prepared for the purpose. It had previously remained in the vault occupied by the mortal relics of the various members of the Washington family. On removing it, the leaden coffin was found to have sunken in and become somewhat fractured, so as to expose to view the head and breast of its tenant, which seemed but little affected by the influence of time. The forehead was still broad and massive, the eye sockets were spacious and profound, and the chest that of a man of unusual size. The grave-clothes had disappeared. The removal, which was performed by torch-light and without any ceremony, lasted but a short time; the leaden coffin was closed again and finally deposited in the sarcophagus, no more, as we trust, to be disturbed.

The tomb even more than the mansion of Washington bears the marks of neglect and decay. The paths leading to it are uncared for and overgrown with weeds and brambles, which nothing seems to disturb, except the feet of pious visitors. The indifference of the Nation to the home and the last resting place of its most illustrious patriot is loudly and justly complained of, and appeals are sometimes made to the people to purchase the humble estate of Mount Vernon and have it suitably kept at the public expense. But these appeals have never been so efficacious as to lead to action on the part of Congress, and even if this venerable locality be redeemed from the encroachments of decay, and caused to bloom, as it should do, with the varied beauty of art and nature, we fear that it must be through the combined contribution of private individuals. It is a fact worthy of attention, that the American democracy does not pay a very ardent *personal* devotion to its heroes and sages. With their best wisdom incorporated in its institutions, and their noble examples shining along the paths of its history, there seems after all to be an instinct which ascribes honor more to principles than to persons, and which in urging forward the republic to a destiny of untold power and usefulness does not linger to offer incense on the altars of the past. It cannot justly be said that this is a new proof of the base ingratitude of republics, for no name is more dearly cherished and beloved by any people than that of Washington by Americans. But it would appear to demonstrate that, as the mass of men have been elevated, the age of hero-worship, of the domination of single individuals, of the towering of isolated persons over the crowd of small and grovelling beings at their feet, has passed away. Such seems to be the true cause why such apparent neglect is shown to the abode and the

MOUNT ETNA

grave of the mortal Washington; it is that the immortal spirit which he breathed into his country and the vast destiny on which he so nobly helped to send it forth, impel the people to other duties and to more productive efforts than the guardianship of ancient houses or of tombs, no matter how great and memorable their inhabitants. Democracy, in the large and comprehensive sense, — is no respecter of persons and devotes itself solely to the service of humanity.

But whatever be the reason of this negligence it is none the less painful to every visitor to Mount Vernon, and we cannot but hope that if the matter should continue to be neglected by the Federal Legislature, private persons of liberality and patriotism will come forward and not only render Mount Vernon the property of the people, but at the same time provide for its being appropriately kept and repaired. But we must confess that our hope even of this, is not very sanguine.

MOUNT ETNA AND CATANIA.

As the greatest minds are born from the lowest strata of humankind, so are the highest mountains the children of the abyss. They were generated by Plutonic power in the depths of the earth, and their rise to the clouds was frequently the gradual work of many ages. Children of the Earth, they are like all earthly things subject to change. The mountains of older date are, indeed, in most cases mere ruins, around which destruction, during the long space of time which separates the grand mutations in the earth's crust, has heaped masses of rubbish. Instances of it are the Alps, the Rocky Mountains, the Pyrenean and the Carpathian chain, the Apennines, and that last stronghold of classic heroism, the Caucasus.

In a better state of preservation are the plutonic mountains of modern date. It is shown in the volcanoes of the two last periods of the earths formation. As the chimneys of mighty furnaces in the bowels of the Earth, they tower from unknown depths up to the sky. To this class of mountains belongs the Etna, the highest elevation in Sicily — the greatest and most remarkable, the most powerful and in its effects the most terrible volcano of Europe. Above 11,000 feet high it consists of a single cone, without a ridge, without high plains or terraces, without valleys or rivers. The enormous mass rests on a basis of twenty four square miles, and its flame-vomiting crater penetrates the region of eternal snow. In all Europe only some peaks of the Alps, and a few points of the Sierra Nevada surpass it in height.

Mount Etna stands with one foot on the plains of Catania, and with the other towards the East, deeply planted in the sea. The base is circular. The conical summit exactly occupies the centre, and the sides spread forth like a roof, in every direction, more or less steep. The peak is formed of the encircling-wall of the principal crater, — a fiery throat which is more than two miles in circumference. Hundreds of smaller craters surround the cone on every side in various shapes, which though large enough when regarded by themselves, appear when compared with the great cone, like mere mole-hills.

The whole mountain is of volcanic origin. It consists of lava, some hundred strata, each varying in thickness and colour, with alternate deposits of gypsum, sulphur and ashes. With the latter the upper regions are entirely covered. A few sulphurous springs run from the lower part of the mountain.

Mount Etna is classic ground for scientific observation. For those who wish to study the influence which elevation exercises upon climate and the vegetable world, no place more convenient can be found in the old world. Probably in no part of Europe are the different zones of vegetation so accurately marked, or so distinctly presented to observation. The peasants and shepherds inhabiting the mountain have indicated these relations by names. They divide the Etna into three regions, the cultivated part, the forest, and the waste. The first extends to the height of twenty five hundred feet. Here the most luxuriant vegetation prevails in numberless vineyards, superb fields of wheat and barley, and in groves of southern fruits. The flora on the sunny slopes of the central-side is truly tropical. Sugar-cane and cotton are cultivated with success and a great variety of the cactus-family clothes the black rocks with a splendid array of brightly coloured flowers. The forest or second zone extends to the height of six thousand feet. The children of the tropics, with the orange and olive-tree, are here no longer visible, the tender almond hardly thrives in protected nooks and higher up even the vine no longer embraces the elm. The true lords of this region are noble species of the pine, oak and poplar, forming forests really majestic. In the lower range dominate the olive, the walnut and the chestnut-tree, which attain an almost incredible size. Many of these giants are known by special names for centuries. One chestnuttree is called the tree of the hundred riders; somewhat above the ground it measures one hundred and eighty feet in circumference. Around the upper border of that second zone the forest-vegetation ceases entirely and nothing remains save the creeping juniper, and the barberry-bush with its bunches of red berries. — The third and highest zone extends from a height of seven thousand five hundred feet, to the edge of the crater. Trees and herbs have disappeared. The soil is covered with bare black lava and ashes and some varieties of cryptogamic plants, which occur in the lower part of this region. Although Mount Etna extends above the limit of eternal snow, yet owing to the intense volcanic heat which warms its sides, snow and ice can as little remain on it, as upon the margin of a heated stove. The heaviest snow-storms clothe the cone in white but for some days. — The ascent of the Etna is a difficult undertaking and requires more than ordinary courage and great vigour of body. It is generally made from the sea-side, starting from Catania, and takes a two days' journey. The first night is passed in „The English House“ erected 1811 at joint expense by the British residents of Sicily. It is situated thirteen hundred feet below the centre cone, and near the spot where according to the legend of classic yore Empedocles had his cell. There is a path practicable for mules up to this station and the traveller can ride; the rest of the journey he is obliged to perform on foot. In vain he looks out for a path in the dreary wilderness; frequently he is forced to climb up with hands and feet. In general the ascent is extremely difficult and wearisome, owing to the danger of slipping on the ashes and the loose polished fragments of pumice-stone. The edge of the principal crater is practicable only from a deep chasm formed by a rent in the walls. A look from its margin into the depth of the fiery abyss is truly terrible. The entire inner wall of the crater is covered with sulphur blocks of ghastly shapes, blackened with smoke and soot, and the heated imagination readily forms them into the devilish and misshapen figures of gnomes and dragons, which glare, grinning and threatening, upon the excited traveller. In the deepest recess of the abyss the actual passage leading to the hidden workshop of the earth is visible through volumes of smoke and flames. Orange-coloured sulphurous gas bursts hizzing forth from the orifice, a blazing lava-torrent boils and foams on its banks, and with mysterious groans and dreadful sighs are dashed upward from time to time red-hot masses of rocks and stone against the sides of the crater, as if the rebellious gnomes below in their rage were trying to demolish their prison. The thought of climbing down the inner wall of the crater is of itself sufficient to inspire terror. Yet its has been attempted by many, and by some successfully. The intrepid curiosity of man is stronger than his fear of death and travellers have approached so near the fiery gulf as to cast stones therein, and have distinctly heard the boiling and roaring in the earth's bowels. Mr. *d'Orville*, a Frenchman, was the first who performed, what many before him had attempted in vain. He descended by a rope, one end of which was bound around his waist. To his astonishment and disappointment he found the opening closed, and in its place a vault of glowing lava, from the crevices of which lightnings darted, and flames, bright as those of gas. It is now a well established fact that the crater from time to time changes its form, and the furnace underneath ceases working.

The view from the pinnacle of the Etna is incomparable — „the recollection of it makes Man happy“. On no side chains of mountains frame the panorama — for the neighbouring rows shrink down to hills from Mount Etna, and land and sea with its fairy islands spread out like a plain to the distance of one hundred and fifty miles in every direction. We fancy to soar in the blue sky, though with the happy and ever-present feeling of standing on terra firma. Sicily lies at our feet, as a city seen from her highest steeple. The Liparian isles swimning in the transparent ocean are so clearly defined and seem to be so near that one might be tempted to grasp at them with the hand. The strait of Reggio winds like a silver snake between the separated lands, on the other side hilly Calabria is seen to rise, and far, far away over its mountains our glance sweeps in triumph over the bright Ionian sea, in search of the blue hills of glorious Greece. The gulf of Naples is indicated by the pillar of smoke of Vesuvius, which however from this height and distance appears but a mole-hill. In the extreme North we recognise the summits of the Sardinian mountains, and the rocks of Gaeta, the Gibraltar of Italy, while in an opposite direction, when the atmosphere is clear, the naked eye discovers the coast-ridge of the African Continent.

As the great deeds of great men are separated by long intervals of time, while the exertions of activity manifested by smaller souls rush on in restless, quick succession — so is an eruption of Mount Etna a far less common occurrence than that of its fire-spouting little neighbour. A year seldom passes in which Vesuvius does not delight or terrify with its performances, while the outbreaks of Etna occur in long intervals, three or four times during a century. Its ordinary peaceful state is indicated by columns of white smoke ascending from its summit to the sky; but when the canals to the furnace underneath are choked up and want cleansing, the operation is manifested by the smoke becoming darker, by lightnings darting from its towering columns at night, and a hollow, noise heard for miles around issues from the entrails of the mountain. This state lasts for some weeks, during which time the quantity and blackness of the smoke is constantly on the increase, and the lightnings grow more vivid and more frequent. Then on a sudden, flames some thousand feet high, are seen breaking forth, which gradually form a perpetual column of fire of surpassing grandeur, subterranean roaring and groaning frightens man and beast, thunder rolls, the Earth trembles and seems to quiver with terror. Earthquakes split the sides of the mountain, yellow tinted sulphur-smoke rushes from the rents. By the force of the subterranean fire, new furnaces open here and there on the sides of the mountain; the summits of newly raised cones burst with dreadful explosions and from the orifices blazing fluids are spouted in all directions, huge, glowing fragments of rocks are hurled forth, and clouds of ashes obscure the sun and fall down upon sea and land like a fiery rain. This grand spectacle continues commonly for several weeks without interruption, often accompanied by earthquakes with their terrific and devastating consequences. At last the bubbling lava fills the giant tub of the principal crater to the brim, and forth it streams over the wall, a furious torrent, moving on with incredible velocity, and tumbling down the sides of the mountain. Streams of boiling sulphureous water often break at the same time from the sides, which, when meeting the flaming lava-torrent, explode with detonations like from a hundred batteries, audible in the distance of twenty leagues. The lava-torrents of Etna often have a breadth of several miles, and they continue to flow for months, until their subterranean source is exhausted. Then they begin to harden; a process which often requires a year or two for completion. While the lava is streaming, the flames of the crater, the rain of ashes and stones and the earthquakes never cease. Day turns into night, and night into day. Cities are overthrown, valleys are filled up, forests perish in flames, and where centuries of human labor had created an Eden, a wilderness is left. Yet in the course of a few decades of years a fresh and young life sprouts forth on the rent and dreary black crust which was once a stream of fire, for the porous lava is soon decomposed, and the warmed soil fosters the most luxuriant vegetation. The fertility of the land round Etna is proverbial and so alluring that man, though often chased away by the wrath of the mountain-gnomes, invariably returns into their realm, caring nothing for their tricks and terrors.

Among the recent eruptions of the volcano the most celebrated one happened 1832 which laid waste the vicinity of Bronte, and destroyed vast forests. Of elder eruptions none was more terrible, than that of 1669. The very preparations and warnings of the mountain startled all Sicily. Eighteen days before the outbreak the heavens were black with smoke and lightning flashed and thunder rolled incessantly. At the same time the neighboring volcanoes were in labor; Stromboli and Vesuvius belched forth flames, announcing the crisis of the mightier destroyer. On the eleventh of March, after a pause of two hours, Etna itself burst forth with a sudden and terrible crash toward the direction of Catania, and a fire-torrent, many thousand feet in breadth, at once issued from the vast rent, seeking the plain like a cataract. During the same night the sides of the mountain opened in many places, and from the fissures the melted lava poured down, wasting and burning all in its course. This lasted until the twentyfifth of March, when the volcano was so terribly shattered by earthquakes, that the great cone, a mass 1800 feet high and 3 miles in circumference at its base, fell in with a crash, that made the earth tremble and struck all Sicily with terror. The immense gulf thus formed sent forth a volume of flames, ashes and smoke of proportionate dimensions and spouted the fragments of the cone, either glowing or half-melted, some weighing thousands of tons, like shuttle-cocks to the distance of miles. The lava-flood in a little time reached the plains at the foot of Etna — a paradise, studded with towns and villages and thickly populated. Before its flaming, flashing, thundering waves, towns fell and were destroyed, and villages and forests vanished like dry leaves before the storm. The huge walls of the city of Catania were overturned, and after destroying the town completely, the torrent, on reaching the shore dashed from the high bluffs at once into the deep. The ocean, so rudely attacked, beamed and foamed mountain high, seething and raging and boiling with a noise more terrible than the loudest thunder. Ancient streams of lava, which had been cultivated for centuries, were melted again by the subterranean heat, and with horror the fugitives beheld farmhouses, vineyards, and woodland blazing and floating in the fiery inundation till they vanished in the waves. Within the space of forty days, the period of the eruption, the houses, gardens, and fields of thirty seven thousand families were destroyed, and of the twenty thousand inhabitants of Catania, seventeen thousand perished.

This was not the first time that this ill-fated city had been destroyed by Mount Etna. Thrice already had the lava filled her streets, and thrice had it changed Life into Death. Not less frequently had the God of War visited her. Dionysius conquered and burnt Catania. Ruined and laid waste in the Punic war, Augustus colonised her anew. In later times she fell by turns in the hands of Goths, Vandals and Saracens, destruction following destruction. And yet it has ever and again risen fair and bright. The wonderful fertility of the country, her beautiful situation, and the tropical climate have ever attracted after each overthrow a new population, and at the present day, Catania, with more than seventy thousand inhabitants, is, if not the largest, at least the most prospering and wealthy town of Sicily.

BRESCIA IN ITALY

Published for HERRMANN J. MEYER. 164. William-Street, NEWYORK.

BRESCIA IN ITALY.

The Italians say: „to get forward in the world one must be somewhat of a fool.“ The recipe is a good one. It saves many a tear, and much hard thinking. Another proverb gives the counsel „Wait a while!“ A small dose of folly and a large dose of patience are surely good things in these odd times, and the Italians and Germans particularly may avail themselves of the medicine. When after the expulsion of the French, Austria took half Italy into her iron arms, and almost stifled the poor land with the caresses of her love, when among the people the belief prevailed, that their tyranny would last till dooms-day, fate counselled: „Wait a while!“ And when at the crowing of the French cock excited Italy arose in arms, and hope hang out the return of the golden age on the banners of national liberty and independence, fate counselled again: — „Wait a while!“ And when the drama had played out, and the signal-fires on the mountains had been quenched, and national colours and carbonari-hats taken away, and the long and bristly beards, worn à la Republicaine, had been shaved off, and the Habsburg-gallows erected where the trees of liberty had stood, and councilhouses were turned into barracks and it was called mercy to execute a patriot with powder and lead: — fate again whispered: „Wait a while; for the bow which is too tightly bent will certainly break.“

Brescia, — matron in mourning — a time will come when thou wilt lay aside thy black widow's garment, and all Italy will haste to clothe thee like a bride for the bridal. The blood which a hyena in the form of man has poured forth in streams, has not washed out from memory the seed which thou hast strewed in the storm of inspiration and sacrifice, and in far distant times history will yet speak of thy martyrdom for the noblest cause!

The City of Brescia traces its origin back to the mythic times of Greece. She claims Hercules as her founder. Laid waste by the first invasions of the Gauls, Brennus restored her. Having become large and wealthy during the days of the Republic and under the Emperors, it flourished until taken by the Huns under Attila, who entirely extirpated all vestiges of Roman life. Then the Goths governed her, and the Lombards settled on her ruins making her the capital of a dukedom. Brescia rose and fell during that eventful and sombre period, in which Upper-Italy — after a century of repose, — was afflicted with all the evils of war and desolation attendant upon a frequent change of government and conquerors. It found the German yoke too heavy to be borne, and Brescia was one of the first Lombard cities which valiantly rose against the Emperor. Its strife for independence abounded in heroic deeds, and the Brescians manifested in defending their city the same bravery which they displayed on the field of battle. In the fourteenth century six thousand citizens resisted a German army six times as numerous, commanded by king Henry of the Luxemburgh dynasty. In 1412 the women of Brescia, headed by the heroine Brigitta Avogadro, successfully defended their city against the besieging army under Piccinino, during the absence of the men who were at that time engaged on another field of battle. In 1429 Brescia fell in the hands of the Venetians, who, too weak to guard their new acquisition, surrendered it after the battle of Aguadello in 1509 to the French. After three years oppression the place shook off the foreign yoke; but a French army under Gaston de Foix, advanced against it, and took it by storm. The fate of the conquered town was terrible. The wild, foreign soldiery gave themselves up to every excess. Nine thousand Brescians were slain in the streets, and after a sackage of seven days, their city was burnt to the ground.

It rose again from its ashes, thanks to that energy of soul and will which is the inheritance of the inhabitants. Their Freedom was lost; but their industry created a new prosperity, and this has been maintained and continually increased until the most recent times. Even the hand of the infamous Haynau, which punished with terrible cruelty the Brescians for their obstinacy in maintaining the late struggle for Italian independence, and gave over the conquered city to the sword and the flames, though able to throw every family into mourning, could not dry up the springs of industry. These are to be found in the breeding of silk-worms and in extensive manufactories of iron and steel goods.

Brescia is situated at the foot of the Rhaetian Alps, on the margin of the fertile plain of the Po, surrounded by pleasant scenery, with a mild southern climate, and sheltered by mountain walls from the rough winds of the North and East. All the country in the circumference of many miles is like a garden where the fig and orange ripen in the open air, and where the olive and the mulberry tree, clad with grape vines, cover all hills and fields. The town itself ranges among the most magnificent of Italy. Intersected by broad streets, Brescia contains a multitude of public squares and places, adorned with monuments and fountains, many of which are of marble and masterpieces of Art. The Brescians are said to be quarrelsome, passionate and brave even to rashness. True it is that their love of liberty is the „red thread“ which connects the eventful history of the city. The love of liberty has often given them success and glory, at times dreadful chastisement and not unfrequently destruction. The number of inhabitants in Brescia exceeds now forty thousand. The old castle on the nearest hill is, by the Austrians, converted into a fortress, to keep the citizens under an iron yoke. Brescia is the seat of a bishopric, of a seminary, gymnasium, lyceum, athenæum, musical academy, and contains beside many valuable collections, a museum of natural history, a botanic garden, a public library of fifty thousand volumes including many manuscripts of the middle ages, a picture gallery, and a cabinet of engravings. Its most remarkable

PALAIS DE LA LEGION D'HONNEUR

(Paris)

Published by HERRMANN J. MEYER. 164, William-Street. NEW-YORK.

BIRMINGHAM IN ENGLAND

Published for HERRMANN J. MEYER, 164, William-Street, NEW YORK.

of all every fact in public life is brought to light and cannot escape discussion; every invention, wherever made, is soon made the property of the public; every event becomes notorious, and is discussed and decided in reference to its causes; every expressed opinion finds its adversary, who submits it to correction; and the inexorable genius of criticism, which penetrates every subject with its sharp analysis, purifies the judgment.

In this judgment we see manifested the power of public opinion. It is a power before which all the potentates of the civilized world, either with „*bonne mine*“ or with gnashing teeth, are bowing. By its judgment all those falsehoods, by which the worn-out craft of diplomacy has so long deceived the credulous crowds, are brought to nothing. All the plausible, hollow phrases of hypocrisy appear before its bar as „very nothings“; all the masks which have been hung around the face of truth are drawn away, and those who move in the darkness of royal antichambers and cabinets, enveloped in the broad mantle of court-craft, are pilloried by the names, which they receive from an enlightened public opinion, long before they are called away to receive their last judgment; facts and events, purposes and endeavors, which the tyrants think concealed in the most profound obscurity, are exposed to the eye of the world; and what is not less remarkable, those who are most concerned in keeping the secret, often break it themselves by the futile attempt of a justification of their cause, even before it is called before the public. It is of no avail to think, that by fettering the press, or purchasing its organs, the verdict of public opinion may be falsified. On the contrary, it is only the more severe against those, who despotically forbid the free expression of thought, and thus deprive themselves of even the means of defence.

Among the different moving powers, which characterize the age, none is stronger than that which is properly called the industrial. Its spirit is a creative one, destroying for the sake of reconstruction, and putting the old to death in order to bring the new to life. Industry strives to take the lead in the affairs of the present, and it is conscious of its high position in the empire of the future. Devoted constantly to progress, it attaches little importance to the present, or the past, and every positive influence which obstructs its restless activity arouses its hatred. The spirit of industry, begotten by the day which gave it birth, and entertaining little estcem for past facts and men, can scarcely avoid arrogance in the consciousness of its strength and it openly asserts its claim to the highest position in a future reconstructed society.

The pressure of the times and the general discontent that arms the desire to bring about a change by revolution, throw the majority of monarchical rulers in conflict with the wants and demands of the age, among which the claims of industry stand in the first rank. We see some governments reluctantly making concessions in the attempt to avoid the storm, and others resolved to face it in downright opposition. Phrases, which have long lost their nominal value, are profusely lavished for a compromise by the former; favors which cost nothing are perpetually paraded by them, and concessions made in one moment, which are taken back in another; while by the downright opponents the most humble claims are denied with scorn or prosecuted as crimes.

But the spirit of Industry is not that of a baby, which is satisfied with toys, or terrified with hard words. It has outgrown the children's dress; it confronts government as a man; it sternly demands a wise economy from the State, a just and honorable disposition to advance every thing good, and constant readiness to satisfy all equitable claims for the support of the useful. As the due representative of national labor, Industry is constantly urging the Legislatures for due protection.

While in this respect an excited, violent, constant commotion prevails on the whole Continent of Europe, we look almost with envy on the quiet and cheering spectacle presented by Great Britain, which is produced by the harmonious co-operation of the intelligence and power of the government and of the people. In England, the questions of Industry have long been solved and its high position established beyond doubt; it is recognised as the most conspicuous fact in the history of the century; it is honored as the Genius that constantly breathes invigorating life into the heart of the mass of the population and as the groundwork of the political glory of Great Britain.

A fine image of the creative power of British Industry is presented in the view, which we are going to describe.

As Thebes was once called the city of the hundred gates, Birmingham may be called the city of the hundred thousand anvils. „Its streets ring with the blows of the hammer“, said old Camden long ago. „But those anvils and those hammers“, observes Kohl, the Economist, „with which the ancients mastered the resisting metal, have been transformed, on the one hand, into such powerful machines, and on the other, into such small and nice tools, that the poetical expression of Camden is no longer appropriate.“

If we go back to the early condition of the English manufacturing cities, and examine the source of their present world-embracing activity, we shall usually find an establishment for the working of iron. Even Manchester, the city of Cotton, took its rise in this branch of industry. Its master-spinners and weavers have succeeded the smiths, who in their turn have been transformed into mechanics.

The metallurgical manufactories of Great-Britain are generally divided into three classes. The first refers to the construction of large, heavy, and coarse articles of Iron, such as rails, boilerplate, ships, iron bridges, chain-cables, and so forth. Their principal seats are the Clyde and Wales, where Merthyr-Tydvill is famous as the most extensive establishment. The second class embraces all kinds of machinery large and small, coarse and fine. This branch is chiefly cultivated in Newcastle, Glasgow, Manchester, and for the manufacture of tools, in some towns of Lancashire.

Cutlery, including every possible variety of cutting-instruments, is chiefly confined to the industry of Sheffield; and that city which furnishes half the world with different other kinds of iron-, copper-, brass-, plated-, silver- and gold-wares, is Birmingham. Twenty thousand different articles are manufactured in this town alone. A description of them would fill an Encyclopedia of many volumes. Every people, every country, every degree of cultivation finds in Birmingham a ready supply of its needs. Some hundred and sixty jewellers furnish ornaments to the fair princesses of Europe, and to the sable queens of Africa, and even the poorest slave who cultivates the hot soil of Brasil under the lash of his driver, finds in Birmingham a busy hand, which for a few paras will place a glittering ornament in his ear, striving to please his rude taste, and give him an agreable article. What a profound and comprehensive study of the manners and the customs of the inhabitants of the globe is required to do this well, and to offer nothing but what is appropriate to every zone and every degree of human culture! What a mass of ethnographic knowledge must be brought to the service of speculation, where a single error may cause ruin!

The division of labor is the key to the riddle why Birmingham can offer its wares cheaper than any other place, although manual labor is nowhere paid better. Almost every article has its special manufacturer. The maker of spurs for fighting-cocks, and the maker of coffin-nails will make no other kind of spur or nail. Their whole industrial ingenuity and effort is confined to improving or cheapening a cock's spur or a coffin-nail. It is surprising for what diminutive and apparently unimportant articles, manufactories are erected, and what immense capitals are devoted to ingenious machines which have no higher object than to save manual labor in some detail of the process, and to lessen a small fraction of the cost of the manufacture, hardly amounting to a shilling in several thousand pieces. Steel-pens, for instance, which so rapidly have come into general use are at present an extensive article of manufacture in Birmingham; they employ 2500 workmen, steam-engines to the amount of 400 horse powers, and a million Sterling of capital. One workman with the aid of the machinery makes about a million of pens in a year, 2500 millions are accordingly annually manufactured in Birmingham, and there are some establishments using above 50 tons of steel-plate in the business. Of no less importance are the fish-hook makers, who now almost exclusively supply the whole world with their article. The manufacture of plated ware supports several thousand workmen, and the quantity of silver which is used for plating is almost incredible. Sixteen thousand are employed in the manufacture of *papier maché*, 14,000 in the manufacture of buttons, and a still larger number in the manufacture of fire-arms with which Birmingham, the rival of Liège, provides not only most of the European armies, but with some exceptions, the armies of the rest of the world in every zone and clime. The show-rooms of the manufacturers exhibit weapons of every form, and for every taste, from the long, richly ornamented musket of the Tscherkessians to the short rifle with which the Abyssinian kills the gazelle of the desert. The manufacture of fire-arms in Birmingham furnishes about 6000 pieces a week; but there is sufficient machinery and power, to produce more than three times that number. Within the present century above 28 millions of fire-arms have been made at Birmingham — a sufficient number to arm the whole population of Europe capable of bearing arms.

Birmingham, a city of more than 200,000 inhabitants, and at least twice as large as Boston, with its forest of gigantic chimneys, the true signs of extensive mechanical industry, presents an imposing appearance in the distance. Its interior is of humbler cast and does not confirm the impression from a far. In architectural splendor, it is inferior to many other manufacturing cities of England, especially Manchester. While Manchester abounds with proud and extensive establishments and colossal warehouses, displaying great beauty of construction, and the magnificent stations of a dozen rail-ways often erected at an extravagant expense, rise in imposing splendor, — industry appears in Birmingham in the simple costume demanded by necessity, and the rail-ways that concentrate in that city are but few. The manufacturers, generally speaking, have seldom more capital than is required for carrying on their business, and they are therefore not willing to erect costly buildings. The greater part of the independent population consists of small manufacturers whose property amounts to 1000—3000 pounds sterling. They are employed, moreover, in a kind of business, which puts the construction of such monstrous establishments, as cotton-spinning and weaving require, out of the question. Astor-fortunes are unknown in Birmingham: and where wealth exists, it is not exposed to view. A comfortable living, equally distant from opulence and from poverty, is universal.

The City covers a space of about nine English square miles. The streets are kept clean, and regularly laid out; showing great uniformity. You may often walk for a quarter of an hour, without seeing a building, that impresses you by its magnitude or elegance. Even the public edifices bear the character of simplicity; very few are able to compare with those of York or Philadelphia in style and vastness. They are crowded into the centre of the City. Within the space of half a mile, the principal church, the town-hall, the high schools, the large hotels, the exchange, the museum have their sites. Birmingham is destitute of a river-communication which would enliven its environs. A small brook feeds a little lake; but the foul water does not contribute to the attractions of the Landscape.

The establishments of metallic manufacture, of which Birmingham is the centre, extend far beyond the limits of the City proper. Those of nails, lamps, candlesticks, hooks, screws, files, buckles, needles, rings and buttons are of the greatest extent imaginable. The hardware-business is carried on chiefly in the neighboring towns of Dudley, Wollsall, Wednesbury, Wolverhampton, Bilston and Stourbridge. Immensity is the character of this industry and a description of its details would surpass belief.

Gez. v. C. Reiss

LIÈGE AND SERAING

Published for HERRMANN J. MEYER, 164. William-Str. NEWYORK

LIEGE AND SERAING.

Motion is the Genius of the day. Religion and Science, government and property, ideas and opinions are in perpetual fluctuation. We might say, nothing is constant, save inconstancy. As the principal motor of this general movement the press is conspicuous, the press — in spite of the thousand fetters laid on it. When Gutenberg and Fust took the first printed sheet from their press, church and state exclaimed: „crucify the traitors!“ They were persecuted and their first press was destroyed as a tool of Satan. What did it avail? In the stead of that one, a hundred thousand presses are now at work, and the hand of time is rubbing, gnawing and rusting at the chains so incessantly, that however busy the hammers are to rivet the broken links and re-unite them, it is evident, that the liberty of the press will become general in the course of time. Though its legal emancipation be yet denied on the European Continent, the glorious day which will make the free press a gift common to all civilized nations can be not kept back for ever. That day will dawn in spite of all resistance, and night will never again celebrate a permanant triumph, though all the owls be fluttering with the air of victory and all that dread the light join joyously in their screams. The emancipation of the popular intellect by the power of the press may be stopped a while;

but it cannot be annihilated. The old tricks of monarchy have lost their craft. For centuries the nations were educated to national hatred, as the surest way to make them blind instruments to their rulers. This stupid hatred became the mother of robbery, murder and theft on a grand scale, what in the dialect of kings is called war and conquest. The intelligence spread by the instruction diffused by the press, has removed from the peoples' eyes the spectacles of colored glass, which the cunning of the princes had put on them, so that no people was able to behold the other in its true shape and light. Nations are now interweaving their interests, like the weaver his threads by the shuttle, and the general welfare unites kingdoms and continents more firmly than solemn pacts. Not only are national feelings strengthened, but intelligence ennobles them at the same time. In our days a conqueror like Alexander or Napoleon is an impossibility.

The leading ideas of trade and manufactures are immeasurably widened. The life of the tradesman was once shut up within the limits of his guild. The guilds stood firmly rooted in society, like a tree, which bears one kind of fruit from generation to generation. The guilds clipped the wings of the laborer's soul, so that the most endowed individual could not lift himself above a certain level. When this system fell into decay, when no one could find comfort any longer under its screen, time sent an angel of death, to rid the earth of it the quicker. Industry came, building up with one hand and destroying with the other, sowing terror, hatred and mourning amongst the bands, that stood by the old colors, while to those, who embrace her with true love, she holds out her horn of plenty, and is praised by them as the pride of the present age. The negative part of her sway has, it cannot be denied, something demoniacal. It has in the states of the old world taken the last morsel of bread from the mouth of millions; from millions more it will take the last penny, and the last hope of earning an honest subsistence by manual labor. On them, to whom Industry and Capital closes the accustomed paths of earning a livelihood, falls a heavy destiny; but the introduction of machinery-work in competition with manual labor makes it unavoidable. That the living may find room, the dead must be buried. Every Present walks over the graves of the Past, and it would be folly to curse and to sacrifice Industry for the sake of the restoration of guilds and other institutions that have outlived their time.

Industry is the true daughter of the age. What the Guild-system suppressed, she has restored. She has opened to men, especially to gifted men in private stations, the long barred career; she makes it possible for them to turn their faculties and talents to account in wider spheres and raise them to a value which they never had before. She has wedded Intelligence and Genius to Labor; whereas under the old guild-system they had been divorced. By Industry the influence of labor has become greater than ever, both on individual prosperity and on the weal of society at large.

Of course every industrial toils next for himself and his family. But the individual is a part of the whole and man exercises an influence upon Society, whether he have any consciousness of it or not. He cannot entirely escape this consequence even by his death. Therefore the manufacturer on a large scale contributes to the progress of modern civilisation, which shows its peculiar character in the rapid change of the social relations. This change goes on in spite of all endeavors to restore the past. It is as little to be stopped as the course of the planets. As the earth cannot through all eternity return twice to the same point in space, so little will futurity bring back society to the state that has passed away.

No political power is strong enough to hinder effectually the development of industry. Industry has now the ascendancy over kings and governments. Even an autocrat, who would declare war to industry, could not escape ruin. Such an experiment would be attended with worse consequences for his empire than the loss of a hundred battles, than pestilence and famine. A civilized state without industry would soon be the prey of the industrious one, without even the chance of an effectual resistance.

This is acknowledged by all intelligent governments. At present no enlightened nation is inclined to sacrifice herself for the passions of dynasties; none is inclined to the advantage of princely avarice and lust of dominion, pride or revenge, to make war on other nations, as was the case in former times. Good governments have taken cognisance of this change in the popular mind, they try to reconcile their ambition and interests with it, and strike into paths which lead not constantly over grave-mounds and fields drenched with blood. Enlightened governments carry on their feuds less with the sword, than with the pen. Custom-houses are their strongholds, the tariff is their battlefield, commercial congresses exchange and unite interests, and industrial treaties set diplomacy in motion. Industry and Commerce are the arena of the rivalship of nations on which they shew their strength and skill.

In such warfare England was constantly the only victor, and therefore she became so great. But the secret of her motives and her ends, of her strategical art and skill has transpired; other nations learned by sad experience, and victory has ceased to be a British monopoly. Great Britain's industry has found a powerful rival in North America, and on the European Continent it has ceased to hold the sceptre of exclusive dominion. Every day it loses a province, every day the circle of its rule is narrowed, every year is marked with some defeat and loss in the old empires of her sway. Continental Europe is resolved not to relax in the constant war against British supremacy, and it will not make peace ere it has shaken off the yoke of British labor completely. Industrial independence of England is now the war-cry of the Continent, and even the most exhausted States take it up and arm themselves for resistance.

In that war France and Belgium have hitherto earned the greatest advantages, especially the latter. This state, though small, and not one half as large as the state of New-York, has within thirty years, under a wise government, raised itself to the character of the most industrial country and deserved the name „Little England“.

Among the elements of Belgian industry, those of the mineral kingdom are the most important. Coal and Iron stand at the head. Belgium extracts above 5 million tons of coals annually from its three great coal-basins at Mons, Charleroi and Liège. The Belgian coal-region extends over a stripe of Land from five to ten miles broad, beginning with the border of France and stretching to the coal-beds of the lower Rhine and Westphalia, with which it is probably connected. The richest coal-basin is that of Mons, which contains not less than a hundred and thirty coal-strata separated by layers of slate and sandstone. In the next line stands Liège. It contains above 80 strata, of which 64 are worth mining, some reaching a thickness of 6 feet. The greatest working-depth here is 1000 feet. A little distance from the coal-districts, the bountiful and provident hand of the Creator has concealed immeasurable treasures of iron-ore in the lap of the earth. So it is near Charleroi, Namur, and Liège. In these cities the iron manufacture preponderates so much, that nearly all the other trades are directly or indirectly dependent on it.

Especially at Liège. This great city announces herself to the traveller at the first sight as a residence of Vulcan. Hundreds of towering chimneys emit pillars of smoke, supporting a black cloud, under which the city lies as under a canopy. In the environs all around project the furnaces, like giant altars, from whose summits blaze the sacrificial flames: a majestic spectacle at night-time!

The interior of Liège does not discredit its outward appearance. Massive houses of 5 or 6 stories blackened with smoke; narrow, irregular streets; a robust, broad-shouldered, large-boned, sooty, busy population; everywhere blazing, crackling furnace-fires, groanings of steam-engines, and the clink of hammers; everywhere metallic wealth, loading and unloading; rattling trains with bars of iron and full coal-carts in all the streets. Of architectural beauty there is little to be seen; now and then a middle-age-palace, or a Gothic church; occasionally a modern showy edifice, the dwelling of a wealthy manufacturer: the ensemble being an image of life wanting not that air of wealth and comfort, which are the offspring of honest industry and labor.

Liège produces every year about 160,000 fire arms. They are exported to all quarters of the globe; for even the manufactories of Birmingham can neither sell cheaper nor of better quality. There are some gun-factories in Liège, that employ more than 1000 workmen.

The population of Liège numbers about 65,000. In earlier times it was greater. In the 14. century 24,000 burghers marched fully armed against the enemy. Feuds and labor at that period divided the time of the citizens; now they were fighting with their bishop, now with the neighboring cities, now with the princes of Burgundy, and their love of war and bravery made them universally respected and dreaded. But from this propensity to broils proceeded [at the end of the 15. century] their ruin. The allied kings of Burgundy and Scotland, to avenge the murder of a prince-bishop of Liège, Louis of Bourbon, besieged the city in 1486, and after a long and heroic resistance they carried the place by storm upon a Sunday, after having, by hunger, reduced the besieged to extremities. All men capable of bearing arms were put to death, the city given up to a six-days' plunder and to the brutish cruelties of the rude, blood-thirsty warriors, and after all, the town was fired at a hundred points at once and completely burnt. The fate of Carthage was not more terrible than the fate of Liège. Only a few convents, whose preservation by penalty of death, the crowned destroyers had commanded out of affected piety, were left standing amidst the ruins. But as young saplings spring up from the roots of an oak shattered by the storm, so in the course of years the streets again rose out of the rubbish, and if the splendor of those earlier days could not be wholly brought back, yet the city is one of the most flourishing in the land.

About a mile from Liège, close by the bank of the river Maas, and on the edge of a beautiful park, lies an old castle within a walled square, which the eye can not see beyond, out of which a multitude of slender towers peep forth, like the minarets in a city of the East. It is Seraing, the world-renowned establishment of John Cockerill.

Seraing has been called the Escurial of Industry. It is in fact still larger in compass than that famous palace of indolence, though it betrays nothing of the lavish splendor, which would be ill applied, where only utility is sought for or is appropriate. According to the original plan, Seraing was to contain a population of 4000 laborers, including the families of the married. At present, and since the care of its creator has been withdrawn from it, the establishment entertains about 900 workmen, and in the coal- and iron-mines, which belong to it, some 3 to 400 laborers are employed. It was Cockerill's plan, to unite in Seraing all processes of iron manufacture beginning with mining the ore, and ending with the construction of all kind of machinery. There are three furnaces here, capable of yielding 175 tons of raw iron weekly, which in the different ateliers goes through all the processes of working. It was calculated that Seraing would produce for 800,000 Doll. per annum and the profits pay all expences of the establishment within 9 years. Now it produces for about 300,000 Doll. per annum, mostly engines and rails for railroads. The raw iron partly passes the different puddling- and melting-furnaces and the hammering- and rolling-machines by which it is made into bars of all dimensions and qualities; or it is melted in cupola-furnaces for castings of the different parts of machinery. Fire-proof-walled rooms contain the brass-founderies and the forges. All imaginable tools for machine-making are to be found here in the highest perfection. Of boring-machines, lathes, metal-planing machines &c. &c., of every size and variety there is no want. Railroads render all communication from one end of the establishment to the other quick and easy. Five and twenty steam-engines stretch their arms through the vast buildings, and when they are all in simultaneous action, they exert the power of 1200 horses and 2500 men. Discipline and order bear sway everywhere, and the greatest cleanliness is conspicous. All the machines shine as if they had just come from the workshop. Of late years only heavy articles, especially steam-engines of all sorts, locomotives for rail-roads, and iron steamboats are made here, all of superior quality and durability. Nothing gives a more striking idea of the enormous mass of machines of every sort, which have come out of this establishment, than the model-magazines, which fill the greatest part of the old castle and several accessory buildings. One of the large halls serves solely for the preservation of patterns of cog-wheels; all models are beautifully arranged according to their dimensions and kept in the strictest order. The making of models and patterns occupies five work-shops of 200 feet in length, where there are always 100 or more joiners, modellers &c., in activity. Good workmen in Seraing earn 6 to 8 Doll. per week. As a branch establishment serves the great factory in Liège, where the nicest machines, as for cotton mills &c., are made. The principal markets for the products of Seraing are Germany, Italy, Russia, the Orient and South America. Under all changes of fortune and time the establishment has maintained the reputation of its machines unimpaired.

Over the principal door the visitor reads within a wreath of stars the inscription: John Cockerill. It was not chiselled by a paid hand, but by the love and veneration of his workmen, when they heard of his death in a distant land. In the still midnight, so runs the tradition, the ghost of the great industrial chief walks over the yard, and when he comes to the door, he stops and looks up thankfully at this modest free-will memorial.

Cockerill's life may be told in a few words. He was a Briton by birth and pennyless. He had nothing but his genius and his manual dexterity. He was of unsteady mind; there was no rest for him anywhere. He wandered about like a comet; as a machine-builder he went from one workplace to another, willing to command, unwilling to obey, and doing what he pleased. Manhood came and with it the desire of setting up for himself. The honest, intelligent, enterprising man found confidence, credit, support. He erected an establishment for machine-building in Belgium and bore it up with eagle's wings. After some years he was enabled to give his plans a colossal extent. The spirits of Boulton and Arkwright seemed united in him. The happiest gift of combination helped him in whatever he undertook. His genius gave a new stamp to Belgian industry; but not confining his gigantic projects to the limits of a single state or kingdom, his cosmopolitan feeling embraced the whole globe for his sphere of activity. Country and people were alike to him; distance and climate of small account; if anywhere he discovered the germ of a great industry, worth his nursing, he cherished it and brought it up, entirely indifferent, where it was, and seldom asking any thing else from Governments, but the „Laisse moi faire!“ He melted copper on the North Cape, iron in Dalmatia; he spun in Berlin, in Cottbus; he built machines in France and Italy and maintained establishments in Aix la Chapelle and in three Belgian cities at the same time. Misfortunes and catastrophes crowded upon him; storms, hail, thunderbolts: he withstood them unbowed. Constantly he marched at the head of industrial enterprise, stimulating, projecting, guiding. The rapid changes in the processes of labor caused many of his undertakings to become obsolete during their very birth; in such cases he did not hesitate; he gave them up, as soon as the pledge of their durability was lost. Several times he started something new, and deliberately abandoned it before it was put in operation. No failure or mistake disconcerted him, terrified him, or unnerved him. His activity, creative and productive in many directions, played as it were with Fate and laughed at the mutability of mercantile results. It was no secret, that on several occasions he lost hundreds of thousands; another time he gained millions. So he went on till the days came when the body begins to bridle the spirit, and when man is inclined to make a plan for filling up the remainder of life. Cockerill meditated, and his project for Seraing was born! It was the mirror of a harmoniously developed thought of the gigantic mind, and gigantic and harmonious was his work. At Liège, in the vicinity of the richest coal- and iron-deposits, an old castle with a park, called Seraing, once the residence of the prince bishop of Liège, was for sale: — Cockerill bought the estate, purchased fields and wood-lands besides, began to build a city for his laborers and workshops, and while above ground thousands of hands were digging at his command, he set hundreds of miners in motion in his subterranean operations. He sunk 600,000 Doll. in mining works, out of which were to be drawn the elements of industry aboveground; 1,800,000 Doll. more the building and outfit of Seraing cost him. Cockerill, the millionaire, borrowed millions, to carry out his great design. 1843 the work was ready, productive, a miracle to all who saw it. 2000 laborers in the workshops obeyed his will; like a prince he stood among them, like a father he was beloved by them; to the whole land he was a benefactor by his works, an example by his conduct: the king prized him higher than a prince, and by the world he was esteemed higher than kings. On a sudden, there fell a thunder-stroke from the inclouded sky: — the Belgian Bank, the institution, whose credit Cockerill had used to the amount of several millions, broke! — Cockerill was at this critical moment in Norway, busily engaged in his copper-mines: when he returned, the flood was past control. He called upon the king for help; but — whether the power or the will was wanting? — King Leopold suffered the first man of his kingdom to fall. Cockerill with a surplus-property of 1,400,000 Doll. was constrained to suspend payments and assign all his fixtures and establishments for the benefit of his creditors. Cockerill's fate created universal sympathy among all men of judgment. When the emperor of Russia heard of the event, he summoned the great industrial to Warsaw, to take his counsels for the construction of a net of railroads over all Russia and he opened for him a credit at the Polish bank for the erection of new establishments in the kingdom. A grand career seemed re-opened to him; but Cockerill was soon convinced, that with the personal elements assigned to him for co-operation, success was more than doubtful. He saw himself in a false and untenable position.

ON LAKE GEORGE

His spirit, imbued with the doctrines of civil liberty, could find no contentment in the realm of tyranny, and once in opposition with it he encountered stumbling-blocks at every step. Chagrin at this, still more than at his earlier misfortunes, consumed his energies, and he died in Warsaw, ere he could execute the emperor's commission.

Cockerill has received from his contemporaries no tablet of stone, no statue. He needs none. His finest monument is Belgium's industrial greatness; for his example has created it.

LAKE GEORGE.

(BY GEORGE WILLIAM CURTIS.)

„Sabrina fair!
Listen where thou art sitting
Under the glassy, cool, translucent wave."

Exquisite and poetic are all the associations of deep, still water. „In the Caribbean sea," related the old Mariners," we look deep down, and see the mermaids wreathed with sea flowers chasing among the coral reefs, — and the Spanish children that listened enchanted to their stories, sailed for those wondrous regions, when they became men, to find the flower-wreathed mermaids, but wrecked in the tropical storms that vexed those oceans, found the haunted sea only, the gulf of oblivion." The same poetic instinct re-appears in the German legends of fairy life, and of water nymphs, — in the story of the Fisher who was fascinated by the beautiful form that sang to him, and clasped him in wave-like arms, and drew him down, enchanted, to death. In Tieck's Melusina also, who one day in every week disappeared from her husband upon his solemn pledge not to attempt the discovery of her secret; but his curiosity mastered him, so that looking through a crevice he saw her, as a mermaid, playing in the water — and in the delicious story of Undine, and of the knight in the French picture, who, following the hunt, was left at twilight alone and perplexed in a morass, and beheld, glistening among the water grass and tall reeds, the unearthly and overpowering beauty of the Lady of the Fields: — these are all dreams of the realm of water, children of those sweet fancies, which the eye sees, as it muses upon the Summer calm, even as the old Mariners saw the mermaids in the Caribbean.

Pure water is the type of the divine spirit. Therefore in the Christian service it is the sign of regeneration, of birth in the beauty of holiness. Therefore, in sacred history Jesus goes down to the river Jordan and is there baptized, while the dove hangs in the air and the voice speaks out of the tranquil heavens. Life is figured as a flowing river in whose pellucid depths shine gems and flowers, — a clear river, calm or perturbed, flowing out into the broad ocean of Eternity. The cold transparency of mountain tarns has, also, its fascination. They live a spectral life in the shadows and lights that flicker and dart across the surface. They receive in its colossal perfection the majestic mountain-outline around them, thus imaging the genius which mirrors the splendor and heights and depths of noble thoughts. The charm of water, quiet or moving, is endless but sure. The most flexible of visible agents, nature moulds it at her will, in glassy calm to paint her summer repose, or in dashing fury to image her tremendous force.

But hardly upon Lake George would the Poet dream of tempest or fury. It lies nestled among the lonely and wild hills of Warren county in New York. It is thirty six miles long and at its lower extremity from two to three miles broad. But ascending toward the head of the lake, the hill shores crowd more closely in, vary the outline of the water, and form a strait of extreme picturesqueness, studded with bits of isles some of which seem but the green pedestals of groups of trees. The legend of the lake tells of three hundred and sixty five islands, so that whoever would tarry a day upon each would occupy just a year in circumnavigating this small Pacific. One of these islands, called Twelve-mile island, because it is that distance from Caldwell, the insignificant village at the foot of the Lake, contains twenty acres and is elevated twenty or thirty feet above the level of the lake; and there is a little Tea-island, so named from some unknown reason, but doubtless from the beverage drunk in the rustic temple among its groves.

The scenery of Lake George is not grand, but it is solitary and wild. The hills that surround it are low, and covered with monotonously dark foliage. There is no settlement upon its shores but the small town of Caldwell at the lower point, which was so named from a gentleman who owned vast tracts of territory upon the lake, and was very averse to any one's settling there. There is good fishing in its waters, and it is a delightful change after the whirl of Saratoga life. The northern traveller should not miss this secluded sheet of water across whose thirty six miles a neat little Steamer will carry him to the isthmus which separates it from Champlain — the Crown-Point, upon which the ruins of the old fort are among the most romantic in America. Lake George has its historical fact, for upon its lower shore Sir William Johnson fought the French and Indians. The remains of the fort he built and called William Henry are still to be seen near Caldwell. But so unchanged is its wildness that the summer traveller as he strolls along its green shore at twilight would not be surprised of a light canoe shot across the gleaming surface, or the sharp crack of the Indian's rifle rang thro' the dark forest upon the mountains.

THE ALCAZAR IN CORDOVA.

The brilliant reign of the early Moorish Khaliphs in Spain has no parallel. The splendor of their great cities surpassed all that Europe had witnessed before. Poetry, science, philosophy and architecture owe a high degree of perfection to the zeal and learning of the Moors, and the genius and munificence of their Almanzors and Abderrahmans spread their renown from Europe through the remotest East.

But while in the other half of Spain, the German institutions, introduced by Charlemagne, obtained the ascendancy in the course of time, the Saracenic sway declined and its era of civilization, refinement and luxury rapidly passed away. No longer supported by its former fanaticism, the Moslims were unable to resist the enthusiasm of chivalry awakened for the glory of the Cross. The fire of the Crescent was extinguished by the armed hand of knighthood, aided by the church militant.

Within half a century after this event the social condition and the prosperity of the country underwent a fearful change. The flourishing Moorish kingdoms, now provinces of the christian conquerors, fell a prey to the desolating system, which the pride of victorious and religious hatred

ALCAZAR in SEGOVIA

Published for HERRMANN J. MEYER, 164 William-St. NEWYORK

dictated. Before the spirits of barbarity, cruelty and fanaticism the populations thinned, towns and cities fell to ruins, palaces and castles tumbled from the crest of their hills and the busy, stirring life of industrious men was no longer to be seen. The great centres of Moorish splendor and wealth fell rapidly to decay. In the streets of Granada herds were pasturing and the population of Cordova „the queen of the earth“ dwindled from 300,000 to 20,000 within less than a century.

Time appeared as jealous of the monuments of the Khaliphs, as christian fanaticism. Of the proud castles of the Moorish grandees, on the banks of the Guadalquivir, of the celebrated palace of Abderrahman himself beyond the walls of the city, not a wreck is left behind.

To the „Alcazar,“ the oldest palace of the Khaliphs, the fate of destruction would not have been spared but for its being selected as a stronghold of the conquerors from which they could overawe the capital. It received the twofold destination of citadel and prison, and in the course of time its outward appearance changed accordingly. During a period of more that 300 years the courts of the Alcazar witnessed the shocking rites of the inquisition and from the terrific dungeons underneath thousands and thousands of victims, tortured to death, were sent to heaven. The holy Inquisition is abolished; but the new tenant of this gloomy monument of Moorish sway Christian Royalty, is not short to the former in craft and cruelty. The „Alcazar,“ is now Spain's most dreaded prison of State, and in its dungeons the noblest champions of truth, right, and liberty, pine, and hope for release.

BENEVENTO IN ITALY.

Benevento the ancient city of the Samnites, whose magnificence during the days of the Emperors was envied by Rome herself, is now a quiet place of fourteen thousand inhabitants. Though surrounded by Neapolitan territory, it belongs to the Papal Dominions. Here in this pleasant paradise man still slumbers in the arms of blind Faith, and an archbishop with about four hundred priests and monks, guard like cherubim this Eden with its sleepers.

Benevento possesses several relics of antique architecture, the principal of which is a triumphal arch of marble dating from the better periods of Roman Art. Trajan erected it in the year one hundred and fourteen. It is in excellent preservation and still used as a city gate. Its sculptures represent events which occurred during the emperor's reign, and they may be ranked, both as regards style and execution, among the noblest works of Antiquity.

TRAJANS _ ARC

AT BENEVENTO IN ITALY

Published at HERRMANN J. MEYER. 6 . North William-Street NEWYORK.

WALL - STREET

New York

WALL STREET, NEW-YORK.

BY PARKE GODWIN.

Streets have their characteristics as well as men; a physiognomy and physiology which show them to be as distinct, as they are sometimes distant; or a peculiar life and form that hinders them from even being confounded with others. Let us then inquire into the character of *Wall Street.*

Its name is just one hundred and ninety-nine years old, and was given, when in 1653 our good Dutch ancestors were thrown into a fright by the reported approach of a hostile force of cunning New Englanders. They found their habitations, including their „*vrows*“ and children, wholly unprotected from the wicked designs of the „*Yankees,*“ and threw up an embankment to shelter the infant colony. It was flanked and sustained by formidable wooden palisades, and every night saw a considerable troop of brave citizens, armed cap-a-pie, gather in its shade, to watch the coming on of the enemy, and to give timely notice to the volunteer defenders.

In the process of time, the embankment or wall was taken down, and the place, where it ran, was converted into a street, which took the name of „*De Waal*“ or Wall Street. Its principal occupants then were Carel Van Bruggh, Garret Jansen Stavast, Jacob Hendrickson Vanavanger, Hans Stein, and Renier Rycken. But alas! the descendants of these gallant Dutchmen have now quite forgotten their names.

The City Hall, or town-house, was formerly in this street where the Custom House now stands, and, if we mistake not, the first Congress under the administration of Washington assembled in that building, and the new Constitution was sworn to by that illustrious man, — so lately the General of a victorious army, — but now the quiet citizen, almost dragged from his home, to be made the First Magistrate of Peace. But in December 1790, the seat of the government, already prosperously organized and set in motion, was removed to Philadelphia, and subsequently thence to Washington.

About that time, Wall Street was the fashionable quarter of the city; rich families had their residences there; the *belles* and *beaux* walked and flirted there, as they now do in Broadway; and there the grand balls were given and merry-makings took place. But precisely because it was fashionable, it became a favorite abode of business. Boarding-houses and shops soon elbowed the substantial mansions of the citizens into other localities. The store, the office, the bank, the counting-house, the exchange, rose upon their ruins, or rather absorbed and converted to their own more noisy uses the old and quiet family-mansions. Then in a little while, Wall Street became, what it is now, the centre of nearly all the commercial transactions of the metropolis. Its growth, therefore, during the last fifty years, has been prodigious and almost incredible. From the mere winding-lane of a new settlement, it has expanded into the most thronged thoroughfare of the third city of the civilized world, in regard to population, and the second in regard to trade. But in its rapid development, it is only a type of the city itself and of the nation.

The principal buildings in Wall Street, at this time, are the Merchant's Exchange, the Custom House, and the Offices of the several Banks. Trinity Church which overlooks it, like a solemn monitor, or which stands at the head of it, stately and grim, as a dread spiritual watchman, belongs rather to Broadway. We shall not notice it, therefore, in our architectural description of the street.

The *Merchant's Exchange* occupies the whole of an angular „block" or square, and is a very large building, but it is so shut in by other structures, that neither its proportions, nor its size are visible. It is not artistically attractive; and yet no little taste is shown in its style and arrangement, which, if it were not buried as it is, would render it an object of great interest. The building of it was commenced in 1836 and completed four years afterwards, on the site of the former Exchange, destroyed in the great fire of 1835. Its materials consist of the Syenite stone of Massachusetts, which has taken the name of Quincy Granite. The principal front has a colonnade of twelve Ionic columns, thirty feet in height, with an interior range of six columns, which support the ceiling of a recess. The Rotunda, an immense circular room on the inside, is surmounted by a dome some eighty feet in diameter, the effect of which is grand.

It is in this Rotunda that the merchants gather at high noon to make bargains and talk of the state of trade; here too, the auction-sales of real estate and town lots are held every day at Meridian; and here formerly the „New-York Stock and Exchange Board", which means the Stock Brokers, assembled to make the vaults reverberate with their eager trafficking. They have since removed to a less conspicuous part of the building, adjacent to the large reading-room which is maintained in the second story. Lawyers' and agents' offices occupy the other parts.

A more showy edifice is the white marble one, with a Grecian portico, which is known as the Custom House, where more than two thirds of the entire revenue of the United States is collected, where five thousand vessels are entered and cleared in a year, and where nearly two hundred millions of exports and imports are annually passed through their accounts. But the building, though a pleasing one in its external aspect, is internally wholly unfitted for its purposes; besides not being large enough to accommodate the crowds who frequent it, it is miserably ventilated and badly arranged. Its original cost was 1,175,000 Doll. The steps on the Wall Street side are famous for two kinds of out-door traffic, that of penny newspapers, and that of puppy-dogs.

The buildings used by the Banks, Insurance Offices, Lawyers and Brokers are large, but not remarkable for their architecture; those most recently constructed, however, as the Bank of the Republic at the corner of Broadway, have more pretensions, than the older ones; and we may predict with safety, such is the rapidity of progress in the new world, that in a few years Wall Street will boast of a great many structures worthy of its enormous wealth.

What that wealth amounts to, it is difficult to ascertain precisely; for, it not only fluctuates from time to time, but it is derived from kinds of trade respecting which we have no statistics. The incorporated Banks in Wall Street, for instance, about fifteen in number, have an aggregate capital of near 20,000,000 Doll.; the Fire and Marine Insurance Companies, of which there are above twenty chartered by the State, have a capital of 10,000,000 Doll. more; while the Life Assurance and Trust Companies have some 5,000,000 Doll., — but these do not include the private bankers, who are supposed to have more money than the banking companies, — nor the agencies of foreign insurance companies, — nor the great railroad, canal, mining, and coal companies, to say nothing of the stock-brokers, the real-estate agents, the auctioneers and the lawyers. It would, therefore, scarcely be an exaggeration to estimate the capital of all kinds in Wall Street at 100,000,000 Doll. — Of the amount of business daily transacted there, we have no method of getting at any information.

It is from ten o' clock A. M. to three P. M. that the busy season prevails in this street, and then it is one of the most active, bustling, restless, „go-a head“ streets to be found in the world. Indeed, we do not suppose that it has its equal out of London. Such a rushing, crowding, shuffling and crushing is there, that a quiet man is inclined to believe that the world is gone mad. Every body seems intent on his own errand; scarcely one man stops to speak to another; women are never seen there, while the faces of all have an anxious, almost fearful look. Gamblers, at their insane vocation, can hardly look more wildly absorbed in the object before them, than many whom you encounter in this street. But it is only a temporary abstraction; for when once the clock of Trinity has told three, their brows relax, the color comes to their cheeks, their eyes laugh again, and they adjourn to the restaurants of Delmonico or Frederick, or ride up to their splendid palaces on the Fifth Avenue, to recreate their exhausted faculties over a fine dinner and generous wine. In the evening, when the doors and windows are all closed, and the last clerk has gone to his home or the theatre, the street has so deserted and forlorn a look, that it is painful to walk its silent ways.

We have said, that at three o' clock the frequenters of Wall Street, dissmissed their anxieties, and went to dine. But this is not universally true; for there are many of them, who, at that hour, are only plunged into a more sure and deeper misery. These are the unfortunate members of the flock, such as merchants who have not paid their notes, when the fatal hour falls, and who can not pay; speculators, who are „bulls“, — as the curious phraseology of the market goes, — in a fall of prices, or „bears“ with prices up; young clerks, who have robbed their employers to sport a trotting-horse on the Third Avenue, and have just been detected through the bank-account; and, finally, the Presidents, Secretaries and thousand and one subordinates of fat incorporations, with a new directorship just coming into office; to all these, the fatal stroke of Trinity clock brings weeping and wailing and gnashing of teeth. For a time thereafter, if not for ever, they are shut out of the enchanted realm, where they were once the nabobs and great men.

Fortune, however, is well represented by the wheel, for while she turns some men down, on the one side, she turns other men up, on the other side, and Wall Street therefore sees merry as well as broken hearts. Poor fellows who left an ill-digested breakfast in the morning, with nothing in the world, except Micawber's hope that „something would turn up", go home at night, unlike that persecuted individual, with the beginnings of wealth in their pocket, made through a lucky hit in the stocks. Wall Street has been their California. It has suddenly, and as if by magic, poured its horns of plenty on them; they stagger with the intoxication of success; they lie down amid golden dreams. Wonderful, miraculous, astonishing is their prosperity. But how long does it last? That is another mystery of Wall Street which we will not here reveal.

The street, indeed, is an epitome and type of our whole modern civilisation, — of that civilization, which gathers into the hands of the few, out of the hands of the many, which rears stupendous piles of money amid extensive and barren plains, like Alps rising out of deserts, — and which repeats materially, in so many forms, the old spiritual truth of the Lord, that that to him that hath, shall be given, while from him that hath not, shall be taken away even that which he hath. When we look over the tables, representing the distributions of riches, in Great Britain, and other aristocratic nations of the old world, we are surprised to learn the fewness of the number to whom it is secured. But it would surprise us a great deal more to be told, that in this land of more equal laws, where legal privilege has long since been prostrated, the same fearful contrasts of possession are rapidly growing up. Wealth, by a peculiar centripetal force, gravitates into the pockets of the few, — while poverty, by an adverse centrifugal action, is diffused over and among the many. Equal chances do not yield equal successes. If here and there one reaches the golden goal, there are thousand that „by the road side fall and perish." A singular fact that, — involving a variety of considerations, moral, political, social and religious, — which we have no space here to touch upon! Yet the reader, by a close scrutiny, may discover some profitable truths.

Knowledge, says the index to Bacon's works, is power; but there is a force almost as great, which is — *Money*. Wall Street has a power, scarcely second to that exercised by Washington. Indeed, we fear that Wall Street sometimes controls Washington. It is the ganglionic centre of our whole social system, — the centre, from which all the delicate and sensitive nerves of commercial influence radiate, — towards which the entire telegraphic apparatus of trade tends. A blow, struck in Wall Street, trembles along all the lines of communication to the outermost extremities of the Union. It sends a thrill through the hearts of great cities; it arrests the solitary hunter of the western wilds; it startles the busy Californian in his mine. Great is the sympathy, as well as mystery, of commerce. Money is well-named the circulation. It is the blood of the frame. He that regulates money, regulates the world. Rothschild is mightier than the Czar, — mightier than the Pope. Ministers of State kneel in his antechambers — Emperors are his supplicants. Those old barons of the feudal-times, who pounced from their castles on the solitary crags, down upon the frightened villages, — the Knight-hawks, as Hood humorously calls them, — were men of vast and almost resistles strength, — but the barons of the moneybags — the Feudal-Lords of trade — who sit quietly behind their counters, dictating laws to their dependents thousands of miles away, — boweling the earth by their locomotives, and beating down the wild ocean with the steady tread of their steam-ships, have a wider, sturdier, more gigantic power. In the midst of all injustice and corruption, too, — much as it wearies and worries the poor laboring-man, — fearful as may be the inequalities it works in our social relations, it is not to be doubted that it is a nobler power. But Heaven send the time, when Money shall accomplish its good, without the terrible desolation which accompanies its present workings.

THE NAPOLEON COLUMN IN PARIS.

(PLACE VENDOME).

When we contemplate the banished Emperor, the man with the giant heart, upon the rock of St. Helena, musing upon the fate of the world, which had cast him out; or when we behold him moving victorious through the continent at the head of his legions, trampling upon the necks of nations, overturning thrones which had stood thousands of years, and establishing others, where none had existed; or follow him returning homeward in triumph at the head of his armies; or view him surrounded by kings and princes, his vassals, granting crowns and laying out kingdoms as if they were but toys: — we feel that there is something tragic and superhuman in the spectacle. It recalls Antiquity, the scenes of Eternal Rome, the triumphs of the Caesars with their trains of captive kings, the mighty deeds of Alexander; it calls up the remembrance of Marius sitting among the ruins of Carthage, of Hannibal, who found treachery and death, where he had sought a refuge. But it is not alone the personal fate of Napoleon, which recalls the mighty impress of Antiquity; the works of public utility and the monuments, which he left hehind him for the astonishment of future ages recalls it too. Visit Paris and behold its marketplaces, its halls and cellars for corn and wine, its slaughter-houses, its aqueducts, its hospitals, its quays, its bridges its streets, its canals; mark its triumphal arches and its monuments intelligible to every one, placed in

C.Reiss del. B.Metzeroth sc.

THE NAPOLEON - COLUMN

ON THE PLACE VENDÔME IN PARIS.

of the market places, exposed to every eye and every judgement, standing in full view of the people, and you must exclaim; Here too, exists the spirit of ancient Rome, here too we feel the inspiration of the mighty past! Even Rome and Greece can show nothing nobler than the „Arc de l'Etoile“, and the Colnmn of the Place Vendôme is the peer, both in design and execution, of the greatest works, which excited the wonder of antiquity.

This column of Victory, raised to commemorate the French triumphs, was cast out of 1200 Russian and Austrian cannon, taken in the famous campaign of 1805. Its model was the column of Antoninus at Rome. The foundations were laid in 1806. In 1810 it was finished. Its height, exclusive of the pedestal, is 118 feet; its foundation-walls are sunk to the depth of 30 feet; and their thickness is 12 feet. It rests upon piles, which in a spirit of contemptible adulation, had been sunk a century before to support a colossal equestrian statue of Louis XIV. One million and eight hundred thousand pounds of bronze were used in casting the shaft. The pedestal, 25 feet in height, exhibits upon its four sides bas-reliefs of the trophies of war. Above the pedestal garlands of oak and laurel are wreathed, which at the four corners are upheld by eagles. A spiral bas-relief, wrought in bronze, winding up the shaft represents the triumphal career of Napoleon and his army, from the march out of the camp at Boulogne to the peace which followed the great day of Austerlitz. Within, a winding staircase of 176 steps leads to a gallery, which rests upon the Capital. Above this rises a circular lantern, which ends in a cupola, on which this inscription is to be read: —

MONUMENT ERECTED IN HONOR OF THE GRAND ARMY.

BEGUN, AUGUST 25. 1805. COMPLETED, AUGUST 25. 1810.

On the summit stood formerly a statue of Napoleon by Chaudet — represented as the Caesar, in imperial robes, the toga over his shoulders, in his right hand a statue of victory, at his feet an eagle. „Thousands of years will pass over this statue and the children's children of world-ruling France will point upward to it, and relate the history of their Hercules and their Solon!" — Thus spake the orator at the inauguration of the monument. And ere a single lustre had passed away — it was lying, an object of contempt and ridicule, in the dust! — How was this? Let me relate.

Treachery and cowardice, rather than their victorious arms, had in 1814 given Paris into the hands of the allies. Napoleon himself was at Fontainebleau and was collecting together the remnants of his army. A few faithful adherents were with him. But most of those, who owed their greatness to him — Ministers, Marshals, Senators, — in that golden age of baseness, swelled with their treachery the power of his enemies.

On the 31. of March, a proposition was made by some of those, who had welcomed with cheers the ostentatious entry of the allied armies into Paris and in whom the tones of the Prussian bugles had awakened fanatical enthusiasm against the heroic age of Napoleon — to hurl his statue down from the Vendôme column. Obsequious tools were found ready to mount the column and fasten ropes around the head of the Emperor. Twenty four horses were attached to these to pull the statue down. It did not yield. Then the corrupt and excited rabble of Paris seized the ropes; thousands laid out their strength; the statue mocked the efforts of these creatures — it stirred not from its place. Mechanics were then send up to saw it off at the base. But owing to the hardness of the metal and to the fact that the extremities had been cast solid, this attempt proved also vain. At length a new scheme was invented; no less than to blow up the monument with gunpowder. Casks of powder were actually brought to the column for that purpose, when a Russian General, more jealous for the fame of France than the Parisians themselves, and indignant at the thought of abandoning one of the noblest monuments of modern times to utter destruction, raised his voice in opposition to the mad design. Russian Cossacks now took the column under their protection, and the instigators of the shameful proceeding were obliged to seek some other means of obtaining their ends.

They accordingly addressed themselves to the leaders of the allied armies, and requested the immediate removal of the statue, whose original, as they expressed it, had now become an object of execration and abhorrence to all France. In consequence of this request, the celebrated artist, Lunay, in whose foundry the statue had been cast and by whom it had been erected, received from the Russian commander in chief an order „under penalty of military execution“ to take down the statue and to have the work finished „by midnight of the 6. of April!“ On the margin of the order was written, „To be executed immediately. Pasquier.“

Lunay executed the task. The statue was taken down without injury and the founder received it into his charge, as a security for longstanding demands, which he had on the public treasury.

The 30. of March 1815 came. The Bourbons fled, the Emperor again sat upon his throne. On the 31. of March Lunay asked permission of General Bertrand to re-place the statue on the column, and in answer received an order to deliver it up to Denon — which was done. It was probably intended at some future time, to make the replacing of it the occasion of an imposing ceremony; this, however, the battle of Waterloo frustrated.

The Bourbons returned. The restoration soon turned its attention again to the statue of Napoleon. Lunay had received it back from Denon, for the purpose of repairing the injuries it had received in the attempts to hurl it to the ground and to saw it off. Since then he had carefully preserved it. On a sudden he received a royal order, to break this noble work of art to pieces and use the metal in casting the horse of an equestrian statue of Henry IV., intended as an ornament to the Pont Neuf. Lunay offered double the price of the metal for permission to keep the statue; and under pretext of the love of an artist for the works of his hand, he at last offered to pay its entire original cost. All was in vain. He was obliged to execute the royal command. „After it was already in pieces“ (such was the account, which Lunay gave in the newspapers of this singular affair) „to prevent at least the utter destruction of what remained, I offered 20,000 pounds of bronze for the fragments, which weighed but 6000. This was also refused.“ Lunay now cast out of the bronze of the emperor's statue, the horse of Henry IV, but made at the same time a statuette of the Emperor, which he placed in the hollow of the right arm of the new statue, and in the belly of the horse he hid a casket containing a full account of the work which had been destroyed and a collection of the songs, speeches, inscriptions, &c. which this disgraceful affair had called forth — eloquent memorials of the spirit of the times in which it occurred, and of the meanness of those, who had shared in it.

After the removal of the statue of the Emperor, the inglorious Restoration planted its white standard upon the column. During the hundred days the tri-color waved there, once more followed by the white. The July-revolution tore down those rags and again the tri-colored-flag floated in the breeze. Louis Philippe snatching at everything, which for a time might amuse the vanity of the nation, after his elevation to the throne, was struck with the idea of raising upon the place of the old, a new statue to the Emperor. Not the ideal Napoleon so grandly conceived by Chaudet, was this to be — not the colossal genius of conquest and victory, not the hero so like the heroes of the old world, — but the so-called historical Napoleon, the man in schoolmaster style, with cocked hat, gray coat and knee-breeches, precisely as he appeared in his campaigns or when reviewing his guards in the court of the Tuileries. And that nothing might be wanting in the correctness of the external appearance, Bertrand was directed to sent to Seurre, the sculptor, who was commissioned to make the model, a full costume of the Emperor's. It may now in truth be said of the hat, the uniform coat, the epaulettes, the over-coat with its facings, the high boots and the spyglass, which he holds in his hand — „Thus they looked exactly!“ The sword was modelled from that which Napoleon wore at the battle of Austerlitz. But is there not a higher historical truth in monumental art, than that which gives the rags in which occasion and accident clothe the hero of an epoch? The most biting criticisms were those silent ones made by the effects of light and shade. For when the statue, the legs of which stand somewhat apart, was raised to its place, it was found that the tree-trunk intended as a support to the figure, when seen from below, gave the whole the appearance of a one-legged invalid. This was to be removed. Fresh difficulties! It was then found, that the light which passed between the legs, gave them such an queer appearance, that they were hardly visible, and the entire figure looked not unlike a paper-kite held fast by cords. To correct this second trick of the airy critic a bombshell and a heap of cannon-balls were piled up between the feet. —

The new statue was cast from 16 Austrian and Russian cannon, trophies of the campaign of 1805. Its height is eleven feet; but in spite of its colossal dimensions, when seen from the ground, it appears not unlike a dwarf.

Considered from an artistic point of view, this monument will ever remain a conspicuous mark of scorn for criticism; nevertheless it will be for ever a subject of pride to a nation, which esteems military glory so highly and which has for ages made such sacrifices to obtain it.

To conclude on such grounds, however, that the present generation will tolerate any prolonged or permanent return of the imperial system, would be a great error; on the contrary, nothing has in a greater degree lost its power and magical influence upon the hearts of the nation, than Napoleon's system of conquest. The day of fruitless trophies has passed by, and those which have been won in the African war, and in the expeditions to the American coast and to Rome, are but wretched parodies on the grand deeds of the Empire, and can never awaken in the people any deep-rooted sympathy. In the present state of Civilization, and when the interests of peace have, universally in the civilized world, become so powerful, no important war can arise without a much more powerful motive than mere conquest; a motive power is necessary which goes far deeper, or which reaches and affects the highest social interests.

Without some such lever, the shock of huge masses of armed men, such as occurred on the battle fields of Napoleon, is no longer possible. Hence, whatever be the triumphs of the moment, all attempts, projects and plans of Louis Napoleon, to sway France with the sword of the hero of the column Vendôme, can only end in the discomfiture and disgrace of the faithless and contemptible usurper, if not in the ruin of the land that he seeks to enslave.

CUMAE IN THE „CAMPAGNA FELICE“, ITALY.

Campagna Felice! Is this the happy land that Horace sung and Virgil praised? I look down upon a waste tract, upon the extinguished furnaces of the Cyclops, upon piles of ashes and heaps of lava, upheaved and scattered by volcanic power; — I look upon the grave-grown grass of ruined cities, where once Amazement paused before the marble palaces of world-robbers, and where thousands glutted their eyes with gladiatorial games. Now it is all waste and deserted. Whence this change? Is nature altered? Has the curse of God struck this land with sterility, or since the days of Trajan is the fire quenched, which warmed this region into thriving, blossoming and fruitbearing luxuriance? Nothing of all this. The hand of nature has never withdrawn her gifts, — nothing is changed but — Man, without whose zeal and care even a paradise would wither into a desert. Italy lies

ENVIRONS of CUMA and LAGO D'AVERNO with LAGO DE FUSSARO

Published for HERRMANN J. MEYER, 164, William-Street NEWYORK.

in the dusk of her day; after a long, dim day her sun of developement is setting. Blood-red stream the fading rays along the horizon, black night of Barbarism threatens to settle over the land, and its degenerate people is tossing about between Despotism and Anarchy. When the night is passed, then only may a still sabbath-morning be hoped for; a new race, a new people may then seize the exhausted land and scatter the seeds of a new harvest. Then upon the grave mounds of fallen cities will rise other cities fair as they. Everything on earth is moving in a circle. Everything blooms, withers and blooms again.

The now desolate region of Cumae was once the most populous one of the Campagna Felice. Every step on it reveals this fact. Corn covers the fields, and woods are green upon the ruins of Roman villas and summer-houses which crowned the heights. Six sister-cities surrounded the great Cumae which was founded by the Greeks in the days of Hercules and in the reign of Augustus was one of the most flourishing cities of the Empire and provoked even the jealousy of Rome. But no city of Antiquity has been more utterly destroyed than Cumae, which, on account of its fortifications, constantly attracted the desolating storm of war. In the fifth century the Vandals under Genseric ravaged it; later the Saracens burnt it. Cumae rose once more from its ashes and in the 12th century felt itself strong enough in population to take up the gauntlet which the Neapolitans, who regarded the prosperity of their neighbor with jealous eyes, had thrown down before them. Conquered upon the battle field, Cumae long with-stood a siege, until, reduced by famine, the city was taken by storm, and met the fate that Rome had inflicted upon Carthage. Cumae, which had given an asylum to the destroyer of its proud rival, was erased from the face of the earth. Its inhabitants were slain, the city plundered and burnt, the walls levelled to the ground and the fields laid waste. So entire was this destruction, that a traveller in the 15. century found nothing but a wilderness of which tradition said „Here stood Cumae.“

Outside the city, are still visible the substructions of an Aqueduct, a temple and a famous amphitheatre in which the populace amused themselves with gladiatorial games and the combats of beasts, after their Greek customs had been supplanted by those of victorious Rome. The amphitheatre afforded seats for 42,000 spectators and was larger than the Coliseum at Rome. Another relic, a semi-circular structure of masonry, appears to have been a seat for the thousands who promenaded among the open places, monuments, temples and columns of the environs of the city. Wherever the plough or spade turns up the ground, traces of its old magnificence are revealed, and wherever excavations are made, they are amply rewarded. Cumae with its suburbs occupied a large part of the space between the lake Avernus and the lake of Licola (the former is the sheet of water in the crater at the left of the picture, the latter, the water on the right, which the profile of the Monte Barbaro, the mountain with the square tower, intersects,) and extended to the Monte di Cumae (the pointed hill in the distance) which bore the Acropolis upon its summit. At the foot of this mountain, the reader will observe a small, white arch. It is the remnant of the famous *Arco Felice,* a magnificent triumphal gate, — once the proud entrance of the city. The sculptures which adorned it, have long since disappeared, and even the slabs of marble that covered it, are gone. Nothing is left except the naked skeleton of the structure, but this is so firm that it will yet endure for ages. Concealed by Monte Barbaro (the Gaurus of the Ancients) is the spot where Scipio Africanus — who derived his surname from the continent he subdued — had a Country-house — the asylum whither he retired from the ungratefulness of Rome. There too is his tomb. Of the inscription upon it — „Ingrata patria nec ossa mea habebis,“ (Ingrate Country! thou shalt not even have my bones), only the word patria is legible and this gave the name to the estate. Cicero, also, had a house at Cumae, and after the fall of freedom, he lived there a long time in the deepest sorrow over the hopeless state of liberty in Rome. „When the senate is annihilated“ he writes „what remains for a man to do?“ Cicero was no Scipio, who constantly insulted by his enemies, deemed it beneath his dignity even to justify himself. Never did a murmur escape Scipio's lips. In him we recognise the type of the great Roman, which was manifest also in Brutus and dis-

GENERAL POST-OFFICE

WASHINGTON

Published for HERRMANN J. MEYER. 8. [illegible] William-Street NEWYORK

appeared with Cato. After the ruin of the republic the Emperors reigned over slaves, and the spirit of ancient Rome had been long quenched when barbarians made the palaces of the Cesars their habitations.

The summit of the square tower which crowns Monte Barbaro (Gaurus) commands the finest view of this memorable region, with which are entwined so many historical recollections and which is consecrated by so many great names. At its foot lies the extinct volcano whose water-filled crater forms those lakes over which the myths of the ancients spread their mysterious veils. Upon their banks dwelt the Sybils, who foretold the destiny of men, and there also were the mouths of the secret paths trodden by the Gods and messengers of the lower world. Peaceful, clear and transparent are those lakes; but no tree droops along the shore, and vague, melancholy silence broods over the water. To the West and South stretches the Mediterranean into the distance, and vessels float upon its surface like white gulls, and islands dot it with graceful forms. But the rocky cliff of Cumae rises like a lofty grave-stone — like the sepulchral urn of the races, heroes and great men who died here, or whose deeds illustrate History. Backwards flows the stream of Time, — the musing loiterer remembers Greece and Rome, and the ghosts of the Sybils, of Hercules, of Eneas, of Scipio, Cicero, Seneca and of Horace hover around him and fade in empty air.

THE GENERAL POST OFFICE — WASHINGTON.

BY CHARLES A. DANA.

In no other Department of public affairs in the United States is the principle of centralisation so completely and extensively established or so rigidly enforced as in the administration of the General Post Office. It is true that the Custom House establishment is equally derived from, and dependent upon, the central Government, but its operations are confined to the sea board and the frontiers, and come directly into contact with the mercantile class alone. The General Post Office on the other hand, has its dependencies and agents in every hamlet and performs its services and levies its revenues among the people of every community in the land. The number of Post Masters, agents, clerks and contractors throughout the country, all either subject to removal from office at the pleasure of the Head of the Department, or more or less dependent upon him, is not less than twenty seven thousand; and it will readily be seen that this vast machine, when wielded by an unscrupulous and skilful Executive must exercise a very potent control over the elections and may be so used as considerably to hinder if not altogether to neutralize the true will of the people. And as the country grows in extent and population, this executive instrument must become more powerful and dangerous. Indeed, no man, who is not blind to what passes before every eye, can fail to perceive the degree of influence which the Post Office Department already has in every canvass, nor how keen is the stimulus which partisans find in the hope of keeping or obtaining possession of its patronage. If the pernicious tendency of Centralization as exhibited in this Department and that of the Custom House, is balanced and overcome by the influence of other more democratic institutions, it is certainly strong enough and active enough to cause serious anxiety to the thoughtful patriot. With so great a number of offices in the gift of the Federal Executive and with the habit of turning out political opponents from all places, lowest as well as highest, in order to make way for political friends on every change in the party hue of the Administration, there has arisen a large body of men whose business is the pursuit of office, gamblers in politics, speculators in principle, seeking the triumph of this or that party solely for the sake of the public spoils, and at the easy sacrifice of every consideration of the public welfare. Thus a large amount of profligacy and corruption is kept in existence and exercises a baneful influence upon the political morality of the land, while the public service suffers from frequent changes in its agents, no degree of capacity or experience being secure against proscription. As a remedy against these growing evils of Executive influence in the elections and these pretorian bands of office-seekers and jobbers, it has been proposed to render the office of Post Master elective by the people of each locality. This reform would strike at the very root of the evil, for it would make the place dependent on capacity and the esteem of the aspirant's acquaintances and fellow citizens, and not on the favor of a distant official, looking for a shrewd political agent or bent on rewarding some political service quite as much as on securing an honest and efficient discharge of public duty. But as yet the reform has found few supporters among the adherents of either of the great parties, possibly for the reason that both fear the loss of so potent an instrumentality of accomplishing their cherished objects; and there seems little reason to hope for a change until the excess of the evil shall render the people at large alive to their true interests. But it appears certain that the Government would be more beneficially and honestly managed if it were stripped of its present enormous patronage and rendered more truly the servant of the country.

The growth of the postal establishment well illustrates the astonishing progress of the Republic itself in power, population and reading-habits. Its first commencement was about the year 1700 when the British government issued letters patent to Thomas Neal authorizing him to set up Post Offices and convey mails in the American colonies for twenty one years. Mr. Neal however subsequently ceded back this monopoly to the crown which consolidated the American establishment with that of Britain and in 1753 appointed no less a person than Benjamin Franklin to the office of Post Master General, which he held for twenty one years, when he was dismissed for lack of sufficient reverence in answering some interrogatories before a commitee of Parliament. In his time the mails were carried on horseback, but so skilful and economical was his management that the expenses were more than covered by the revenue. It was a principle with him to make every mail route pay its own way; in 1756, for example, he wrote to Gen. Washington that the mail from Philadelphia to Winchester Va. would have to be stopped unless the Legislature of Virginia would contribute toward its expenses.

The Colonial Post Office was virtually brought to a close in December 1775 by a notice from the Deputy Post Master, Francis Dashwood to the effect that as the revolutionary authorities had stopped the posts, he should send out no more. In the month of July previous, the Continental Congress had passed a law for the appointment of a Post Master General with a salary of 1090 Doll. a year, authorizing him to appoint such assistant deputies as might be necessary. To this office Benjamin Franklin was unanimously chosen with authority to institute a line of Post offices from Falmouth (now Portland Me.) to Savannah Ga. with such cross routes as he might deem advisable. At the same time beside other assistant offices, an Inspector of dead letters was provided for with a salary of 100 Doll. which he was to earn by a quarterly examination of matters in his department. Franklin held the office about a year and a half when he resigned it for more important duties. He was succeeded by Richard Bache, whose ledger up to the year 1779 is still preserved. It contains the accounts of eighty post offices, all that were in existence during the time mentioned and three quires of foolscap-paper comprise the whole.

The first ordinance for the regulation of the Department was passed by Congress in Oct. 1782. By this the salary of the Post Master General was raised to 1500 Doll. and an extension of the establishment provided for; the rate of letter postage was fixed at about $5\frac{1}{2}$ cents for not more than 60 miles; $12\frac{1}{2}$ cents for not more than 100 miles &c.; newspapers were not taken by the mails, but might be carried by postriders outside the bags, on such terms as the Post Master General should fix.

When the federal constitution came into operation there were only 75 post offices in the Union; only 2000 miles of postroads, all upon the Atlantic coast; the expenditure of the Department for carrying the mails was only 22,000 Doll. a year; and the receipts of the New York Post Office, now the largest, were but 5537 Doll. At that time the postage on a letter from New-York to Savannah was 36 cents.

offices and the total receipts were but 46,000 Doll. In 1792 the rates of postage were first fixed in federal money, and newspapers were taken into the mails. An excellent clause was now introduced into the law, allowing newspapers to exchange with each other by mail free of charge. The salary of the Post Master General was also raised to 2000 Doll. Seven years afterwards the number of Post offices had increased to 700 and the length of post routes to 15,000 miles. Then it took forty four days to send a letter from Philadelphia to Nashville and receive a reply; but in 1810 the Post Master General announced to Congress with great satisfaction that such was now the perfection of the service that only thirty days were required for that operation! In 1814 there were 3000 post masters, 43,000 miles of post road and the revenue of the Department had grown to 730,000 Doll. In 1816 the rates of postage were fixed at 6 cents for letters going less than 30 miles; 10 cents for less than 80; 12½ cents for less than 150; 18¾ for less than 400; and 25 cents for all greater distances. In 1845 in compliance with a universal and long unsatisfied want of the people, these rates were reduced to 5 cents for letters not going over 300 miles and 10 cents for greater distances. At the same time another judicious change was introduced, namely the reckoning of postage on the weight of letters instead of by the number of single sheets or pieces of paper, as before. In 1851, thanks to the efforts of the Hon. N. K. Hall, Mr. Fillmore's Post Master General, seconded by the press and an enligthened majority in Congress, these rates were still farther reduced and a system of genuine cheap postage established. According to Mr Hall's suggestions letter-postage was reduced to three cents for prepaid letters and five cents for letters not prepaid, for all distances. When Mr Hall came into office in 1850 there were 19,000 post masters and 5590 different post routes in operation; the revenue from postages amounted to 5,495,000 Doll. of which 919,484 Doll. were derived from newspapers. In 1851 the number of Post Offices had increased to 19,796, and the length of mail routes to 196,290 miles. Since then the increase of mail routes has been very great; these lines of communication now ramify not only through the elder states of the Atlantic coast and Mississippi valley, but strike boldly across the continent to New Mexico and the Mormon communities in Utah, and spread far and wide along the Pacific shore and in the remote valleys of California and Oregon.

We give the above statistics in their exactness, because they are redundant with a vitality and interest not often belonging to figures. They are eloquent with the spirit and the power of the Republic. They are the foot marks and signs of its astonishing progress. In seventy five years, while the population has increased only eight times, the post office establishment, the first of public institutions for the diffusion of intelligence and the facilitation of intercourse between the different sections of the country, has become two hundred and fifty times as large as it was at the beginning of the period, and the amount of service performed by it, the mass of letters and newspapers which it distributes has grown in a proportion infinitely greater still. In no country under heaven, not even in England, the land of cheap postage, are any thing like so many letters and journals carried by the mails; in none is there so much writing and reading in proportion to the population, as in the United States. We say this in no spirit of boasting, or as a peculiar honor to the American people; the honor belongs to Free Institutions, whose unspeakable blessings the American people enjoy.

The edifice represented in the engraving was first occupied by the Department in 1841. It is one of the best of the Government buildings at Washington; it extends the length of an entire block between Sixth and Seventh streets and has its front on E street. It is of white marble now yellowed by the weather, and cost 600,000 Doll. Up to 1836 its site was occupied by the old General Post Office, which was originally built for a hotel and passed into the hands of the Government in 1812. It was burned down in 1836.

www.ingramcontent.com/pod-product-compliance
Lightning Source LLC
LaVergne TN
LVHW020113110826
845151LV00001B/147

* 9 7 8 1 4 2 5 5 4 3 2 7 3 *